Communications
in Computer and Information Science **1117**

Commenced Publication in 2007
Founding and Former Series Editors:
Phoebe Chen, Alfredo Cuzzocrea, Xiaoyong Du, Orhun Kara, Ting Liu,
Krishna M. Sivalingam, Dominik Ślęzak, Takashi Washio, Xiaokang Yang,
and Junsong Yuan

More information about this series at http://www.springer.com/series/7899

Rens Brankaert · Wijnand IJsselsteijn (Eds.)

Dementia Lab 2019

Making Design Work: Engaging with Dementia in Context

4th Conference, D-Lab 2019
Eindhoven, The Netherlands, October 21–22, 2019
Proceedings

 Springer

Editors
Rens Brankaert ⓘ
Eindhoven University of Technology
and Fontys University of Applied Sciences
Eindhoven, The Netherlands

Wijnand IJsselsteijn
Eindhoven University of Technology
Eindhoven, The Netherlands

ISSN 1865-0929   ISSN 1865-0937 (electronic)
Communications in Computer and Information Science
ISBN 978-3-030-33539-7   ISBN 978-3-030-33540-3 (eBook)
https://doi.org/10.1007/978-3-030-33540-3

This Springer imprint is published by the registered company Springer Nature Switzerland AG
The registered company address is: Gewerbestrasse 11, 6330 Cham, Switzerland

Preface

We are proud to present you with the first proceedings of the Dementia Lab conference, 2019 edition and 4th to take place, organized around the theme 'Making Design Work: Engaging with Dementia in Context.' These proceedings contain papers and ideas presented at the Dementia Lab 2019 conference.

Dementia Lab is a growing community, established in 2016, which builds on a legacy of work done for and with people living with dementia and their surrounding context. The Dementia Lab approach to dementia is inclusive, participatory, and person-centered. Where in other venues it might be challenging to convey the experience of working with people with dementia, or the urgency of working in this field, Dementia Lab allows for a focused discussion around this topic with like-minded designers, researchers, carers, and other professionals operating in this area. Design is important in the wider dementia context. The number of people with dementia is still vastly increasing, presenting us with various challenges. Technology, services, environments, and engagements can alleviate some of these challenges, and contribute to the quality of life, care, and wellbeing of people living with dementia.

The theme for Dementia Lab 2019 is 'Making design work: Engaging with dementia in context.' This theme focused on research and design happening in direct engagement with people living with dementia, and their wider network. 'Making design work' zooms in on what 'works' or 'does not work' in terms of design, technologies, services, environments, or design methods in these contexts of living, caring, and working. These design challenges are addressed through a variety of contributions, both emerging from academic work as well as sharing hands-on experiences. We focus, amongst others, on the relational character, that is, the sustained relationship that a designer or researcher may develop and nurture with people living with dementia, the challenges of materiality, for example, what visual, tactile, olfactory, or other materials 'work' for and with people with dementia in context, or temporality, that is, what engagement in time is needed to let design or research work have a sustainable impact on people with dementia. In Dementia Lab we try to avoid regarding people with dementia as the extensions of their physical or cognitive limitations, or as a singular, undifferentiated collective defined by a common syndrome, but rather focus on their personal history, identity, and lived experiences. In doing so, we hope to be considerate and sensitive to the active and deeply personal role people with dementia can play in the design process.

This year's edition took place in Eindhoven, at the Eindhoven University of Technology, hosted by the departments of Industrial Design and Industrial Engineering & Innovation Sciences. Eindhoven has a legacy of work in context of working for and with people living with dementia, and has established the Expertise Centre of Dementia & Technology to address these challenges. Additionally, the organization of this year's edition is supported by Vilans, the national Centre of Expertise for Long-term Care in the Netherlands, Alzheimer Nederland - the Dutch Alzheimer Association, University of Leuven, LUCA School of Arts, and Fontys University of Applied Sciences.

During Dementia Lab 2019 we aimed to have a diverse offering of work for the fields of design, art, and health. The selected papers come from researchers from around the world including Australia, Canada, Mexico, South Africa, and of course from various locations in Europe. This highly diversified audience gave us the opportunity to achieve a good level of understanding of the interests, approaches, and ongoing studies in the context of dementia.

The topics included in these proceedings are divided in three sections: (i) Inclusion & Participation – these papers elaborate on engaging with people living with dementia through various approaches and methods, (ii) Technology & Experience – in which technology examples are proposed and evaluated to support people with dementia or their family members or enhance the experience of living with dementia, and (iii) Dementia Lab Ideas – short papers which propose a new concept, technology, or idea to work further on in future studies. All papers were peer-reviewed by three qualified reviewers chosen from our Scientific Committee based on their qualifications and experience.

The proceedings editors wish to thank the dedicated Scientific Committee members and the Organizing Committee for this hard work in realizing this year's edition and these proceedings. We also thank Springer for their trust and collaboration in publishing the Dementia Lab 2019 proceedings. Let this be the first proceedings in a long lasting series!

October 2019

Rens Brankaert
Wijnand IJsselsteijn

Organization

Scientific Committee

Gail Kenning	University of Technology Sydney, Australia
Kellie Morrissey	University of Limerick, Ireland
Rita Maldonado Branco	Universidad Portugal, Portugal
James Hodge	Newcastle University, UK
Sarah Foley	University College Cork, Ireland
David Unbehaun	University of Siegen, Germany
Berry Eggen	Eindhoven University of Technology, The Netherlands
Eveline Wouters	Fontys University of Applied Sciences, The Netherlands
Liselore Snaphaan	Tranzo Tilburg University, The Netherlands
Rens Brankaert	Eindhoven University of Technology and Fontys University of Applied Sciences, The Netherlands
Wijnand IJsselsteijn	Eindhoven University of Technology, The Netherlands
Niels Hendriks	KU Leuven, Belgium
Andrea Wilkinson	KU Leuven, Belgium
Sandra Suijkerbuijk	Vilans, The Netherlands
Henk Herman Nap	Vilans, The Netherlands
Minke Kooistra	Alzheimer Nederland, The Netherlands
Ans Tummers	Eindhoven University of Technology, The Netherlands
Maarten Houben	Eindhoven University of Technology, The Netherlands
Myrte Thoolen	Eindhoven University of Technology, The Netherlands

Organization Committee

Rens Brankaert	Eindhoven University of Technology and Fontys University of Applied Sciences, The Netherlands
Wijnand IJsselsteijn	Eindhoven University of Technology, The Netherlands
Niels Hendriks	KU Leuven, Belgium
Andrea Wilkinson	KU Leuven, Belgium
Sandra Suijkerbuijk	Vilans, The Netherlands
Henk Herman Nap	Vilans, The Netherlands
Minke Kooistra	Alzheimer Nederland, The Netherlands
Ans Tummers	Eindhoven University of Technology, The Netherlands
Maarten Houben	Eindhoven University of Technology, The Netherlands
Myrte Thoolen	Eindhoven University of Technology, The Netherlands

Contents

Inclusion and Participation

The Relevance of Involving People with Dementia in Design Research

Niels Hendriks[1,3]([⊠]) [ID], Karin Slegers[2] [ID],
and Andrea Wilkinson[1,3] [ID]

[1] Dementia Lab, Inter-Actions, LUCA School of Arts, Genk, Belgium
niels.hendriks@kuleuven.be
[2] Tilburg School of Humanities and Digital Sciences,
Department of Communication and Cognition,
Tilburg University, Tilburg, The Netherlands
[3] Institute for Media Studies, Mintlab, KU Leuven, Leuven, Belgium

Abstract. Multiple researchers and designers have attempted to involve people with dementia in the design research process. This paper tackles the relevance of doing so. It discusses how society can benefit from involvement of people with dementia in the design process. In addition, it looks at how people with dementia experience such involvement (and how relevant it is to them). The paper consists of theoretical reflections complemented with experiences from a case study and an educational module on design and dementia. The paper ends with providing concrete suggestions on how to increase relevance using the agonistic qualities of design and the way participation in design can help to meet unmet needs of people with dementia.

Keywords: Involvement in research · Participatory design · Involvement in research · Design research

1 Involvement of People with Dementia in Design Through Participatory Design

In recent years many researchers and designers have attempted to involve people with dementia in the design process [3, 4, 14, 17, 20]. Such an approach links to participatory design (PD) aiming to involve all stakeholders in the design process. Quite a few challenges exist when involving people with dementia due to the absence of adequate PD methods, tools and techniques. This paper is based on a PhD project that focused on finding such methods, tools and techniques. The PhD study set up (and analysed) explorations in a series of design projects and an educational module on design with people with dementia. These projects and the educational module all involved individual designers collaborating with individual people with dementia, both in residential care as well as in home care. The authors of this paper were either the designers or researchers (in the projects) or the coaches of other designers (in the educational module). The basic premise was to (collaboratively) create designs that 'make life more pleasant' for the person with dementia.

© Springer Nature Switzerland AG 2019
R. Brankaert and W. IJsselsteijn (Eds.): D-Lab 2019, CCIS 1117, pp. 3–11, 2019.
https://doi.org/10.1007/978-3-030-33540-3_1

This paper aims to answer questions on the relevance (of the involvement of people with dementia). Throughout the PhD project, the authors of this paper questioned whether involvement of people with dementia in the design process holds any relevance for society. Will this involvement help change the negative perspective on people with dementia? Next, at several occasions, the authors were critical towards the research question, namely whether it is relevant for people with dementia themselves to be involved? The authors of this paper believe in the relevance of the research question at stake both for society as well as for people with dementia and discus in the next section why this is the case.

2   Relevance for Society

In general, the representation of people with dementia in society is quite negative both in fictional [6, 16] and also in non-fictional accounts [8] as these tend to focus on decline, loss, degeneration, etc. [19]. This is evident from the language used: dementia is seen as a 'tragedy' [12] and people with dementia are denoted as 'dementia sufferers' [1], getting the diagnosis of dementia as 'social death' [9]. Society's view on the self and on the role cognition plays might be part of the underlying reasons for this negative connotation. The perception of the self and cognition is heavily influenced by the Locke-Parfit vision (LP) [5]. The LP vision distinguishes the physical self ('man') from consciousness, self-reflection and reason, which makes up the 'person'. Without the 'person', there is only a physical body, a 'man'. The LP vision also foregrounds connectedness and continuity: the ability to link the 'person' of today to the 'person' of the past. Without a memory of causes and effects that created the person, there is no self. The LP vision regards a person with dementia –with a distorted consciousness, frequent memory failures, etc., less as a 'person' and more as a 'man', not recognizing the person with dementia as 'full'. Despite all good intentions of campaigns like the Belgian "Onthou mens, vergeet dementie" ("Remember the human being, forget about dementia") or the Irish "Forget the Stigma" (using "I have dementia. I am still me." as a slogan) that try to stimulate the general public to overcome the medicalized view of people with dementia, this still exist [19].

As explained above the design projects and educational module described in this paper did not deal with awareness campaigns to change society's perspectives on people with dementia, but dealt with a participatory design process with design outcomes that should make the life of a person with dementia more pleasant. We will look at how the outcomes of these PD processes show the relevance of involvement of people with dementia for society. The central element in the discussion is the 'agonistic quality' of the design outcomes. The agonistic quality of design comes, according to Markussen [10], through the fact that via its conception, attraction and use a design tries to disrupt "socio-culturally entrenched forms of belonging and inhabiting the everyday world" [10, p. 4]. Applied to dementia, the outcomes of the design process may redefine society's vision on (the person with) dementia and draw attention to the participatory process that lies at the base of the outcome of the design process, as such showing the value of people with dementia (as fully respected partners of a design process).

This paper provides ample space to discuss the large collection of design outcomes created in the design projects and the educational module, but we will zoom in on two, the "Do Nothing Box" (Fig. 1) and "Collect for Later" (Fig. 2).

2.1 The Do Nothing Box

Fig. 1. The "Do Nothing Box"

The "Do Nothing Box" provides a series of activities with step-by-step instructions that a cognitively able person (family member or caregiver) can do with a person with dementia. The suggested activities -such as walking in the care facility for half an hour-are at first no different than what is to be expected: the family member is asked to take the hand of the person with dementia, walk out of the door of the room of the person with dementia, etc. It is only after a couple of minutes walking that the instructions ask you to stop, hold each other more tightly and stand silently. The aim here is to help caregivers and family members understand (through this activity and a small reflective booklet) that a person with dementia might 'just' enjoy your company and that a conversation is not needed (or even wanted). In this sense, such a tool reflects on re-defining the relationship between the caregiver or family member and the person with dementia. As a son, daughter or caregiver, you might feel the need to use 'words' as a way to interact and you might want 'something to do' in order to feel that you are having a meaningful time. The "Do Nothing Box" challenges such feelings. On a larger scale, the object tries to stir the discussion on what is normal (it feels normal to talk with someone, it feels normal to respond to our urge to do something and not do nothing) and to stimulate us to redefine our notion of what is normal. The project was created by Jean, who has dementia, and designer Dorien. Dorien tried to have Jean work on a set of playful assignments consisting of a game combining math exercises with photos of the past. While she was explaining what she expected Jean to do, he suddenly grabbed her hand, with a faint smile looked her in the eye and held tight. It was at that point that she not only understood she could use his physical interactions as a way of involving him in the design process, but also that he 'needed' the presence and the'warmth' of another person.

2.2   Collect for Later

"Collect for later" was created through a PD setup with resident Mia and designer Els. For 4 years, Mia had been living in a nursing care home. Even though she was at ease in the care home, there were moments that she felt alone and became emotional. After being with Mia for quite some time (joining for dinner, chit-chatting, etc.) designer Els noticed that Mia would be distracted every time one of Els's male colleagues, Rik, passed: Mia would eagerly observe all of his movements, smile as he smiled and comment on his presence both verbally (e.g. "That is a guy I like!") and non-verbally (e.g. by giggling, winking multiple times at Els in a conspiratorial way, etc.). Mia expressed that she missed a man in her life. Els then worked out a design process in which she created several magazines with pictures of men, clothed, nude or wearing swim suits or boxers and used Mia's response to select among these. In the end, Els developed a set of cards and a colourful folder to collect the cards. The set of cards had attractive men (a nice balance between clothed men and more 'erotic' pictures of men in underwear) photoshopped into scenes that depicted other themes that were of interest to Mia (scenes of popular holiday places, animals, etc.). The cards were given to Mia at times when a negative mood would struck her. She had a colourful folder to keep the cards in (collect for later) and would keep the folder most of the times nearby.

Fig. 2. Collect for later

The design stirred quite some discussion with the family of Mia and the caregivers who were unsure whether they were pleased with the 'erotic' pictures of males in their underwear being given to Mia. Amongst the group of caregivers, the design also generated debate on how to deal with the longing for intimacy and sexuality at a dementia ward and initiated a first step in setting up a protocol on this.

The feeling of 'awkwardness' that a design such as Collect for Later brings, confronts us with our vision on the person with dementia as an ill, frail or 'lovely' old person, but not as a human being with desire or lust. The design outcome 'works' as it helps Mia to break boredom and to not get her into a melancholic or bad mood, but it is also critical towards society's attempt to 'desexualize' older people and certainly people with dementia [21].

Both projects, through their design outcomes and the design processes, re-valued the person with dementia as a 'full person' who once was and still is a person with wants, needs, dislikes and desires and, in this way, the process and its outcomes challenge society's preconceptions on people with dementia. The next section will zoom in on the relevance of people with dementia to be involved in the design process.

3   Relevance of Involvement for People with Dementia

There are few accounts of people with dementia reflecting on their experience of being involved in research. McKillop [11] and Robinson [15], both having dementia, explain in detail how they experienced being involved in research. McKillop thinks his participation has helped him to better express himself and gain confidence. He also sees that his voice might trigger some reflection with the researchers or even the recipients (readers of the papers on his participation for example) of the research. Robinson finds that it is an obligation -not only to those who set up the research project, but also to the people with dementia - to be involved in research: "after all, who else would know what it is like to have the disease?" and she continues "What a hugely missed opportunity it would be if people with Alzheimer's were excluded from the very thing that could be used to gain a fuller understanding of their disease" [15, p. 104]. For her personally, being part of research lifted her morale and gave her the opportunity to meet a variety of people with and without dementia all interested in her story.

The benefits of participation McKillop and Robinson experienced, seem to be in line with some of the (unmet) needs by people with dementia found in research. Commonly reported unmet needs of people with dementia (both at home or in a nursing care home) include the need for coping strategies and the need to accept their condition, as well as the need for social and meaningful activities and company, and the need to be accepted and respected as they are [2, 13, 18]. At least two of these unmet needs could be met by involving people with dementia in the design process, as was also expressed in the examples of McKillop and Robinson as both the social aspect (meeting new people and being involved in meaningful activities) and the idea of being respected stand out in the stories on their participation. Kenning [7], working with people in later stages of the dementia process, also experienced that involving a person with dementia in the design process provides 'in the moment'- pleasure for the person with dementia, and thus meaningful and social activities. Next to this, the actual pleasure experienced when using the artefacts resulting from the (participatory) design processes can't be neglected either. The "Collect for Later" card set, for instance, gave Mia a much-needed distraction as she was, at times when a melancholic mood struck her, given cards of handsome men which she could collect for later in a folder.

During the research and design processes of the projects and educational module, it was never explicitly tested or verified what participation entailed for people with dementia and how they experienced being involved in the research and design process. However, similar to the positive views of McKillop and Robinson, we saw people with dementia to be enjoying the moment: a person would shift from being quite apathetic to being enthusiast when scrolling through old photos used in a design; a woman living at home would say she looked forward to our meetups; designer Dorien reported that Jean, in the example of the Do Nothing Box, would be fast to get up whenever he saw Dorien enter the room, eagerly wanting to start working with her (or at least physically expressing his positive feelings towards them working together); a lady confined to her wheelchair would be intensely 'busy' for a couple of minutes using her fingers to explore the pieces of cloth brought to her as part of creating an aesthetic piece of clothing that would allow fidgeting.

The major difficulty for us, as designers and researchers, was to communicate what people with dementia could expect from our working together. With an abstract design goal ('to make life more pleasant'), the actual benefits of their participation were not always that easy to predict. Whenever this was possible, we used examples of previously created objects to show people with dementia and carers what type of design outcomes one could expect. This was also done in order to avoid unrealistic expectations and showing the 'prototype'-state most design outcomes were in. Participants however hardly expressed any disappointment (with final outcomes) and we had some participants (in more early stages of the dementia process) who eagerly indicated that whatever would come out of it would be fine. They explicitly referred to our participation as a learning moment for us, the designers and researchers, and hoped we could become better at designing for "others, just like me" (Jeanne, living at home with dementia). This too links to the above-mentioned unmet needs of the feeling of being respected and taking part in a meaningful activity. Working with people in late stages made us explicitly focus on the in-the-moment-pleasure: how can we as designers and researchers make sure that they are having a good time. As a demonstration of this, numerous selfies of people with dementia with a designer, as a snapshot of the 'fun' they were having, were taken, stories of listening and singing along to music together were told by designers in the educational module (and the amazement or enjoyment the person with dementia expressed listening to the designer who also shared 'their' music with them).

4   Conclusion: How to Enhance Relevance

The question on the relevance of involvement of people with dementia in the design process has been tackled in this paper on two levels: the relevance for society and the relevance for people with dementia. The paper shows how the agonistic quality of what came out of a (participatory) design process aids in changing the vision on people with dementia. It also tells what 'needs' of the person with dementia such a participatory approach can meet.

Before going into a series of 'lessons learned' on how to enhance the relevance, a critical reflection needs to be made. It cannot be fully proven as such, that relevance on both levels has been attained merely through the participatory approach. It seems highly unlikely, however, that working only with proxies (caregivers or family), or without stepping 'as deep' into the collaboration with the person with dementia as the designers in our projects did, would lead to such a taboo-breaking result as with the "Collect for Later"-project or would provide such a clear understanding of the wants (for closeness and warmth) as was the case in "The Do Nothing Box".

To conclude, we formulate a series of 'lessons learned' in order to support designers and researchers to enhance the relevance of their PD processes. First of all, in order to enhance the relevance for the individual with dementia, we believe that for each PD project one should first question how to provide **in-the-moment pleasure**. This means that the designer should be critical towards making sure the moments together/**the moments of participation will be pleasant and joyful**. This is not a straightforward act, but will require from the designer and researcher to focus not so much on the goal of being together (namely creating a design) but on the means and context to facilitate this (creating an atmosphere where the person with dementia feels comfortable). This would see the designers and researchers often spend time on non goal-oriented activities such as having dinner together with the person with dementia, joining them in physical therapy, going to church together etc. Next to this, the design process should work towards fulfilling a person with dementia's unmet needs. It will be most rewarding to work with the need for social and meaningful activities and the need to be accepted and respected for who the person with dementia is. In our projects, we did this by **showing explicitly (through posters which were hung up in the nursing care home and setting up a fair where process and outcome were showcased) how the design outcome was part of a collaborative process** where both (designer and person with dementia) had a share in. On top of that, at the end of each project, the designers were asked to wrap up the collaboration by **making explicit what they had learned from their collaboration** and by making sure that they **left behind the design outcome** or -if it was in an early prototype stage- a derivative that shows this collaboration. What is left behind should be of value to the person with dementia (in use or through its meaning). Next to this micro level, the design outcomes and processes can work on a meso and macro level and several actions can be planned to enhance the relevance on each of these levels. Creating relevance on a meso level, the level of the care organization and those surrounding the person with dementia, was done by **showcasing the design outcomes and the process** not only in a designer's portfolio's, but also at a fair and poster event set **in the nursing care home**. Showing the way the collaboration between a designer and a resident unfolded and what it led to, helped stir discussions between carers and management on topics such as sexuality and intimacy (as happened with "Collect for Later" leading to the setup of a first version of a protocol on this) or on how to provide a meaningful activity in 'dull' moments (when staff is busy). To support this debate on a meso level we suggest **to be transparent about the collaboration between a person with dementia and how this led to**

certain design decisions and outcomes, and to communicate this in a clear format (using posters and informal conversations at a fair rather than long-winding paper reports). Trying to challenge society's preconceptions on people with dementia (i.e. the macro level) had us **showcase artefacts and the participatory process** which preceded it, not only inside nursing care homes, academic or design events, but more importantly, **at places where caregivers, family of people with dementia, (health) policy makers and the general audience come together** (e.g. seminars for future dementia reference persons, showcases organized by the Alzheimer League, network events for health professionals and industry, a city's biennale etc.). Implementing these lessons learned in the participatory process will help designers and researchers to enhance the relevance for society and people with dementia.

References

1. Cheston, R., Bender, M.: Understanding Dementia: The Man with the Worried Eyes. J. Kingsley Publishers, London (1999)
2. Hancock, G.A., et al.: The needs of older people with dementia in residential care. Int. J. Geriatr. Psychiatry **21**(1), 43–49 (2006). https://doi.org/10.1002/gps.1421
3. Hendriks, N., et al.: Challenges in doing participatory design with people with dementia. Presented at the Proceedings of the 13th Participatory Design Conference: Short Papers, Industry Cases, Workshop Descriptions, Doctoral Consortium papers, and Keynote abstracts-Volume 2, Winbdhoek, Namibia (2014). http://dx.doi.org/10.1145/2662155. 2662196
4. Hendriks, N., et al.: Valuing implicit decision-making in participatory design: a relational approach in design with people with dementia. Des. Stud. (2018). https://doi.org/10.1016/j. destud.2018.06.001
5. Hughes, J.C.: Views of the person with dementia. J. Med. Ethics **27**(2), 86–91 (2001)
6. Ignatieff, M.: Scar Tissue. Macmillan, London (2000)
7. Kenning, G.: Making it together: reciprocal design to promote positive wellbeing for people living with dementia. UTS (2017)
8. Keulen, C.: Vulnerable Love (2017)
9. Lopez, O.L., et al.: Psychiatric symptoms vary with the severity of dementia in Probable Alzheimer's disease. JNP **15**(3), 346–353 (2003). https://doi.org/10.1176/jnp.15.3.346
10. Markussen, T.: The disruptics aesthetics of design activism: enacting design between art and politics. Presented at the Nordic Design Research Conference 2011, Helsinki (2011)
11. McKillop, J.: Did research alter anything? In: Wilkinson, H. (ed.) The Perspectives of People with Dementia: Research Methods and Motivations. Jessica Kingsley Publishers, London (2002)
12. McParland, P., et al.: Dichotomising dementia: is there another way? Sociol. Health Illn. **39** (2), 258–269 (2017). https://doi.org/10.1111/1467-9566.12438
13. Miranda-Castillo, C., et al.: Unmet needs, quality of life and support networks of people with dementia living at home. Health Qual. Life Outcomes **8**, 132 (2010). https://doi.org/10.1186/ 1477-7525-8-132
14. Morrissey, K.: "I'm a rambler, I'm a gambler, I'm a long way from home": exploring participation through music and digital design in dementia care. University College Cork (2017)

15. Robinson, E.: Should people with Alzheimer's disease take part in research? In: Wilkinson, H. (ed.) The Perspectives of People with Dementia: Research Methods and Motivations. Jessica Kingsley Publishers, London (2002)
16. Roca, P.: Wrinkles. Knockabout Comics, London (2011)
17. Rodgers, P.A.: Co-designing with people living with dementia. CoDesign 14, 188–202 (2017). https://doi.org/10.1080/15710882.2017.1282527
18. van der Roest, H.G., et al.: Subjective needs of people with dementia: a review of the literature. Int. Psychogeriatr. 19(3), 559–592 (2007)
19. Van Gorp, B., Vercruysse, T.: Frames and counter-frames giving meaning to dementia: a framing analysis of media content. Soc. Sci. Med. 74(8), 1274–1281 (2012). https://doi.org/10.1016/j.socscimed.2011.12.045
20. Wallace, J., et al.: Making design probes work. Presented at the (2013). https://doi.org/10.1145/2470654.2466473
21. Ward, R., et al.: A kiss is still a kiss?: the construction of sexuality in dementia care. Dementia 4(1), 49–72 (2005). https://doi.org/10.1177/1471301205049190

Towards Dementia Things

How Does Participatory Research and Design Improve Quality of Life in Contexts of Dementia?

Carolin Schreiber[1](✉), Jan Üblacker[2], Diana Cürlis[1],
and Nora Weber[1]

[1] Folkwang University of Arts,
Martin-Kremmer-Straße 21, 45327 Essen, Germany
carolin.schreiber@folkwang-uni.de
[2] Research Institute for Urban and Regional Development,
Brüderweg 22-24, 44135 Dortmund, Germany

Abstract. In the early stages of dementia, care often takes place at home. In the project Dementia Things we form competence teams consisting of designers, professional caregivers, persons with dementia and their care giving relatives. We ask for the everyday problems of persons with dementia and their relatives in private environments and use methods of field research and participatory design to understand the specific contexts of dementia and improve the quality of life. From the ongoing field work we were able to identify four factors influencing the participatory design process: building up trustful relations in the field, the role of the professional caregiver, the surplus of overcoming verbal barriers with design methods, and the overall benefit of changing perspectives and knowledge transfer within the competence team.

Keywords: Dementia · Participatory design · Field research methods

1 Introduction

In the early stages of dementia, care often takes place at home. In contrast to a stationary environment with professional staff, routines and equipment the care of people with dementia by their relatives at home is characterized by a multitude of different problems concerning not only the material environment but also the inter-personal relationships. Therefore, creating a social and material environment which meets individual needs and resources is the key to enable people with dementia to live longer in their known environment and allow them to lead a self-determined life.

As the progress of dementia is difficult to predict and depending on the persons daily form, the need for versatile offers and solutions is essential. These have to concern, among other things, aids for orientation (day and night) in the home and in the neighborhood or for communication with the overall environment. Since problems often change according to the patient's daily form, solutions should be customizable and spontaneously modifiable by people without professional background, most of all for the care giving relatives. The development of such products, services or measures

© Springer Nature Switzerland AG 2019
R. Brankaert and W. IJsselsteijn (Eds.): D-Lab 2019, CCIS 1117, pp. 12–23, 2019.
https://doi.org/10.1007/978-3-030-33540-3_2

often comes up against economic limits and therefore there are almost no individually designed products and solutions to purchase.

In professional care, a phenomenon can be observed in which experienced nursing staff try to help themselves with self-constructions and easily accessible products. Many of these ideas, which arise out of necessity, have the potential to be professionalized to a certain degree and made accessible to a wider audience. As we expect the problems arising out of contexts of dementia to be highly individual so have to be the solutions: the dementia things. As dementia things we understand products, services or social routines that emerge from a process-oriented, participative development that takes place in the domestic environment of the person with dementia. The aim of the process as well as of the dementia thing itself is to sustainably improve the quality of life of persons in contexts of dementia.

In the participatory research and design project Dementia Things we seek to answer the following questions:

1. What are the problems faced by persons with dementia, their care giving relatives and (professional) caregivers in their domestic environment and what strategies do they use to deal with these problems?
2. How can participatory design methods contribute to the quality of life in contexts of dementia? What are hindering and supporting factors of the participatory design process?

While the first question requires a social scientific approach to the subject the latter clearly states a transformative goal, which might be achieved by the discipline of (participatory) design. In the project Dementia Things, we gather designers, professional caregivers of the discipline of social work/geriatric care and social scientists to form interdisciplinary teams and participate in everyday life situations in contexts of dementia.

With this contribution we want to share first experiences from ongoing field work with people with dementia and their caregivers in their domestic environment. After clarifying our methodological approach in the next section we move on to discuss four topics: (1) entering the field and establishing trustful relationships, (2) relationship work and professional care givers, (3) the role of design in coping with cognitive impairments and (4) the deficit focus of care giving relatives. In each section we address distinct problems of participatory design research in the field of dementia, link them to additional studies if necessary and provide our own experiences and solutions. With this we hope to advance our knowledge and methods on how to better work and design in contexts of dementia. We close with a conclusion and outlook on further topics.

2 Participatory Research and Design Methods

To conduct the participatory research and design process we form competence teams which consist of one designer, one professional caregiver (geriatric care/social work), the person with dementia and the care giving relative or volunteer assistant (see Fig. 1). Once established the competence team meets approximately once a week over a period of three to six months in the domestic environment of the person with dementia in order to develop a dementia thing in a participative co-creative process (Sanders and Stappers 2008; Sanchez de la Guia et al. 2017; Suijkerbuijk et al. 2019). Following the usual product or service design processes, the development of each dementia thing can be divided into three, sometimes iterative phases:

(1) Research and analysis: After the successful formation of a competence team the members start with regular meetings on a weekly basis. The first task for the designer and the professional caregiver is to build a trustful relationship to the person with dementia and the care giving relative in order to gather reliable information on the everyday life in this particular context of dementia. This is typically done by applying several methods of qualitative empirical social research, such as narrative interviews (Hopf 2008; Helfferich 2011), group discussions (Bohnsack 2008) or participant observations (Jorgensen 1989). Since the competence teams mostly pay short visits to the field of approximately one to two hours, the overall style of this research may best be described by what Hubert Knoblauch termed focused ethnography (Knoblauch 2005). It is important to note that in this phase of the process the designer and the professional caregiver do not have a specific topic or question in mind when entering the field. They rather rely on the open character of the methods and the reactions in the field. Over time and especially with the improvement of the field relations potential topics and problems will occur. If so, the fore mentioned methods are used to gain a deeper understanding of the issue and draw up a thick description of the phenomenon.

Fig. 1. Composition of the competence team

(2) Transformation and conception: Throughout the first phase the competence team usually identifies several topics and problems. In the second phase the competence team jointly selects one problem and starts developing concepts to solve it. For the further process it is particularly important that the chosen topic is highly relevant to the person with dementia and the care giving relative since this raises the motivation and continued use of the dementia thing after the completion of the process. By using creative and design methods the findings from the first phase are translated into simple tangible things (mock ups, prototypes) and tested in everyday life. The aim of the conception phase is to carry out first samples and experiments in order to observe

whether these can be helpful in dealing with the problem identified in the research and analysis phase. It should be noted here that solutions are designed to be as low-complex as possible, so that they can be implemented and further developed with simple manual skills and simple materials in the best possible way, if necessary even by using ready-mades by non-professionally trained designers, namely the professional caregivers and relatives in the competence team.

(3) Implementation: In the last phase the competence team creates the product, service or social routine and implements it in the everyday life of the person with dementia. Parts of this phase may take place in external workshops to be able to work on the necessary materials. To keep up the motivation and foster identification with the final dementia thing the person with dementia and the care giving relative participate in these finals steps as much as possible.

In order to make cross case comparisons we work in three independent competence teams at the same time over a total duration of one and a half years. Up to now we successfully entered field work with 7 families.

We document the whole process with field protocols to be able to analytically identify hindering and supporting factors of the participatory design process. After each meeting with the competence team the designers and professional caregivers complete a field protocol. The protocols were developed within the interdisciplinary project team and collect information relevant for social scientific, nursing science and design research. Besides information on the people participating in the meeting, place, time and duration, the field protocols also cover the following aspects:

- description of the course of the meeting
- description of the interaction between the participating persons
- particularly special things (positive/negative)
- materials used
- applied creative or design methods
- objectives of the meeting and expectations of the team members
- results of the meeting
- significance of the result for the further process

Through the comprehensive recording of the meetings from both the point of view of the designers and the point of view of the professional caregiver it is possible to compare the different perspectives and skills that are brought into the process. The topics and experiences discussed below are derived from the information contained in the field protocols.

3 Entering the Field and Gaining Trust

Since we aim on working with families in their private environment our first goal was to achieve public attention for the project in the city of Essen. This was important because compared to other projects (e.g. in senior homes) we had limited possibilities to acquire cases from stationary environments. In the first-place flyers, posters and a website were created and distributed at various events of general public interest (e.g. local festivals). In addition, our project partners supported us with articles on the project that were published in subject-specific journals and newspapers with high reach (e.g. municipal newsletters, local newspapers, Caritas Magazine). Through this public attention and with assistance of the professional caregivers in our team we got in contact with more specialized people in the field that introduced us to dementia cafés, day care and self-help groups, in which we then presented the project.

A basic prerequisite for the development of a dementia thing is the access to the context of dementia: the private home, the care giving relatives or the voluntary care givers and the person with dementia. Especially the caregivers are important contact persons since they manage everyday life and know the personal history and habits of the person with dementia (Palmer 2013). What makes access particularly challenging is that the family caregivers are often self-taught laypersons and do rarely have any professional knowledge on dementia care. Hence a lot of care giving relatives are often overburdened with the situation and emotionally strained. Simply coping with an ordinary day without special activities demands their highest level of attention and patience.

Nevertheless, as experts of the living environment their willingness to participate is vital for the development of a dementia thing and the success of the project. The acquisition thus proved as a large hurdle. While in a stationary environment a formative and to a certain extent creative project[1] is perceived as a welcome distraction of everyday routines of people with dementia and professional caregivers, we found it difficult to motivate care giving relatives to take part in the project and at the same time convey information to prevent the following common misunderstandings:

- Answering the question, what a dementia thing could be.
- The explanation of the sustainable benefit of a dementia thing and thus the added value of participating in a project as well as the short-term benefit of our presence in the family.
- Explanation of the time schedule of the project.
- The work processes or activities of the competence teams in the private premises.
- The wish that those affected actively participate in the design process and do not see the project as an opportunity for a short break for the nurse.
- Reassurance that it is possible to withdraw from the project at any time (e.g. if you move to an inpatient area, stay in hospital, changed care situation, death or simply if the project does not suit you).

We could identify some factors that were helpful to build up trustful relationships to potential participants. Firstly, providing material to illustrate the ongoing process and its outcome for the families (e.g. storyboards, exemplary products from other stationery projects) was crucial to overcome irritations and misunderstandings about the aim and use of the project. Secondly, we got the impression that in particular measures in which we engaged in direct personal contact with families had the highest chance of successfully acquiring households. Thirdly, while presenting on public events and publishing articles in local newspapers helps to generate public attention for dementia, the

---

[1] The previous project "Do we know each other" took place in a stationary environment; demenz-lab. folkwang-uni.de.

most efficient way to gain participants was to use gatekeeping institutions, such as dementia cafés or day care, and professionals already working in the field of dementia, as some of our project partners do. This also highlights the importance of working in interdisciplinary teams.

4 Relationship Work and Professional Caregivers

Several studies on participatory design in the field of dementia question the reliability of information gathered from persons with dementia and their caregivers, thus making it difficult to engage in participatory work with them (e.g. Meiland et al. 2012; Hendriks et al. 2014). Although we can confirm these problems, there were quite some cases in which we made different experiences.

Gaining reliable information in field work is a common problem in qualitative research (Jorgensen 1989). To strengthen the reliability of the information our teams focus on developing and sustaining field relationships in the first phase (see above). Establishing trust and cooperation, reciprocity and exchange and finally gaining acceptance may help the designer and professional caregiver to better evaluate the verbal and nonverbal information gathered in the field. Another problem frequently faced in working with care giving relatives is their emotional and psychological state. This is where the specific role of the professional caregiver comes to play.

The professional caregivers can respond professionally to the everyday life of the affected persons and empathize with them and thus meet the expectations of the families. Often the relatives or caregivers describe their everyday lives in initial conversations and experience the professional caregivers in our team as specialists who are familiar with the care situation, can assess it and, through professional questions and answers, convey a feeling of security to the families who are often self-taught in the field of care. This seems to be much in line with the role of empathy in bridging the gulf of experience reported by Lindsay et al. (2012). In addition, they can identify problems in the area of care and activation (in the home context) and may help define initial questions for potential design fields. By asking appropriate questions, the caregivers are encouraged to reflect on their own (care) situation right from the start, thus opening up the project. Furthermore, there is often the phenomenon of unpredictable reactions of the person with dementia during project meetings. Depending on their daily constitution, people with dementia react aggressively, with a general lack of interest or reject the collaboration. In these situations, the professional caregivers give the designers security. They are able to explain unclear situations and mediate (even non-verbally) between designers and patients. A tension-free atmosphere is the basis for a successful joint project.

Basically, the involvement of professional caregivers as "dementia experts" in the participative design process increases the level of subjective security for all participants. In this way, a strengthened relationship of trust can be built up in a short period of time, which will endure during the cooperation and can be intensified.

5 Design and Cognitive Impairment

People with dementia experience a loss of memory, difficulties with communication and verbalization. Combined with the loss of abilities, skills and competencies this gives them a feeling of losing autonomy and independence (de Boer et al. 2007). In sum this makes it challenging to integrate persons with dementia into the participatory design process (Hendriks et al. 2014). Studies on the interaction with persons with dementia highlight that while language skills and abilities to verbalize interests decrease throughout the progression of dementia, persons with dementia may be activated by emotional or tactile stimulations (Kim and Buschmann 1999; Skovdahl et al. 2007). Research on the function of transitional objects for people with dementia (Loboprabhu et al. 2007; Kenning and Treadaway 2018).

Within the process the designers make the development of dementia things possible through their experiences with the visualization and implementation of practical and haptic things. By going beyond verbal communication and focusing on material and emotional aspects all affected people and their needs are included in the design (human-centered approach). The products, services or social routines must represent an increase in value and an improvement of their everyday life for both the people with dementia as well as for their caregivers. Designers can contribute an extensive knowledge, e.g. about ergonomic studies, which concern the handling, as well as about the psychology of perception of the dementia things. They also have the ability to visualize initial ideas for everyday helpers with the help of easy-to-process materials (e.g. cardboard, plasticine, pencil, paper, wooden sticks, photos), with which even inexperienced co-designers, e.g. people with dementia and caregivers, can express themselves in order to test them in everyday life (mock-ups, functional prototypes). Here, designers often take on a moderating, guiding role (design empowerment).

6 Changing Perspectives Without Neglecting Needs and Wishes of the People with Dementia

A recurring phenomenon in the working process was what we further describe as the caregiver's focus on the deficit of the person with dementia. In almost all cases, the descriptions of the person with dementia remaining abilities and interests that were given by their relatives and caregivers are more negative than the impression our team received throughout the meetings. One factor for the more negative perception of the remaining resources of the person with dementia may be due to the strain and excessive demands placed on the care giving relatives or caregivers: the increasingly comprehensive care of a person who is regressing in his or her abilities demands many people to such an extent that the laborious maintenance of activating activities cannot always be achieved (Gräßel 1998; Müller et al. 2009). An example: If the patient needs a lot of support during dinner preparation cutting cucumber slices, to the care giving relative it seems more efficient to prepare the dinner themselves rather than having to deal with a labour-intensive integration of the person with dementia.

Existing resources and remaining manual skills of the person with dementia are thus increasingly disappearing in everyday life. In general, it is not possible to offer the same degree of confirmation and stimulation in the private environment as would be possible in a stationary care facility. The necessity to uncover the resources of the patient and (primarily) to use them for stimulating activities (e.g. games, assistance in everyday life, daily planning) is already one of the most frequent questions in the cases dealt with so far. The relief of the caregivers that can be achieved by these measures shows first positive effects. Less frequently than expected by the research team, those affected miss tools and products for better coping with the basic needs in everyday life, e.g. related to food preparation or body care.

Some of these improvements may also be due to the fact that in a research team consisting of at least two persons there are more possibilities to separate the person with dementia and the care giving relative. Thus, giving the opportunity to openly exchange ideas with the caregivers while the person with dementia is busy at the same time. So far it has often been the experience that in a meeting the care giving relative or caregiver did not openly talk about possible problems in everyday life or deficits in order to not expose the person with dementia.

However, one of the most important advantages of the competence teams is the adaptation of each other's perspective and expertise. Professional caregivers start communicating creatively and designers interact (verbally) more sensitively with the person with dementia. The voluntary caregivers may be able to professionalize their skills and reduce the labor intensity by the help of the designed dementia things. The work in competence teams allows more freedom for testing different ideas and approaches, as possible critical situations, which always arise in the course of working with people with dementia, can be solved more quickly and effectively together.

7 Conclusion

The purpose of this contribution was to share first experiences from our current field work in contexts of dementia in the pre-stationary sector. We wanted to find out what problems people with dementia and their care giving relatives face and how the quality of life in these private environments may be improved by the development of dementia things. Since we report from a project with ongoing field work, no final result can be reported yet. Nevertheless, due to the comprehensive documentation of the field work we are able to identify four factors that contribute to a successful research and design process. When working in domestic environments it is particularly important to build up trustful relationships right from the beginning to maintain motivation and initiative of the care giving relative and the person with dementia. The influence and experience of the professionally trained caregivers on the care giving relatives is of crucial importance when it comes to dealing with problematic and complex situations. Within a more tension-free atmosphere the skills and methods of the designer may help to overcome the barrier that often arises from the cognitive impairment of the person with dementia. Overall the work in competence teams supports the transfer of knowledge, experiences and skills between care giving relatives, designers and professional caregivers.

Yet, with regard to the actual outcome of the process - the dementia thing - there are still a number of questions to be answered. The team is currently facing the fundamental questions of what dementia things should be, what classifications, forms or shapes they should have. What significance do materials and artefacts really have? Is a dementia thing possibly a new attitude or the impetus for reflection and if so, how does this relate to the role of design in the process?

Acknowledgements. The project is planned for three years and is financed by Stiftung Wohlfahrtspflege NRW. Together, three partners, Folkwang University of the Arts, Theresia Albers Stiftung and Katholische Pflegehilfe carried out the project. The project is currently in its first phase, in which the interdisciplinary competence teams and families jointly develop dementia things. In the second phase the scientific documentation and analysis of these processes is used to develop a training program to transfer the knowledge towards professional and voluntary caregivers, care giving relatives and people with dementia. The target groups will be able to develop own dementia things in a participatory and creative process.

Appendix

Fig. 2. Writing field protocols

Fig. 3. Preliminary concept of a dementia thing

Fig. 4. Using the dementia thing

References

Suijkerbuijk, S., Nap, H.H., Cornelisse, L., IJsselsteijn, W.A., de Kort, Y.A.W., Minkman, M.M. N.: Active involvement of people with dementia: a systematic review of studies developing supportive technologies. JAD **69**, 1041–1065 (2019). https://doi.org/10.3233/JAD-190050

Müller, I., Hinterhuber, H., Kemmler, G., Marksteiner, J., Weiss, E.M., Them, C.: Auswirkungen der häuslichen Betreuung demenzkranker Menschen auf ihre pflegenden Angehörigen. Psychiatrie und Psychotherapie. **5**, 139–145 (2009). https://doi.org/10.1007/s11326-009-0079-8

Hendriks, N., Huybrechts, L., Wilkinson, A., Slegers, K.: Challenges in doing participatory design with people with dementia. In: Proceedings of the 13th Participatory Design Conference on Short Papers, Industry Cases, Workshop Descriptions, Doctoral Consortium papers, and Keynote abstracts - PDC 2014, Windhoek, Namibia, vol. 2, pp. 33–36. ACM Press (2014). https://doi.org/10.1145/2662155.2662196

Sanders, E.B.-N., Stappers, P.J.: Co-creation and the new landscapes of design. CoDesign **4**, 5–18 (2008). https://doi.org/10.1080/15710880701875068

Kenning, G., Treadaway, C.: Designing for dementia: iterative grief and transitional objects. Des. Issues **34**, 42–53 (2018). https://doi.org/10.1162/DESI_a_00475

Helfferich, C.: Die Qualität qualitativer Daten. VS Verlag für Sozialwissenschaften/Springer Fachmedien Wiesbaden GmbH, Wiesbaden (2011)

Lindsay, S., Brittain, K., Jackson, D., Ladha, C., Ladha, K., Olivier, P.: Empathy, participatory design and people with dementia. In: Proceedings of the 2012 ACM annual conference on Human Factors in Computing Systems - CHI 2012, Austin, Texas, USA, p. 521. ACM Press (2012). https://doi.org/10.1145/2207676.2207749

Knoblauch, H.: Focused ethnography. Forum Qualitative Social Research **6** (2005)

Bohnsack, R.: Gruppendiskussion. In: Flick, U., von Kardorff, E., Steinke, I. (eds.) Qualitative Forschung: ein Handbuch, pp. 369–383. rowohlts enzyklopädie im Rowohlt Taschenbuch Verlag, Reinbek bei Hamburg (2008)

Gräßel, E.: Häusliche Pflege dementiell und nicht dementiell Erkrankter. Zeitschrift für Gerontologie und Geriatrie **31**, 57–62 (1998). https://doi.org/10.1007/s003910050019

Jorgensen, D.L.: Participant Observation: A Methodology for Human Studies. Sage Publications, Newbury Park (1989)

Palmer, J.L.: Preserving personhood of individuals with advanced dementia: lessons from family caregivers. Geriatr. Nurs. **34**, 224–229 (2013). https://doi.org/10.1016/j.gerinurse.2013.03.001

Flick, U., von Kardorff, E., Steinke, I. (eds.): Qualitative Forschung: ein Handbuch. rowohlts enzyklopädie im Rowohlt Taschenbuch Verlag, Reinbek bei Hamburg (2008)

Hopf, C.: Qualitative Interviews - ein Überblick. In: Flick, U., Kardorff, E. von, and Steinke, I. (eds.) Qualitative Forschung: ein Handbuch, pp. 349–359. rowohlts enzyklopädie im Rowohlt Taschenbuch Verlag, Reinbek bei Hamburg (2008)

de Boer, M.E., Hertogh, C.M.P.M., Dröes, R.-M., Riphagen, I.I., Jonker, C., Eefsting, J.A.: Suffering from dementia – the patient's perspective: a review of the literature. Int. Psychogeriatr. **19** (2007). https://doi.org/10.1017/S1041610207005765

Skovdahl, K., Sörlie, V., Kihlgren, M.: Tactile stimulation associated with nursing care to individuals with dementia showing aggressive or restless tendencies: an intervention study in dementia care. Int. J. Older People Nurs. **2**, 162–170 (2007). https://doi.org/10.1111/j.1748-3743.2007.00056.x

Sánchez de la Guía, L., Puyuelo Cazorla, M., de-Miguel-Molina, B.: Terms and meanings of "participation" in product design: From "user involvement" to "co-design." Des. J. **20**, S4539–S4551 (2017). https://doi.org/10.1080/14606925.2017.1352951

Kim, E.J., Buschmann, M.T.: The effect of expressive physical touch on patients with dementia. Int. J. Nurs. Stud. **36**, 235–243 (1999). https://doi.org/10.1016/S0020-7489(99)00019-X

LoboPrabhu, S., Molinari, V., Lomax, J.: The transitional object in dementia: clinical implications. Int. J. Appl. Psychoanal. Stud. **4**, 144–169 (2007). https://doi.org/10.1002/aps.131

Meiland, F.J.M., et al.: Usability of a new electronic assistive device for community-dwelling persons with mild dementia. Aging Ment. Health **16**, 584–591 (2012). https://doi.org/10.1080/13607863.2011.651433

Evaluating Three Validation-Methods for an Architectural Intervention for Seniors with Dementia in the Empathic Design Framework, a Case Study

L. P. G. van Buuren[✉], M. Mohammadi, and O. Guerra Santin

Department of Built Environment, Eindhoven University of Technology,
Eindhoven, The Netherlands
L.P.G.v.Buuren@tue.nl

Abstract. Designing for seniors with dementia is a difficult task, because they are more dependent on the design of the building in order to perform activities of daily life (ADL). The Empathic Design Framework with the four phases (explore, translate, elaborate, and validate) makes it possible to design a suitable building for this target group. Using this framework, developed and translated design principles need to be implemented and tested in order to validate an architectural intervention which stimulates ADL. In the case study presented in this paper, three methods were used to validate the architectural intervention of door decals: performance-based orientation task (M1), fly-on-the-wall observation (M2), and questionnaire-based interview (M3). This paper presents the evaluation of these three methods in order to discover which method or methods suit best the purpose of validating an architectural intervention. In this study, multiple variables were tested; however, it was not possible to test each variable with every method. Based on this case study, we recommend to choose the application of the methods according to the to be tested variables and the type of behavior that needs to be measured: M1 and M2 are more suitable for the measurement of real behavior change of the target group; while M3 suits well if opinions and the level of acceptance need to be measured.

Keywords: Dementia · Validation-method · Nursing home · Door decals

1 Introduction

Dementia is a general term for a decline in mental ability that is severe enough to interfere with daily life and has symptoms like disorientation [6]. Seniors with dementia in a late stage are not able to live at home anymore in the Netherlands and have to move to a nursing home. The seniors find it hard to adapt to the new environment and get lost often. However, the design of the physical environment can support way finding abilities for this target group [7].

Designing for dementia can be done by following the Empathic Design Framework (EDF) [9]. This framework consists of four phases (explore, translate, elaborate, and validate), and transforms research from rational towards sympathetic. The obtained

© Springer Nature Switzerland AG 2019
R. Brankaert and W. IJsselsteijn (Eds.): D-Lab 2019, CCIS 1117, pp. 24–34, 2019.
https://doi.org/10.1007/978-3-030-33540-3_3

knowledge will be transformed into design principles which are processed in social and spatial context and tested in a case study.

Multiple design principles (cues) on the levels of architectural features and the design of the environment with graphic and verbal information have been drawn in order to stimulate way finding for this target group [7, 12]. Examples of characteristics of these principles for the entrance of the individual room of the resident are: room number, difference in color, portrait photograph, name, memory box, or profiling [1, 3, 5, 7, 10–12, 16]. The design of a door decal – a real size image of a realistic door pasted on a door – is a translation of these principles.

Table 1. Studies using validation-methods for interventions for seniors with dementia

	Aim of the study	Method	Variables	Lay-out experiment	Sample
Gibson et al. [2]	Find out which cues are helpful in the wayfinding process	Performance-based orientation task (resident); Structured interview (resident); Tests of psychological function (resident)	Recognition, successful elements	Only post-IM; Recognition: YES or NO (if NO: repetition of task; if YES: interview); Within one week, eight weeks after intervention	n = 19 residents
Gulwadi [4]	The use and usefulness of memory boxes at the entrance of individual room of resident	Environmental walk-through (researcher); Photo-documentation (researcher); Memory box inventory (researcher); Interviews (care professional)	Recognition, identity, memories	Only post-IM; Three facilities with three different types of memory boxes	n = 109 memory boxes n = 3 interviews (care professionals)
McGilton et al. [8]	The effects on wayfinding abilities and agitation by orientation training	Performance-based orientation task (resident)	Recognition, mood/emotion	Two groups: a control group and a treatment group; Recognition: YES|NO; Three times a week, for four weeks	n = 32 residents
Nolan, et al. [11]	The effect of two external memory aids outside individual room on wayfinding	Performance-based orientation task, with direct observation technique (resident)	Recognition	Pre- and post-IM per person (pre-IM: ±20 measurements| post-IM: ±20 measurements); Recognition: YES|NO (NO if not find room & >3 min); Pre-IMs 5½ weeks and post-IMs 2½ weeks	n = 3 residents

(continued)

Table 1. (*continued*)

	Aim of the study	Method	Variables	Lay-out experiment	Sample
Van Asch et al. [13]	First impressions of added value of true doors (architectural intervention: door decals) of company True Doors	Interviews (care professional and family members)	Feeling of home, wayfinding abilities, mood, memories, group dynamics, atmosphere	Only post-IM; Interviews three weeks after implementation	n = 20 interviews (14 with staff and 6 with family members)
Veldkamp et al. [14]	Effect of landmarks in route instruction in wayfinding abilities	Performance-based orientation task with direct observation technique (resident); Questionnaire (resident)	Navigation error, hesitation (3-point scale), acceptance and attitude (7-point scale) (questionnaire)	Two routes with instructions, ±750 m, 13 decision moments (Route 1: left/right directions|Route 2: landmark directions)	n = 6 residents

Following the EDF, the implemented design principles need to be tested in order to validate the intervention. The question arises how architectural interventions for seniors with dementia in a nursing home can be validated. Table 1 shows an overview of studies of validation-methods for architectural interventions for seniors with dementia. These studies show a variety of methods (e.g. performance-based orientation task and interviews), lay-out of the experiment (pre- and post-intervention measurements (IM), only post-IM, and comparison between groups), sample sizes (between three and 32 residents, and between three and twenty caregivers), and variables (e.g. recognition).

In this case study, the intervention of door decals has been examined by three different methods; chosen based on Table 1 and an additional method of the exploration phase of the EDF. This paper presents the evaluation of these three methods in order to discover which method or methods suits this purpose best.

2   Method

2.1   Introduction to the Case Study

In a short term case study of seven weeks, the intervention of door decals was tested in a controlled, however living environment of a nursing home of one organization by using three methods. A single factor between-subjects design (without and with door decals) has been applied.

The facility contains five psychogeriatric departments (three departments at ground floor level, two at the first floor) with fifteen-eighteen residents per department. The building layout has a structure of a "main" road – where the common living room is situated – with "side" streets – corridors where the residents have their individual rooms; distinguished by soft pastel shades. During the pre-IM, the doors of the individual rooms were equipped by a number, nameplate, a brown color, often a portrait photograph (50/81 rooms), and one door of an individual room was already equipped by a door decal. During the post-IM, the doors of the individual rooms were equipped with a number, nameplate, and a door decal of an image of a front door.

The first step in selecting the door decals was by providing a long list made by the researcher of images of (front) doors on the website Shutterstock, which varied by color, composition, and presence of window openings. The common characteristics were not too much detailing and a Dutch appearance. Second, a shortlist was created in collaboration with a psychologist and caregivers of the organization. Lastly, the order of the door decals was chosen by the researcher with attention to contrast between colors and composition between adjacent doors and the door at the end of the corridor.

Table 2 shows the overview of the tested variables and which methods are used to test the variables.

Table 2. Overview of variables of the case study and assessed by method

Variables				Methods		
Variable	Aspect	Aspect elaboration	Source	M1	M2	M3
Wayfinding abilities	Recognition	*Recognition of the room*	[2, 4, 10, 13]	X	X	X
		Time		X		
		Level of hesitation		X		
Behavior	Wandering vs focused walking	–	–		X	X
Social interaction	Between residents	*Talk*	–		X	X
	Resident and care professional	*Informal interaction*			X	X
		Care-related interaction			X	X
	Resident and informal caregiver	*Informal interaction*			X	X
		Care-related interaction			X	X
Atmosphere	Atmosphere in the corridor	–	[15]			X

2.2   Method 1 (M1): Performance-Based Orientation Task with Direct Observation Technique

The first method applied was performance-based orientation task with direct observation technique [2, 8, 11, 14]. The aim of this method was to determine if the residents were able to find their individual rooms.

The measurement-trials were applied once a week; three weeks of pre-IM and three weeks of post-IM (with a maximum of six measurements per resident during the study). The residents were asked to show their own room, starting from the common living room. The moment when the resident grasped his door know, the resident succeeded the task.

The performance-based orientation tasks were held in all five departments (n = 81 residents). Before the case study started, caregivers selected residents who were able to move around by themselves. Only residents who participated in both pre- and post-IM were included in the analysis of the results (n = 22 residents, Table 3). If the resident did not wanted to participate in the study, the resident did not had to.

The variables in this performance-based orientation task are showed in Table 2. The registration was done by notes, while walking and observing the resident.

2.3 Method 2 (M2): Fly-on-the-Wall Observation

The fly-on-the-wall observation technique with a recognizable outsider was used as a second method within the case study [15]. The aim of this method was to measure the real behavior of residents and care professionals in the corridor.

This method has been applied for six days: three days in pre-IM, and three days in post-IM; from 15:00–20:30 h. During this timeframe, residents show a lot of wandering and restlessness and spend a lot of time in the corridor (based on pre-observations and on the opinion of caregivers of the health care organization).

The observations have been applied in one department of the facility (n = 16 residents, Table 3). This choice was based on: number of residents with high mobility skills, more movement within the facility, the opinion from the caregivers of the facility, and the location on the first floor with less disturbance of multiple people.

The variables in this fly-on-the-wall observation are showed in Table 2. The registration was done using floorplans, pictures, sketches, and notes, while sitting on a chair at the end of the corridor. During the execution of M2, the researcher knew where the residents lived. The researcher counted every time when the residents did one of the tested variables.

2.4 Method 3 (M3): Questionnaire-Based Interview

The third method in this case study was a questionnaire-based interview. The aim of this method was to explore the opinions of the caregivers. This method was applied twice; in week one (pre-IM) and week seven (post-IM).

The questionnaire was distributed by caregivers of all five departments during the pre-IM (n = 16 care professionals). Only caregivers who participated in both pre- and post-IM were included in the analysis of the results (n = 14 caregivers, Table 3).

The variables in this questionnaire are showed in Table 2. The questionnaire contained open and closed questions. The registration was done by a form, mostly using a 7-point Likert-scale.

Table 3. Characteristics participants in case study

Method	Participants	Gender	Age	ZZP	Mobility	Department	Living in facility
M1	Residents	16 women 6 men	Born between 1923 and 1947	19 ZZP5 3 ZZP7	6 walk freely 1 walking stick 12 walker 3 wheelchair	3 in dep. 1 3 in dep. 2 7 in dep. 3 6 in dep. 4 3 in dep. 5	Between two and 54 months
M2	Residents	10 women 6 men	(Unknown)	(Unknown)	5 walk freely 5 walker 6 wheelchair	16 in dep. 5	(Unknown)
M3	Caregivers	13 woman 1 man	(Unknown)	(NA)	(NA)	2 in dep. 1 3 in dep. 2 2 in dep. 3 4 in dep. 4 3 in dep. 5	Working in facility: between less than one year and 27 years

2.5   Ethical Aspects

Participants of M1 were chosen in close collaboration with caregivers of the department. The residents were asked if they wanted to participate in the research and their family was informed via email written by the researcher and sent by the responsible caregiver of the department. During the measurements, the researcher was wearing the same t-shirt as the caregivers and a badge of the organization. The responsible caregiver of the department provided the data on the age, ZZP, department, and time living in the facility of the residents; the data on gender and mobility is obtained by observation.

The choice of the department in M2 is elaborated in Sect. 2.3. The family of the residents and the caregivers themselves were notified on the research activities via email written by the researcher and sent by the responsible caregiver of the facility. The researcher was wearing "normal" clothes and a badge of the organization. The residents and family had conversations with the researcher, and the researcher identified herself as a researcher during these conversations. Data on gender, mobility and the room of the participants was obtained by observation.

During pre-IM, the researcher approached all working employees at that day if they wanted to participate during M3. The participants were notified the research beforehand by email from the researcher and the manager, and face to face. The participants knew the researcher, who was wearing "normal" clothes and a badge of the organization. Data on gender, age, which department and time working at the department was provided by the participants themselves on the response form.

The participants in this study were not asked to sign a consent form, but they were always informed on the research taking place and participation was voluntary.

3   Data-Analysis and Results

The obtained data of the three validation-methods have been analyzed, using statistical t-tests (Table 4) and chi-square tests. The results of M2 are, at this stage, only shown in percentages. Unfortunately, almost none of the results are statistically significant, which could be caused by the small sample size. However, the following paragraphs describe some trends.

3.1   Wayfinding Abilities

The recognition of their room was tested by the three validation-methods. Based on the average of all participants, we can conclude that there was no difference between measured pre- and post-IM with method M1 ($X^2(2) = 0.53$, Not Significant; and based on the percentages of residents finding their room: both pre- and post-IM of 82%); a small increase was found during post-IM of recognizing their own room with M2 (during pre-IM 41% residents entered their own room when entering a room, to 58% during post-IM), and a small decrease during post-IM with M3 (Table 4). The expectations measured with M3 were higher than the actual result (Table 4). The results on the time spending locating their room measured with M1 show a trend of a small decrease (Table 4), meaning that residents found their room a little bit faster. In addition, a trend based on the results of the level of hesitation measured with M1 show that residents had more confidence in finding their room during post-IM (Table 4).

3.2   Behavior

The behavior of the residents, in the form of wandering versus focused walking, was measured with M2 and M3. The results of M2 show a small increase of wandering during post-IM (76% of movement in the corridor by residents during pre-IM was wandering behavior, to 83% during post-IM), while the trend of the results of M3 (the opinion of the caregiver) show no difference ($X^2(2) = 0.00$, Not Significant).

3.3   Social Interaction

The variable social interaction was measured by M2 and M3. A trend of social interaction between residents in the form of a conversation measured by M2 and M3 do not show a difference (37% of interaction between residents were conversations during pre-IM, to 38% post-IM; Table 4). However, caregivers expected that the door decals would have led to more interaction in the corridor (Table 4). Results of M2 do show that during post-IM more moments of contact were reported (an average of 33 moments during pre-IM, to 45 post-IM). Trends of social interaction between residents and caregivers show by M2 an increase of care-related contact during post-IM (12% of the moments of contact was care-related during pre-IM, to 47% post-IM), while a small decrease, both care-related and informal contact and in expectations by M3 can be seen (Table 4). Social interaction between residents and informal caregivers do show a trend in M2 of a decrease of informal contact (100% pre-IM, to 97% post-IM), and a small increase of this type of interaction in M3 (Table 4).

During all three methods, quotes of residents, caregivers and informal caregivers about the door decals have been noted. Some examples are: *"I like that green door, do you?"*, *"You live behind the yellow door"*, '*a resident tried to ring a doorbell, he thought that they were real*', and '*a resident noticed that all the doors were painted, which was very well done. However, at a 'worn out' door, she joked that the paint had run out*'.

3.4   Atmosphere

The variable atmosphere was only measured by M3. A trend can be seen that the caregivers experienced a small increase of a positive atmosphere in the corridor after the door decals were implemented (Table 4). However, the results of the expectation and the real experience on the question if the door decals would have a positive influence on the atmosphere showed no difference (Table 4).

Table 4. Statistical results using t-test

Method	Variable	Aspect	Mean		n	r	df
			Pre-IM	Post-IM			
M1	Wayfinding abilities	Time (unit: seconds)	80,2	70,2	19	0,69	18
		Hesitation[1]	5,8	6,2	19	0,23*	18
M3	Wayfinding abilities	Recognition[1]	3,9	3,6	14	0,32	13
		Recognition expectations[1]	4,2	2,9	14	0,09**	13
	Social interaction	Between residents (chat)[1]	3,4	3,4	14	0,48	13
		Between residents (expectation)[1]	4,1	3,7	14	0,02	13
		Resident-care (informal)[1]	4,6	4,5	13	0,61	12
		Resident-care (care related)[1]	4,6	4,4	13	0,51	12
		Resident-care (expectation)[1]	4,5	4,4	14	−0,24	13
		Resident-inform. care (informal)[1]	4,2	4,4	13	0,33	12
		Resident-inform. care (care related)[1]	3,5	2,8	13	0,42*	12
		Resident-inform. care (expectation)[1]	4,6	4,6	14	−0,14	13
	Atmosphere	Atmosphere in the corridor[1]	4,1	4,6	14	0,06	13
		Atmosphere in the corridor (expectation)[1]	4,8	4,8	14	0,19	13

Notes: [1] 7-point likert scale; * < 0,05; ** < 0,01

Caregivers were asked to describe the atmosphere in the corridor during pre- and post-IM in M3. During pre-IM, descriptions such as 'dull', 'monotonous', and 'nice' were mentioned. While during post-IM, descriptions such as 'more domestic', 'more flowery', and 'a little busy' were mentioned. In addition, the caregivers reported that some of the doors were not matched properly for the specific resident.

4   Discussion

A number of limitations were found in the methods followed in this study. The first limitation is the level of active involvement of the residents and informal caregivers by selecting and implementing the door decals. It is recommended to involve the residents and the informal caregivers actively in this processes in order to shape a better relationship with the researcher and the level of acceptance.

A limitation on the effectiveness and impact of the door decals is the short timeframe of the study. The study only took place within seven weeks, with one week of time for the residents to adapt to the intervention. A recommendation on the short term study is to extend this adoption time and have a follow up study a couple of months later in order to measure long term effects.

The sample size is the next limitation. The sample size is rather small; only 22/81 residents participated in this study, one department have been observed, and fourteen interviews has been carried out. In addition, the participating residents were in quite good shape and had the capabilities to go independently to their own room. The amount of measurements is also rather small.

A limitation of M2 is the possibility of the Hawthorn effect [15]. During this case study, this was solved by the researcher by staying for a long time at the same place. It would be a possibility to observe the real behavior – avoiding the Hawthorn effect – by using sensor-based technology (for example sensors in the door and wearables for entering a room, or facial recognition to measure the mood).

In order to carry out this kind of studies, it is important that the health care organization – both management as well as the caregiver – supports the researcher. The top-down importance can be found in financing the door decals, the relationship between management and caregivers, relationship with the client council, "approving" that this case study is allowed to be carried out, and provides integrity to the researcher. The bottom-up importance is shown in the willingness to help the researcher, and participating in the interviews. It is important as a researcher to make yourself visible and clear.

5   Conclusion

Using the four phases of the Empathic Design Framework, it is possible to design a suitable building for seniors with dementia. The fourth phase is the validation phase. The aim of this study was to evaluate three validation-methods to examine an architectural intervention (in this case study: door decals) for seniors with dementia in an inpatient residential health care facility. The methods in this case study were:

performance-based orientation task (M1), fly-on-the-wall observation (M2), and interview by questionnaire (M3).

The results showed that the intervention did not have a statistical significant effect on the variables measured (except for three variables). However, as mentioned in the discussion, this could be caused by the small sample size or timeframe of the intervention. Comparing the results of the methods and the variables, the results show that a difference can be found in the measured real behavior of the residents (M1 and M2) and the opinions of the caregivers about the behavior of the residents (M3) in the variables of recognition (wayfinding abilities), wandering vs focused (behavior), and care-related interaction between residents and caregivers and informal interaction between residents and informal caregivers (social interaction).

The three methods are compared on four aspects: variables tested, participants, real behavior vs expected behavior, and time (Table 5).

Table 5. Comparison of the three methods

| Aspects | Methods | | |
	M1	M2	M3
Variables tested	A very specific task makes it possible to measure only a couple of variables	Registration of all activities makes it possible to measure a large number of variables	The questions and length of the questionnaire makes it possible to measure a large number of variables
Participants	Involving residents	Involving residents	Involving caregivers, asking questions regarding the perspective of the resident
Real behavior vs expected behavior	Measures real behavior	Measures real behavior	Measures opinions of the participants (expected behavior)
Time (using a three-point scale; the more +, the more time it costs)	Preparation: ++ Actual performance: ++ Analysis: ++	Preparation: + Actual performance: +++ Analysis: +++	Preparation: +++ Actual performance: + Analysis: ++

Based on the case study the following recommendation can be given. In order to measure the real behavioral change of the target group, M1 and M2 work best in comparison to M3, because M3 measures opinions which can be wrong or biased. M3 only measures the perspectives of the target group, which are valuable if you want to know their acceptance of the architectural intervention. M2 requires a lot of time, but provides insights in real behavior over a longer timespan during a day (and also over weeks). Another recommendation is to enlarge the sample size in order to run statistical tests to measure a statistical significant effect. The sample size of M3 can be enlarged easier and less time consuming, than the enlargement of the sample size of M1. To conclude, the application of the methods depends on the chosen variables and the type of behavior that needs to be measured.

Acknowledgments. This research was supported by RSZK ZorgProfessionals.

References

1. Day, K., Carreon, D., Stump, C.: The therapeutic design of environments for people with dementia: a review of the empirical research. Gerontologist **40**(4), 397–416 (2000)
2. Gibson, M.C., MacLean, J., Borrie, M., Geiger, J.: Orientation behaviors in residents relocated to a redesigned dementia care unit. Am. J. Alzheimer's Dis. Other Dementias® **19**(1), 45–49 (2004)
3. Gross, J., et al.: Recognition of self among persons with dementia: Pictures versus names as environmental supports. Environ. Behav. **36**(3), 424–454 (2004)
4. Gulwadi, G.B.: Establishing continuity of self-memory boxes in dementia facilities for older adults: Their use and usefulness. J. Hous. Elderly **27**(1–2), 105–119 (2013)
5. Innes, A., Kelly, F., Dincarslan, O.: Care home design for people with dementia: What do people with dementia and their family carers value? Aging Mental Health **15**(5), 548–556 (2011)
6. Jonker, C., Slaets, J.P.J., Verhey, F.R.J.: Handboek dementie. Laatste inzichten in diagnostiek en behandeling (2009)
7. Marquardt, G.: Wayfinding for people with dementia: a review of the role of architectural design. HERD: Health Environ. Res. Des. J. **4**(2), 75–90 (2011)
8. McGilton, K.S., Rivera, T.M., Dawson, P.: Can we help persons with dementia find their way in a new environment? Aging Ment. Health **7**(5), 363–371 (2003)
9. Mohammadi, M.: Empathische woonomgeving (2017)
10. Namazi, K., Johnson, B.: Physical environmental cues to reduce the problems of incontinence in Alzheimer's disease units. Am. J. Alzheimer's Care Rel. Disord. Res. **6**(6), 22–28 (1991)
11. Nolan, B.A.D., Mathews, R.M., Harrison, M.: Using external memory aids to increase room finding by older adults with dementia. Am. J. Alzheimer's Dis. Other Dementias **16**(4), 251–254 (2001)
12. Passini, R., Pigot, H., Rainville, C., Tétreault, M.H.: Wayfinding in a nursing home for advanced dementia of the Alzheimer's type. Environ. Behav. **32**(5), 684–710 (2000)
13. Van Asch, I., Voorhaar, M., Willemse, B.: Het verhaal achter de deur. Een verkennende studie naar de toegevoegde waarde van true doors voor bewoners van zorginstellingen. Trimbos-Instituut, Utrecht (2015)
14. Veldkamp, D., Hagethorn, F., Kröse, B., De Greef, P.: The use of visual landmarks in a wayfinding system for elderly with beginning dementia. Global Telemedicine and eHealth Updates: Knowledge Resources, pp. 48–51. Luxembourg: Luxexpo (2008)
15. Zeisel, J.: Inquiry by Design: Tools for Environmental-Behavior Research. Cambridge University Press, Cambridge (1981)
16. Zeisel, J., Silverstein, N.M., Hyde, J., Levkoff, S., Lawton, M.P., Holmes, W.: Environmental correlates to behavioral outcomes in Alzheimer's special care units. Gerontologist **43**(5), 697–711 (2003)

'Build Your Story': A Research Game That Includes Older Adults' Perspectives

Susan van Hees[✉][iD], Meriam Janssen[iD], and Katrien Luijkx[iD]

Tranzo Department, Scientific Center for Care and Welfare, Tilburg University,
PO Box 90153, 5000LE Tilburg, The Netherlands
s.v.vanhees@uu.nl

Abstract. Insight in older adults' own ideals, ideas and experiences is crucial to enable meaningful applied research activities. To increase and enable older adults' perspectives to be heard in academic research, innovative methods are needed. This research presents an analysis of a newly developed research game called 'Build your story'. The aim of designing this game was to develop an innovative, participatory methodology that enables the collection of stories that older adults share about their daily life experiences, ideas and ideals. These are considered important input in setting and renewing a research agenda that attunes to older adults' perspectives on what is important in their life. The game was tested in individual and group sessions with older adults with and without dementia. Despite critique on the design and use, observations and experiences also demonstrate a different method allows different stories to be told. Positive questions and associations offer opportunities for dialogue.

Keywords: Older adults · Ageing · Social design · Research methods · Research agenda · Public engagement · Participation

1 Introduction

In this paper, we present a research game called 'Build Your Story' (in Dutch: '*Bouw Je Verhaal*'). This game, developed in collaboration between researchers and a designer, aims to include (frail) older adults' perspectives concerning their daily lives and needs via novel research activities. Within research and policy, the importance of including the voices of citizens, patients, clients, consumers, and users—also referred to as 'the public'—is being increasingly emphasised, as has been demonstrated by Nielsen and Langstrup (2018), among other researchers. Although there exist various ideas regarding what involvement means, including the public's voice is considered valuable in policymaking as well as a great variety of practices (e.g., knowledge making). However, the practice of including the public's voices (i.e., those of users and potential users) is not self-evident, specifically not when this public consists of frail older adults who are living in nursing homes and dealing with health conditions that possibly constrain their participation opportunities, such as feeling insecure or unable to stress what they consider to be important.

© Springer Nature Switzerland AG 2019
R. Brankaert and W. IJsselsteijn (Eds.): D-Lab 2019, CCIS 1117, pp. 35–47, 2019.
https://doi.org/10.1007/978-3-030-33540-3_4

Within the Academic Collaborative Centre for Older Adults of Tilburg University, care organisations and researchers working at the Department Tranzo of Tilburg University structurally collaborate on applied research projects. Together, they aim to contribute towards improving the quality of person-centred care for older adults. In studying care for older adults, we focus on those living in residential care both with and without dementia.

It is important that we attune the research activities—beginning with the research agenda—according to what older adults themselves consider important. Aside from their demonstrated value, the existing participation methods and tools nevertheless pose limitations. Most solely focus on exploring specific health- and care-related aspects, (e.g., surveys, observations) while participants are not merely care-recipients. Thereby they often draw on participants' verbal capabilities (e.g., interviews, focus groups). In aiming to engage older adults in research practices, various scholars in the health and social sciences have explored methods for engaging this population more actively by, for instance, creating opportunities for 'partnership' or 'delegated power' (Abma and Broerse 2010; Hook 2006). Participation via these methods demands that the participants possess certain skills, including the ability to verbally share their own perspectives. The partnership method even requires that participants become 'empowered' whilst participating. Rather than focusing on empowering older adults to engage in our research activities, we might be able to explore their perspectives by adjusting these activities according to their capabilities. In this paper, we describe how we have aimed to design a research game as a fun, interactive, accessible method for exploring what really matters to a variety of older adults. However, we shall firstly provide an overview of some literature related to participation, public engagement, and design derived from a variety of research streams. This overview is important for the analysis of the game we have developed and will help indicate the opportunities and challenges associated with giving individual voices to the perspectives of the (frail) older adults involved in our research, which can help to come to a more representative voice eventually.

2 Background

Within studies that focus on social, health, and ageing aspects, participation and co-creation in knowledge making are considered to be increasing in importance. It is assumed that engaging the public will help researchers achieve a more thorough understanding of older adults' individual perspectives. Many facilitators of and barriers to public engagement have been distinguished, which also apply to the engagement of older adults—especially those living in residential care (Backhouse et al. 2016). Time and funds, trust and strong relationships, ethical concerns, and ageist stereotypes are merely a few elements that affect the public's engagement.

The practice of involving users (and non-users) for the development of all kinds of technologies is elaborately described in science and technology studies (e.g., Oudshoorn and Pinch 2003). In recent decades, many participatory techniques have been developed with the aim of engaging users. Story-telling techniques are often used in co-design (Kankainen et al. 2012). Stories about possible scenarios, such as an example of issues faced in the house when ageinge, help users to link their experiences, memories, and dreams as they can recognise or relate to these (Sanders 2001). Designers thereby search for opportunities to include experiences that offer insights about the past, present, and future alike (Buskermolen and Terken 2012). Cultural probes (e.g., diaries, cameras) collect stories that are later interpreted by a designer or scholar, while fictional and customer stories create dialogues. In the past, within science and society, various tools have been employed to collect data. Guggenheim et al. (2013) instructed their participants to build scenarios in a sandbox while studying disaster scenarios, while Lego developed its worldwide-implemented Serious Play facilitation methodology to experiment and test ideas within organisations (James 2013). Brandt (2006) compares several exploratory games to find a 'repertoire of possibilities', describing how winning is rarely important (or even possible) in game design and that the kind of materials that are used are less important than what the materials actually create, which is ideally 'a common ground that people can relate to'.

Within participatory design, researchers emphasise the importance of a participatory mindset when involving (future) users in the research and development process of new tools and techniques (Sanders and Stappers 2008). In working on a suitable method for individuals with dementia, Suijkerbuijk et al. (2014) distinguish the following elements of user-centred design lessons that are valuable for our project, as well: (1) in developing (and assessing) a qualitative user-centred research method, a dynamic design that allows various input types because it offers users a sense of control (Bartlett 2012; Nygård 2006); (2) activities that may be split up (to reduce the burden [time and energy wise] for users) and that offer users various opportunities for providing their own input (In the toolkit designed by Suijkerbuijk et al. (2014), the researchers included opportunities for adding written, spoken, and photographed materials.); (3) activities that contribute meaningful contexts (i.e., real situations that matter to each user); (4) questions that are clear, unambiguous, and future directed; and (5) a game-like appearance, which creates an informal setting and a more relaxed experience wherein participants do not feel they are being tested.

In a literature review on participatory design in gerontechnology, Merkel and Kucharski (2018) propose that four levels of (future) users' engagement may be distinguished—none, low, medium, and full—rather than the classic distinctions that are based on Arnstein's (1969) ladder of participation, which involves a participant, an advisor, and a decision maker. Full involvement herein means older adults equally participate in all stages of for instance a policymaking process and are able to actively influence this process. At a low level of involvement, older adults are solely asked about their preferences or are followed through observational study, while a medium level of involvement indicates they are involved in one or multiple stages in which they are able to influence the overall process.

Merkel and Kucharski (2018) argue that full engagement might be considered the most democratic and transparent of the four levels and is thereby the most preferable variant, although recruiting participants who opt for full engagement is not always manageable or feasible. The authors exclude, for instance, individuals who are cognitively limited or impaired due to various challenges associated with participation, although they do emphasise that these voices should not be excluded in future designs.

3 Methodology

Qualitative research methods (e.g., interviews, focus groups, observations) are important to explore and should involve older adults' perspectives, although some are not able or willing to participate via these methods. Interviews and focus groups are primarily based on respondents' verbal capabilities, while observations depend on an outsider's interpretations. To include a more diverse population, new research methods are needed. In co-creation with a social designer, a research game was developed to encourage and enable frail older adults to share stories about whatever they believe is important in their daily lives and in relation to ageing. In this paper, we describe and reflect upon the research game and its opportunities for increasing public engagement and participation in research.

We developed and tested the research game 'Build Your Story' (in Dutch: 'Bouw Je Verhaal') that was designed as a creative research method. During development, we tested the game with individuals and groups; an overview of the different test sessions is detailed in Table 1. During the test sessions, we explored older adults' perspectives concerning what they consider to be important in their daily lives, and these test sessions provide input for this paper in the form of seven observations/interviews and four focus group discussions; additional details about the game are discussed in the following Sect. 4. All test sessions were audio-recorded and (partly) transcribed. In addition to the recordings and transcriptions, the researchers took notes both during and directly after each session. In our analysis, we focus on how the research game enabled our participants to share their stories as well as the various types of stories the game provoked compared to conventional methods.

The Ethical Review Board of Tilburg University approved the design for this study under number EC-2017.88. Informed consent was acquired from all participants prior to each research activity, while their consent was verbally reaffirmed during the activities.

Table 1. Overview of test sessions.

Test session	Number of participants, gender	Location	Duration
1 (day 1)	1 female	Resident of care centre	0:20
2 (day 1)	1 male and 1 female (no couple)	Residents of care centre	0:48
3 (day 1)	1 female	Resident of care centre	0:41
4 (day 1)	1 male	Resident of care centre, verbally impaired due to Parkinson's disease	0:47
5 (day 2)	1 female	Visitor of daycare for people w. cognitive impairments	0:49
6 (day 2)	1 female	Visitor of daycare for people w. cognitive impairments	0:35

(*continued*)

Table 1. (*continued*)

Test session	Number of participants, gender	Location	Duration
7 (day 2)	1 female	Resident of care centre, participating in activities for people w. cognitive impairments	0:42
8 (group 1)	2 female, 3 male (4 of them with their informal caregiver)	Innovate Dementia Network, including people with dementia, their informal caregivers and several (not-participating) coordinators and project-members of the Network	0:42
9 (group 2)	5 female	Daycare activity for people living at home, with and without cognitive impairments	1:17
10 (group 3	5 female	Activity for residents of a care centre	1:27
11 (group 4)	3 female, 1 male	Activity for residents of a care centre, with and without cognitive impairments	1:24

4 'Build Your Story': A Research Game

We collaborated with a social designer for this project, as social designers respond to both the world and the challenges within the world. These individuals are playing an increasingly important role in finding solutions to societal challenges, as they are able to contribute refreshing perspectives by approaching societal matters differently than researchers (Suijkerbuijk et al. 2014) and the public. We asked the designer to create 'something' that could help collect untold stories about people's daily life experiences, ideas, and ideals. These stories should extract insights regarding what older adults consider important and subsequently more closely attune our research to what these individuals believe truly matters.

The design of 'Build Your Story' (see Fig. 1) commenced from a mixture of the designer's previous experiences, the assignment formulated by the research project team, and ideas within social design about imagination and associative thinking. An important criterion was that the tool should eventually be able to collect insights into the many different topics on which we are focusing, which can be roughly categorised using the following descriptions: (1) person-centred care for older adults, including self-management and autonomy; (2) improved quality of care for older adults; (3) social networks and social needs; and (4) meaningful applications of technology. The 'Build Your Story' design includes (1) positive questions that allow participants to dream, (2) construction sites (i.e., game boards), and (3) a set of building blocks; an example of a positive question is 'what does your favourite day look like?' The grids on the game boards are abstract illustrations of a map, a balance board, a timeline, and a totem pole (see Fig. 2)—the idea being that participants may use these grids as a base to build their story on.

Fig. 1. Photographs of final design and a participant

Fig. 2. The different designs on the game board: a map, a balance, a timeline and a totem pole/circle. Design by Malou van Dijck.

All sets of building blocks contain a great variety of blocks in several (and unusual) shapes made from leather, wood, and epoxy. This mixture of materials and shapes was designed to induce participants' associative thinking abilities; for instance, when choosing more common shapes, such as a heart or a star, participants would be more inclined to choose shapes that do not need interpretation or explanation, thereby limiting associative thinking. Through this design—combined with the positive questions we formulated—our participants were invited to interpret the materials in whatever way worked most effectively for them. The availability of a construction set is expected to invite people to build, and as such, the capabilities of all potential participants were considered when designing the set of blocks; for instance, usability must be carefully considered for individuals with tremors, which could hinder their ability to build using the tools provided.

5 Findings

By testing the research game with a variety of older adults, we distinguished some interesting dynamics throughout each test session. We identified an ambiguity between what participants reported of their experiences with this research game and what we actually observed. Most participants emphasised that they enjoyed participating but that they would have given similar answers in an interview or focus group design. Notably, we observed how our design enabled the telling of new stories and the engaging of dialogues.

The participants were instructed to use the provided blocks to build their ideal day, their favorite route, their most valued relationships, and a personal robot that may perform any function they desire'. While building their favourite days, routes, relations, and robots, these older adults demonstrated and shared some of their expectations related to ageing while simultaneously emphasising how their ideals are being increasingly constrained by health-related barriers. During the first test session, we asked a woman to build her favourite walking route, to which she replied that she actually did not like to walk, but that she had always enjoyed bicycling—specifically on a route she used to take to visit her children. When we asked her to visualise her route by building it with the blocks, she focussed on elements other than her children's homes; rather, she zoomed in on the green and built environment, including a viaduct, a soccer venue, a swimming pool, and some surrounding factories. Furthermore, while building her route, she mentioned additional visits, and an excerpt from a dialogue between this participant and the designer is detailed below:

Participant: '*on the way back I went via place, I cycled all day long, via [the houses of] my daughter and son*'
Designer: '*and is it just the route, because you are now giving us all these specific mark points...were the people the most important part of the route, or the route itself, or is it...?*'
Participant: '*the route itself, but yes, also the people, and, like, when I went to my sister['s home] and the car was not there, it meant she was not home*' [T1].

Another woman used the balance board to elaborate upon the three most important relationships in her life by distinguishing them as elements. The main element was her husband, her 'pillar', next to whom she envisioned her sibling and her former general practitioner. She referred to 'a specific life event' that induced this third relationship; although she appreciated her close friends, they were not included in the important relationships symbolised with the blocks. As a follow-up, the woman built her favourite route, a four-day walking event that she had finished several times after surviving cancer. This route symbolised her being a survivor: '*I have had breast cancer. That* [pointing to a block] *is the half that is missing. In December 10th '85* [refers to the operation date] [silence].. *in July '86, I walked the first Four Days March. And I have done that each year since, if it was possible. And that is—was—for me, very important—something that I could accomplish every year again*' (T3). The people she valued most, including the general practitioner and his wife, played important roles in this annual adventure (Fig. 4).

Fig. 3. Photograph of "finding my way out of this maze"

During the first test day, a man and another woman insisted upon testing the game together. They decided to share a board, and both started building their favourite days, which they eventually found out diverged tremendously. The woman seemed happy with her current situation and her daily routines, while the man missed the aspects that he was no longer able to hold onto. The man talked about his partner's impairments, due to which they could no longer enjoy their favourite activity: making city trips. He explained that he hated the daily routines where he lived, with every day being similar to the previous or the next and with co-residents who solely talked about the weather or their (grand)children. Due to his inability to have children (he and his partner were a homosexual couple), he felt he had nothing in common with the other residents. A 'good day' contained some bustle, which was however impossible because his partner's condition required routine. The woman worried instead about the planned renovation of her apartment, due to which she would need to move for some time; this impending event made her feel out of balance.

The 'good day' question also led to a dialogue about different perspectives during a session with five residents of a care centre, one of whom immediately started reminiscing about a visit to a theme park with relatives earlier in the year. She shared how grateful she was for the experience and how she cherished the positive memories. Although she was visually impaired and needed a wheelchair for this visit, she believed being able to go was wonderful in itself, and she had genuinely enjoyed all the perks that accompanied her handicap; for instance, an attraction was paused while she was let on and she received priority access to attractions for which one normally has to queue. Another participant responded that she thought it was naive and meaningless to think back on 'good days': *'let's be honest, we all suffer from being incontinent and how much we may want to go out. We don't go because then we need to bring a pile of "inleggers"* [incontinence materials] *and who wants that?'* (T10). Conversely, the previous participant replied that these very materials enabled her to have the wonderful day she described (Fig. 5).

Fig. 4. Photograph of building stories, re-building and building on stories

Later that morning, we asked each participant to build a robot that would do anything he/she wanted. A sceptical 99-year-old woman replied she would not participate; she did not like robots because she believed they were stupid and dangerous. As moderators, we emphasised that her robot could do whatever she wanted it to do; when she observed the other women building and talking about their ideal robots—those that helped with housekeeping or helped them get to their favourite places—the sceptical participant built one herself and explained that her robot would not be able to do anything because she detested the idea of having a robot in her home (Fig. 5).

Fig. 5. Photographs of test-session: overview, building a good day and a robot (T.ID)

During the test with the experienced focus group (Innovate Dementia). The Innovate Dementia project involves focus groups with people who have dementia, supported by their informal caregivers, who test and evaluate novel ideas and technologies, they or other people with dementia might benefit from. Innovate Dementia has been described elaborately by Van den Kieboom et al. (2019). After a short warming-up, participants were asked to choose to either build their favourite route or the robot. One man chose the robot assignment and quickly collected three blocks that he had used to present himself earlier on: a green block to represent his favourite colour and motorcycle, a purple block for his wife, and a yellow block because he and his wife were 'a sunny couple'. With these three blocks, he was able to reveal a lot about himself with very few resources. His ideal robot would make each day a sunny day, and when his wife suggested that the robot help him remember past experiences, he considered that aspect less important.

Fig. 6. Photograph of 'a sunny couple' and 'let the sun shine'

Participants found elaborating upon specific elements difficult, mainly when we wanted to learn what was needed to improve their daily life experiences. To explore opportunities for improvement, we added some so-called disruption questions. Inspired by Guggenheim et al. (2013), we introduced the questions 'what could have gone wrong?' and 'how could this be solved?' While discussing 'a good day', participants mentioned occasions in which living in a care centre was rather negative. The year prior, they had experienced a period of quarantine, during which time they were unable to leave and the professionals had looked like 'moon walkers' in their protective suits. Finding a care solution without these suits was one opportunity the participants mentioned for improvement.

Our findings demonstrate the opportunities that the research game offers for gaining new and valuable insights into what older adults believe is important. We determined how participants with dementia or cognitive impairments immediately started to build, many of whom came up with interesting creations. Although some claimed building their answers was impossible, they nevertheless demonstrated the opposite. When talking about how and what they had built, they shared ideas related to the original question, elaborated on their thoughts and also shared how the assignment made them feel (for instance excited, insecure, enthusiastic). In group sessions the assignments led to dialogues between participants, while in individual sessions participants either were enthusiastic in visualising elements of their lives, or were enabled by the set to talk about other things. We also tested the set with a man who was unable to speak, and although he needed a tablet to explain what he built, we were able to 'discuss' several topics he found important.

Adjustments and further developments are clearly needed to address the following challenges. (1) A verbal (or written) back-story is necessary to understand the stories being built. (2) A 'game' is normally accompanied by rules, and some participants got lost when determining how to 'play'. They tried to 'fix' the game as they would a puzzle or a riddle (e.g., *'I just want to get out of this maze'* (Fig. 3)), while some believed it was a psychological test. (3) Not every participant liked the design, and some participants mentioned they needed more realistic elements to be able to build their stories because the design was 'childish' or, as one participant asserted, *'this is not real'* [T11]. One man admitted the board made him feel nervous, and he wanted *'to get out of this maze* [on the board] *as soon as possible'* [T8]. (4) The game's context and introduction are crucial for getting participants in the right mood. Some participants felt insecure and expressed that they felt they were unsure whether or not they were doing the activities 'right'; for example, on the second test day, when we asked one participant what she thought of the totem pole-building assignment, she expressed: *'eh, well, I did not really like it because I was afraid I would not do the right thing'* [T6], while another woman responded that she truly enjoyed building, and that *'if it was up to me, they could add another 100 blocks'* [T7].

6 Conclusion and Discussion

We developed and tested an innovative research game to explore and share various perspectives on ageing and ageing research based on older adults' daily life experiences, ideas, and ideals. 'Build Your Story' was created to unravel voices that have not yet been heard, especially those of individuals who are 'hard to reach' for a variety of reasons (Dewar 2005).

We endeavoured to eradicate as many barriers as possible, although the materials do represent the world in their own way—both in themselves and in relation to the questions asked. Our agenda to explore older adults' perspectives is embedded in the game's themes and questions. Although the game can be re-used and adjusted for other purposes, it is not value free. Participants and scholars alike formulate their own interpretations of the game, their own emotions towards the game—including excitement (due to an interesting activity) or suspicion ('am I being tested?')—as well as expectations and assumptions about new insights contributed by older adults' perspectives. 'Build Your Story' succeeds in provoking participants' curiosity and allows them to participate without requiring any prior preparation or training. Although not everyone liked the idea of building their own story, almost all participants did so anyway, thus demonstrating their ability to participate via this research game. For the game's further development, tinkering with the materials and questions will be necessary, and additional data will help us formulate a method for analysing and interpreting the data more systematically.

There were many arguments in favour of involving older adults earlier on in the design process, but we consciously chose to test the game with users after our prototypes had been developed. Moreover, we experienced how older adults often find difficulty expressing what they believe is important when they are not presented with example responses.

Previous studies have demonstrated difficulties associated with giving a voice to frail groups; for instance, Backhouse et al. (2016) provide an overview of barriers and facilitators distinguished in the review of a group of research participants from an elderly care home. In addition, a variety of scholars have described how giving a voice to people in general and marginalised groups in particular (e.g., older adults) is accompanied by the construction of new realities and meanings (Pols 2014; Voß and Simons 2018). However, this difficulty does not mean we should avoid giving a voice to the wider public, but rather that we must do so carefully and whilst remaining aware of the new worlds we consequently create. We would ultimately like to argue that scientific practices are inevitable for making heard the voices of older adults. By encouraging and enabling people to get involved, we also intervene in their daily practices by, for instance, asking them to reflect upon specific themes related to their life experiences . Moreover, we co-construct the world in a way different from how it has been represented thus far (Voß and Simons 2018).

Our findings demonstrate that this different research method proves interesting due to the alternative types of stories it provokes; although some participants hesitated, they eventually started to associate and build (both literally and verbally) their stories differently than they would in conventional interviews—that is, with more detail and in a more explorative way, taking time for the stories they actually wanted to tell. While in interviews and focus groups participants respond immediately, the research game allowed our participants to consider and construct their answers more thoughtfully. Furthermore, the design materials evoked associations by, for instance, influencing a female participant to alter her ideal day while building it, thus demonstrating how 'playing with' the materials can lead to new stories. Although other creative methods are already in use (e.g., Lego Serious Play), we consider our game's ability to provoke participants' open-mindedness' a strength. Although not everyone can be included in research via a single method, we must endeavour to provoke diverse perspectives when representing older adults as 'the public' (cf. Dewey 1991 [1927]) and when unravelling matters of concern that have not yet been addressed. Since perspectives are always dynamic and are affected by the contexts and backgrounds in which they are formed, this game's repeated use can play a reflective role on both an individual level and a group level.

NOTE: Codes used in this paper refer to the sessions listed in the table T1 is test session 1, T2 is test session 2 et cetera.

References

Abma, T., Broerse, J.: Patient participation as dialogue: setting research agendas. Health Expect. **13**, 160–173 (2010)

Arnstein, S.R.: A ladder of citizen participation. J. Am. Inst. Plan. **35**(4), 216–224 (1969)

Backhouse, T., Kenkmann, A., Lane, K., Penhale, B., Poland, F., Killett, A.: Older care-home residents as collaborators or advisors in research: a systematic review. Age Ageing **45**(3), 337–345 (2016)

Bartlett, R.: Modifying the diary interview method to research the lives of people with dementia. Qual. Health Res. **22**(12), 1717–1726 (2012)

Brandt, E.: Designing exploratory design games: a framework for participation in participatory design? In: Proceedings of the Ninth Conference on Participatory Design: Expanding Boundaries in Design, vol. 1, pp. 57–66. ACM, August 2006

Buskermolen, D.O., Terken, J.: Co-constructing stories: a participatory design technique to elicit in-depth user feedback and suggestions about design concepts. In: Proceedings of the 12th Participatory Design Conference: Exploratory Papers, Workshop Descriptions, Industry Cases, vol. 2, pp. 33–36. ACM, August 2012

Dewar, B.J.: Beyond tokenistic involvement of older people in research–a framework for future development and understanding. J. Clin. Nurs. **14**, 48–53 (2005)

Dewey, J.: The Public and Its Problems. Swallow Press, Ohio University Press, Athens (1991 [1927])

Guggenheim, M., Kraeftner, B., Kroell, J.: 'I don't know whether I need a further level of disaster': shifting media of sociology in the sandbox. Distinktion Scand. J. Soc. Theory **14**(3), 284–304 (2013)

Hook, M.L.: Partnering with patients–a concept ready for action. J. Adv. Nurs. **56**(2), 133–143 (2006)

James, A.R.: Lego Serious Play: a three-dimensional approach to learning development. J. Learn. Dev. High. Educ. (6) (2013)

Kankainen, A., Vaajakallio, K., Kantola, V., Mattelmäki, T.: Storytelling group–a co-design method for service design. Behav. Inf. Technol. **31**(3), 221–230 (2012)

Merkel, S., Kucharski, A.: Participatory design in gerontechnology: a systematic literature review. Gerontologist **59**, e16–c25 (2018)

Nielsen, K.D., Langstrup, H.: Tactics of material participation: how patients shape their engagement through e-health. Soc. Stud. Sci. **48**(2), 259–282 (2018)

Nygård, L.: How can we get access to the experiences of people with dementia? Suggestions and reflections. Scand. J. Occup. Ther. **13**(2), 101–112 (2006)

Pols, J.: Knowing patients: turning patient knowledge into science. Sci. Technol. Hum. Values **39** (1), 73–97 (2014)

Oudshoorn, N.E.J., Pinch, T.: How Users Matter: The Co-construction of Users and Technologies. MIT Press (2003)

Sanders, E.B.N.: Virtuosos of the experience domain. In: Proceedings of 2001 IDSA Education Conference (2001)

Sanders, E.B.N., Stappers, P.J.: Co-creation and the new landscapes of design. Co-design **4**(1), 5–18 (2008)

Suijkerbuijk, S., Brankaert, R., de Kort, Y.A., Snaphaan, L.J., den Ouden, E.: Seeing the first-person perspective in dementia: a qualitative personal evaluation game to evaluate assistive technology for people affected by dementia in the home context. Interact. Comput. **27**(1), 47–59 (2014)

Van den Kieboom, R.C., Bongers, I.M., Mark, R.E., Snaphaan, L.J.: User-driven living lab for assistive technology to support people with dementia living at home: protocol for developing co-creation–based innovations. JMIR Res. Protoc. **8**(1), e10952 (2019)

Voß, J.P., Simons, A.. A novel understanding of experimentation in governance: co-producing innovations between "lab" and "field". Policy Sci. **51**(2), 213–229 (2018)

Developing Dementia Personas for User Centered Architectural Design Considerations in Non-specialized Contexts

Izoné McCracken$^{(\boxtimes)}$, Retha de la Harpeand, and Monica Di Ruvo

Cape Peninsula University of Technology, Cape Town, South Africa
izone@ebesa.co.za

Abstract. This paper is concerned with dementia persona development as a research and design tool to help architects and designers to uncover important information towards design processes and decisions in practice. Architects design spaces for specific functions, but do they truly consider integrating these objectives with a focus on creating meaningful spaces for people with dementia while designing and if so, on what grounds. The reason for using dementia personas and not directly approaching people with dementia is due to the fact that it can be very hard to understand the needs of dementia care as people with dementia are dependent on caregivers and family members, in addition to this many designers and architects do not have ethical clearance to work with people living with dementia; as a consequence of their designation. A literature analysis and participatory workshops were used to develop the dementia personas discussed in this paper. The process of developing dementia personas posed many challenges; iterative revisions had to be made to make the personas relatable and concrete enough to be used as a successful design tool. The complex context of the case requires more personas to represent the diversity of persons with dementia in the service provision on different levels and this is the start of the persona development process. The findings are reported herein.

Keywords: Dementia · User centered design · Care · Persona · South Africa

1 Introduction

The impact of caring for persons with dementia is on the increase globally (Ferretti et al. 2018: 2) resulting in many initiatives to address the needs of an aging population. It has been noted that the number of people with dementia in low- and middle-income countries is increasing (Walker and Paddick 2019: 538). However in such contexts where resources are limited it becomes difficult to design appropriate solutions that address the needs of persons with dementia (Khonie et al. 2015). South Africa's diverse population and unequal healthcare systems further contribute to the challenges faced by architects and designers. In South Africa the majority of the population has to rely on under-resourced public healthcare services because they cannot afford the well-resourced privately owned healthcare facilities available to a smaller percentage of the population (de Jager, et al. 2017). Occupation specific architecture, such as buildings specific for people with dementia, remains poorly resolved and almost absent in South

© Springer Nature Switzerland AG 2019
R. Brankaert and W. IJsselsteijn (Eds.): D-Lab 2019, CCIS 1117, pp. 48–61, 2019.
https://doi.org/10.1007/978-3-030-33540-3_5

Africa (Prince et al. 2016: 99). The reason for this may be contributed to the lack of professionals in South Africa specializing in dementia care; with less than ten geriatricians and five old-aged physiatrists noted in 2016 (Prince et al. 2016: 99).

The problem with designing for persons, such as those living with dementia, who may not be able to participate as active co-designers, is their inability to communicate their own perspectives due to their cognitive impairment (Brankaert 2016). The principle of including representatives of all stakeholder groups, including persons with dementia, to design solutions with and not for, is an important consideration for the authors. The problem of doing this in practice is discussed in the methods section. In this paper we describe a persona development method based on secondary data which was used as part of a larger research project; the ultimate aim, to provide guidelines and methods for architects to design human-centered facilities.

The paper is organized as follows: firstly, the theoretical models used for the study are described followed by a brief overview of the literature used to develop the persona templates. The three iterations of the persona designs are presented followed by the findings obtained using the personas. The paper is concluded with a brief discussion and conclusion.

2 Theoretical Models of Place and Occupation

Two theoretical models were chosen as analytical lenses and as a guidance framework for the persona development by obtaining initial themes from the literature. It was important to ensure that the literature reviewed and evidently personas developed would be in line with the type of research anticipated as the study forms a part of a larger research project, architectural research for developing buildings with a placial understanding focusing on people living with dementia as the main occupants of the building, in which the personas will be used as a design and data collection tool. Therefore the two models chosen serve as a guide for understanding what constitutes place as well as how to position people with dementia at the center of place through organizing the literature in accordance to the themes of the models and as a result formulate the dementia personas accordingly.

For the purpose of this paper a distinction is made between place and space. Although the understanding of place is better described in the paragraphs below it is important to note that space refer to a physical contained volume whereas place refer to an all-encompassing environment which enables dwelling. An analogy to explain this notion better is defined by Davidson et al. (2005: 77) as follow: Land is the physical tangible entity, whereas landscape refers to dwelling; where life patterns are uncovered and activities resonate with each other (Fig. 1).

The concept of place has been adopted by architects in attempt to create meaningful and significant spaces (Jordaan 2015: 1). Seamon (2013: 149) argues that place is an ontological supposition in phenomenology; meaning that people and their worlds are interwoven. Place is the phenomenological possibility for enunciating the relationship between people and their worlds (Seamon 2013: 149). Therefore, the notion of *a sense of place* in the architectural field leaves enormous scope for uncovering what constitutes place for people living with dementia.

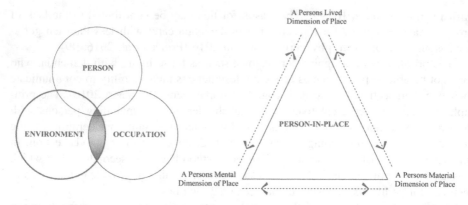

Fig. 1. Conceptual framework based on Jordaan (2015: 53) and Wong & Leland (2018: 2)

Van Steenwinkel (2015: 289) stresses the lack in the articulation of a method which architects can use to understand and design homes for people with dementia that speaks to architectural design methodologies. Jordaan (2015: 224) developed an architectural framework, the placial triad, for understanding place making by specifically looking at the lived dimension, material dimension and mental dimension of place (Jordaan, 2015: 51). The lived dimension is concerned with things happening in and to spaces such as daily routines and the changing of a space purpose; in other words the space was once used as an office but are now utilised for residential purposes. The material dimension of place is concerned with physical objects in a space as well as the materiality of a space. Whereas the mental dimension of place refers to a person's ability to connect to another space or evidently place while not being there, or thoughts and ideas about a space.

Yet the various dimensions of place are always bound to a person. In other words, place must be thought of as person-in-place. In the development of a conceptual framework for this research Wong & Leland's (2018: 2) person-environment-occupation model was therefore also incorporated. The person-environment-occupation model look at how effective a task is preformed considering the environment, person and occupation. The use of the two theoretical models therefore look at both what constitutes place and how effective a place can be, especially in dementia care facilities.

3 Method

For this research, it was decided to focus on the caregivers, who take twenty-four-hour care of the persons with dementia, as the main participants in the co-design sessions. The selected case for the study is a private residential care facility with an entire secure division for persons with dementia. The persons living there are able to afford private healthcare services. In this facility, there are twelve persons with dementia with seven caregivers. In both decisions compromises were needed – there is too little known of dementia care in the public healthcare sector in South Africa (Khonie et al. 2015) to start there and therefore the decision to use a facility already providing dementia care as the case. This is the start of a larger project and more cases will be required to obtain insights in the prevalence of dementia care in South Africa. There is, for example, not even a Xhosa word or term for dementia and the meaning of dementia in different contexts in South Africa need to form an important part of further studies (Khonie et al. 2015). The decision to not include persons with dementia as participants in the co-design sessions was a practical decision and does not imply that their involvement is not important (Swaffer 2014). There was no health professional in the team conducting the research to supervise it to look after the interests of persons with dementia as would be required by the university's ethics board. These initial personas would only represent the case for private healthcare and without the involvement of the persons with dementia. This is an important limitation of this study but with the experience gained in developing the personas, extending the personas to represent the diversity of South Africa and with the involvement with persons with dementia will be the next step. As much as research on dementia is limited in low and middle income countries, researches in such contexts also often do not have access to resources to conduct a study with the involvement of the necessary stakeholder groups.

Literature was reviewed to identify the overlap between the conceptual framework derived and architectural elements of dementia facilities; the challenges that dementia care providers experience; and the underlying characteristics of people living dementia as well as dementia as a syndrome. In preparation for the workshop, eighteen relevant online journal articles listing the possible underlying characteristics mentioned above were reviewed. The content was divided into themes which emerged from the literature including dementia syndrome symptoms, dementia - types, diagnoses, care facilities, care givers, political support, treatment, and therapy for people living with dementia. Three overarching spheres were identified: the biomedical sphere, the social sphere and the political sphere. The literature was summarized in accordance to spheres. The information under each sphere was re-organized into the themes of the two theoretical models and used as a starting point for the workshop described herein as Iteration 1.

The methods used in the co-design session were brainstorming using design probes and scenarios and the affinity method. The affinity method is a creative brainstorming session that enable the collection of a large amount of data and grouping the data according to themes, this method is also known as the KJ method (Scupin, 1997: 233). That allows participants to freely explore and organize information creatively. The following steps were followed: probing questions were used to stimulate a discussion by the participants who then wrote their ideas on sticky notes and position them on a surface. The group then as a collective discuss the ideas to form emerging patterns and to note any surprises. The themes follow from the consensus reached by the group.

Two more iterations took place, in the second one expert input was obtained from an international health care service design practitioner, a local professional nurse and PHD candidate teaching and working with dementia patients, an international PhD student researching dementia care with a visual communication perspective and taking care of persons with dementia in the UK in his spare time and an international Professor specialising in human activity and product design focusing on the elderly. In the last iteration, the persona templates were further refined until they were suitable to use for data collection.

4 Persona Design

4.1 Using the Literature: Underlying Characteristics of Dementia Syndrome and People Living with Dementia

There are few known personas representing people with dementia; most personas are concerned with elderly people focusing on physical and age related deteriorations (Jais et al. 2018: 216). The dementia personas that do exist focus on daily activities but do not necessarily address all placial dimensions as per the proposed theoretical framework (Jais et al. 2016: 3). It has been established that people with dementia have a better quality of life in special care facilities as opposed to traditional care facilities (Marquardt, et al. 2014: 133). Marquardt et al. also suggest that using literature as a basis for research with expert input might be more beneficial as opposed to using focus groups. This approach informed the research process. The three spheres identified in the research are outlined below highlighting the key ideas identified as potential persona informants hat is also in line with the type of research anticipated, and in turn also concurring with the two proposed theoretical models.

The Biomedical Sphere

The biomedical Sphere represents the physical and cognitive aspects of a person with dementia. Dementia is referred to as an umbrella term that defines a set of symptoms manifesting in the social, emotional, private, and daily realms of people's lives. In accordance to Brankaert (2016: 47), preceding a dementia diagnoses, there is a realization phase. This is when people who possibly have dementia, as well as members of society become aware of irregularities and abnormal behavior.

As the dementia progresses it often leads to behaviour and personality changes that impacts the care of persons with dementia (Glasby and Thomas, 2017), especially when the persons with dementia are in denial about their situation (Wiersma et al. 2014: 5). Dementia is progressive in nature increasingly affecting the everyday living of persons with dementia (de Jager et al. 2015). Persons with dementia progressively become detach from their physical place as well as from the people they know. Psychiatrists are the only professionals that can undertake a neuropsychological assessment and consist of the necessary skills to undertake therapeutic intervention. (British Psychological Society Dementia Advisory Group 2016: 6).

Mild Cognitive Impairment (MCI) is seen as the sign sate of dementia. It proves to be problematic; many people displaying signs of cognitive impairment, such as short term memory loss often return to leading a normal life defeating early recognition of dementia (Manthorpe and Iliffe 2016: 17). Consequently a diagnoses, or how the nature of the irregularities is defined is usually only in the late stages of a person's life (British Psychological Society Dementia Advisory Group 2016: 5) In this sphere it is already evident that the biomedical aspect pertaining to dementia is interlinked with both theoretical models, especially to the environment and lived dimension of place, and that the impact on the quality of life of people living with dementia should be closely considered as difficult choices impact people living with dementia predominantly in the later stages of their lives.

The Social Sphere

People with dementia are focused on the here and now opposed to making plans for the future (Wiersma et al. 2014: 5). Hendriks et al. (2016: 12) state that if one looks at how a person with dementia experiences the now, taking into account the person with dementia's subjective interpretation of the world, with their own behavioural- and meaning-giving rituals, one can begin to understand a person with dementia. This notion is very powerful considering an architectural perspective as design for people living with dementia need to serve people with immediate effect while being closely bound up with their perception and interpretation of place. In addition behavioural- and meaning-giving rituals refer to the theoretical models; for example the power of objects, a person's material dimension of place, and routines, a person's lived dimension of place, can give people living with dementia a positive effective occupational output being physically or mentally.

Short term memory loss associated with dementia proves that people might find it hard to understand and navigate their physical environment, consequently leading to disorientation (Grey et al. 2015: 120). Disorientation can cause anxiety and fear that is further heighted when combined with other age related diseases. Loud constant white noise can create difficulties in hearing and lead to further disorientation evidently reverting back to anxiety or even aggression (Grey et al. 2015: 32). In this context, all social and physical displays become interrelated and possibly mental characteristics as well.

Dementia is seldom experienced alone. The effects of dementia, especially on informal or unpaid caregivers are significant. (Brankaert 2016: 32). Informal caregivers are recommended by local authorities as those affected are able to preserve their self-worth in a community (Manthorpe and Iliffe 2016: 21). Although this enables people with dementia to remain in their own homes, the social impacts on care givers are dramatic. Ninety eight percent of informal caregivers develop mental and physical health problems due to taking care of a loved one with dementia (Brankaert 2016: 35). The social occurrence can be further interpreted to be not only highly individual, but also country and culture specific. Various countries have their own pharmaceutical or socially orientated care systems (Brankaert 2016: 36).

The Political Sphere

Care for people with dementia is mostly done by informal carers, also well-known as the informal care phase (Brankaert 2016: 36). The informal care phase can negatively impact the economy as in many cases informal carers have to quit their jobs in order to fulfil the demanding task of caring for a loved one living with dementia (Manthorpe and Iliffe 2016: 22).

Dementia has a financial implication, which is sometimes used to gain political favour. Manthorpe and Iliffe (2016: 12) describe this notion as the medicalization of dementia; it is used to mobilize and to be mobilized within a political argument. In other words the immense stress and focus on the expertise of the medical field becomes a manner in which a government strategizes financial or social favour. This is almost the manifestation of the Machiavellian school of thought; also described by Manthorpe and Iliffe (2016: 12) as Biopower. The Machiavellian school of thought is concentrated on how one is portrayed in certain light in order to gain power; in this instance using the medicalization of dementia (Henaff and Strong 2001: 15). Biopower focuses on the living and strategies for governing life; hence people with dementia become the object of political devices (Manthorpe and Iliffe 2016: 12).

People with dementia should never be or become the object of political- or any devices; however the literature show political interest in the realm of scientific medical treatment for people living with dementia as opposed to other disciplines. Perhaps the focus of governments, especially in the South African context, should look at how to better design for people living with dementia. This can create economic opportunities while improving the quality of life for people living with dementia, especially for South Africans that rely on public healthcare services.

4.2   Iteration 1: Developing a Persona Template

A workshop was done by the authors of this paper for the development of dementia personas. The workshop was introduced by establishing that the goal was to develop an outline of a dementia persona template that could be used for further development into a final template and ultimately a persona. The workshop was based on an extensive summary of the literature. The content was summarized onto twenty one separate pages, each page listing the underlying characteristics that emerged from the texts. Each page was divided into two columns; one listing the possible underlying characteristics of the dementia syndrome and displays thereof by people living with dementia, and the other referring the various stages of dementia to connect the characteristics to specific stages.

The workshop was started with the goal to identify the characteristics of a person living with dementia to develop a suitable persona template and ultimately a persona. Each participant coded a section of the summary writing each code on post-its. The themes were identified jointly from the post-its by grouping them writing a heading on a circular shape note in order to distinguish it from the codes.

During the process of organizing ideas, and characteristics in accordance to a certain heading, theme or domain it became clear that the characteristics overlap in various sections. As a consequence a second layer of information was added in order to establish how these headings, themes and domains can be distinguished and how can it be identified in accordance to the placial - as well as the person-environment-occupation model.

The placial and person-environment-occupation models were used to assist with the grouping of the themes. This resulted in adding more information to the themes about the material, mental, lived, person, place and occupation dimensions.

With all the information gathered from the workshop a draft persona template was developed by one of the authors of this paper. The template identified spatial envelopes and certain domains or themes that fit in the envelopes in order to be relevant to the architectural placial research to follow.

The draft template for the personas was sent for review to the other participants of the workshop. Upon reviewing the personas, and after consultation with post graduate students and a qualified dementia nurse doing research in the same field, it was decided to reduce the dementia stages to three instead of the initial seven, consequently using the CDR scale as opposed to the GDR scale, to deal with some overlapping characteristics. Only persons with moderate to severe dementia are usually referred to a facility for care and therefore the decision to develop two personas, one for each phase.

4.3   Iteration 2: Refinement of Personas

After the dementia persona template was revised, a second workshop was conducted to start the process of getting expert input on the developed persona template. An expert in health care service design, participating in a design project in Canada, provided insight about the dementia personas through discussing how they could be used in procuring data for design purposes. The insight process started with an explanation of the process of developing the persona dementia template.

After the above mentioned discussion the expert in health care service design presented research done for a lighting design project in residential health care and how to involve stakeholders through the building of miniatures. Miniature is the building of a physical environment on a smaller scale by stakeholders using materials such as: clay, recycled materials, blocks, plastic toys and even projections of maps on paper. The use of miniatures was then brain stormed as means of collecting data in dementia facility design research. As a consequence the dementia personas can be used as probes for the building of dementia environment miniatures by stakeholders.

Insight to the dementia persona template came as a result of the discussions around the design informant themes used by the health care service designer in her own research. It was noted that some of the themes made reference to the two theoretical models chosen. Therefore it was confirmed in the workshop that the theoretical models are in fact relevant to the development of the personas as well as using it for architectural design research and design. Further discussion with the expert in health care service design pertaining to the dementia persona information and its visual attributes delivered the following outcomes that were used for further development. Firstly race, gender and cultural background were still abstract in terms of the demographics. This could be that more expert input was needed as dementia demographics in the South African context were not clear from the literature obtained. The figure in the persona template was also gender and race nonspecific; the focus was to present a moderate or severe dementia persona irrespective of race and gender. As a consequence it was suggested that we should draw two different dementia caricatures for the respective persona templates. Additionally the persona characteristics should be further populated and reviewed again.

4.4   Iteration 3: Selection of Personas

Upon sending the reworked template for comment the persona template was again shared with experts as mentioned in the method section of this paper. A third workshop was arranged where the revised dementia persona templates and development thereof was presented to the experts mentioned. The workshop was attended by the same panel of experts with exception the expert in health care service design expert due to other obligations.

After presenting the personas there was various inputs and suggestions from the experts on how the template should be further refined in order to develop two dementia personas. Comments were made regarding the amount of text and legibility, demographic information was provided according to South African prevalence, and the importance of cultural relevance in South Africa. All attendees agreed that the characteristics of the persona templates were thought found to be correct, but needed to be described in an engaging manner. The caricatures used were too abstract and the amount of information is hard to process; hence photographs were included and information condensed in order to provide a sincere connection as the personas would ultimately be utilized as probes.

As a result of the expert input received the dementia templates were developed into two personas. The first is persona, known as Annie, is an elderly female living with moderate dementia according to the CDR scale. The second dementia persona is also an elderly female, living with severe dementia; this persona is known as Susan. It is important to note that the two personas seem quite similar and the reason for that is in South Africa there are limited facilities for people living with dementia due to under-resourced public healthcare services. Subsequently the personas represent the prevalent demographic of people living with dementia in South Africa that are able to afford and to live in facilities specifically for dementia care. Most of the persons in the facility are females and the two personas represent two different stages of dementia. The personas also need to be relevant for the facility where research was conducted, that form a part of the lager study mentioned, as the carers must be able to relate to the personas. The two final personas represent a collective of the characteristics of persons with dementia and are not relating to any specific person (Figs. 2 and 3).

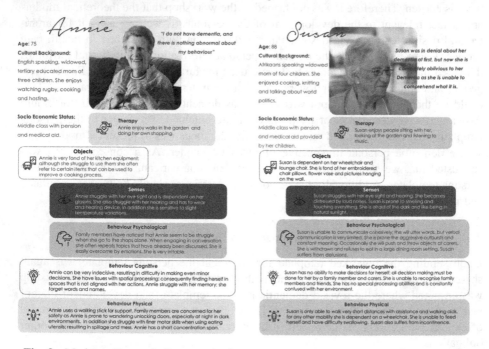

Fig. 2. Moderate Dementia Persona- Annie   **Fig. 3.** Severe Dementia Persona- Susan

4.5   Data Collection with Personas

The personas, Annie and Susan, were used to collect data at a non-government organization dementia facility. The personas were utilised as probes in a co-design session using the affinity method. There were two sessions held that comprised of five caregivers. They were briefed regarding the two personas, their respective dementia stages, dementia syndrome characteristics and respective personalities. It was further explained to the caregivers that the personas are meant as probes in order to relate to patients presenting with similar characteristics and personalities. They were further assured that this is not a test and that their practical experiences are valued. The question for both sessions was structured in line with the conceptual framework for the research in order to gain data that is in line with the models and subsequently, the understanding of place. The questioned posed for the first session was: Identify and write down an object, activity/place and story/emotion that are prominent in the morning and afternoon routines of Annie and Susan. The object, activity and story must be related to each other. The second affinity session comprised of a set of questions where the questions can be answered by drawing, writing or even by imitating dialogue through means of a speech bubble. For the purpose of this paper the question that will be discussed in the findings is: How is the relationship between people living with dementia and family members maintained in the facility? (Fig. 4)

Fig. 4. Affinity sessions with care givers

4.6   Persona Findings

The use of dementia personas in architectural design research to uncover placial understanding proved to be useful, but challenging. The data retrieved from the affinity sessions with caregivers delivered rich, insightful data conveying cultural, placial and occupational significance for a non-specialized context such as South Africa. The data delivered stories of different cultural interaction and understandings; for example the meaning and stories attached to objects and how they are conveyed and remembered.

One of the caregivers in affinity session one indicate that the persona Annie is very fond of her wash cloth; being insistent that the carers at the facility wash her with it every morning. Upon discussing the object and story in the group setting it was evident that for some carers it came across that Annie is very demanding whereas other care takers saw her persistence as admirable while understanding Annie's need for dignity and self-worth. Although Annie is not able to wash herself; hygiene and objects associated with it is very important for Annie as part of her morning routine. Another example for one of the caregivers is the significance of a bowl and spoon in persona Annie's room. The bowl and spoon is considered to be unnecessary items as all meals are prepared by and served in the facility. Nevertheless the carers explained that the bowl and spoon reminded Annie of her love for baking. One of the carers explained that Annie requested the kitchen staff to bake her some cookies as she is not allowed to, but her request was denied. In the group discussion it was noted that the bowl and spoon as objects are not necessarily connected to the morning or afternoon routine; the occurrence of Annie being fond of the objects occur at both. Thought-provoking physical objects do not necessarily refer to permanent objects such as photos or was cloths; for another care giver the persona Susan is fond of sweet treats, such as koeksiters and milk tart, brought to her by her daughter. When referring to the theoretical models and considering Susan is living with severe dementia; the sweet treats is therapeutic to receive even though it is hard for her to eat it without assistance. Accordingly the sweet treat is an example of temporary objects that are true to the South African culture of the persons belonging to that culture and encompass all the dimensions of place, as well as look at the occupational output in a certain environment for Susan.

In the second affinity session care givers gave both positive and negative feedback; mentioning how the relationship deteriorate or how family members as well as carers try to help with the maintenance of relationships. One of the carers explained that some of the family members in the case of the persona Susan do not have a lot of patience with their loved one living with dementia; as a consequence there is a lot of misunderstandings and frustration that sometimes lead to objects and privileges taken away from the person living with dementia. Another carer, also referring to the persona Susan, explained that if a family member visits and is perceived to experience their own difficulties the carer feels obliged to only tell the family members about good things that happened during the day to Susan. The speech bubble below imitates the conversation between a family member and the persona Annie; it's a conversation relayed by one of the carers as an observation of the relationship between Annie and her daughter when Annie was taken for some treats in the dining facility.

Consequently insight was gained on significance for patients and how this is understood by the caregivers. In practice, this level of information would enable architects to better understand a very complex placial configuration for people with dementia whose sense of place is limited and difficult.

The challenging aspect of the use of personas came as a result that the use of such tools in South Africa as a placial architectural design methodology is rare. The concept of a persona needed to be carefully explained to care givers to ensure that the function of the persona as a probe in the affinity session is successful. If the personas were not as relatable as developed in the third iteration, the collection of data would have been even more challenging if not impossible. Nevertheless the dementia persona template developed in the second iteration proved to be an insightful template for the interpretation and analysis of data the collected. As designers we solve problems, therefore the persona templates developed in the second iteration help to access how good or how progressed the problem is. It also helps to identify to what degree of importance or efficiency key objects or therapy measures are consequently informing design decisions.

The fact that the personas were developed informed by the two theoretical models strengthen them as architectural design probes in dementia care design. Other dementia personas might not be able to sufficiently address the complexities of place and occupation.

5 Conclusion and Recommendations

This paper has discussed the development of moderate and severe dementia personas in non-specialized contexts such as South Africa for the purpose of using the personas as an architectural design tool. The development of personas was a trial and feedback process where the final personas were relatable to concrete information based on literature reviews and expert input. Using the personas as probes in affinity sessions was useful to uncover crucial information about place where the person with dementia lives. The fact that the personas were developed in line with the two theoretical models strengthens them as architectural design probes in dementia care design. Other dementia personas might not be able to address the complexities of place and occupation. The use of dementia personas and orientating people to understand the use thereof for design research is an unfamiliar occurrence in South Africa. It is recommended that additional personas are developed and tested for various socioeconomic groups in South Africa. Despite the limitation of only considering a representation of a small percentage of a much larger population the method seems to be a good starting point for using personas in dementia research in non-specialized contexts to obtain important insights in the complexity of such contexts where information about persons with dementia is limited. More research is needed to expand the persona method to include persons with dementia in the persona development process and to incorporate cultural specific aspects in the process to represent the diversity of such contexts.

References

Brankaert, R.G.A.: Design for dementia: a design-driven living lab approach to involve people with dementia and their context. Eindhoven: Technische Universiteit Eindhoven (2016). https://pure.tue.nl/ws/files/15933086/20160302_Brankeart.pdf. Last accessed 2 Apr 2018

British Psychological Society Dementia Advisory Group, Psychological dimensions of dimentia: Putting the person at the centre of care. British Pschycological Society, 1–28 (2016)

De Jager, C.A., Joska, J.A., Hoffman, M., Borochowitz, K.E., Combrinck, M.I.: Dementia in rural South Africa: a pressing need for epidemiological studies R. Coles, S. Costa, & S. Watson, eds. South African Medical Journal, 105(3): 189 (2015)

De Jager, C.A., Msemburi, W., Pepper, K., Combrinck, M.I.: Dementia prevalence in a rural region of south africa: a cross-sectional community study. J. Alzheimer's Dis. **60**, 1087–1096 (2017)

Ferretti, C., Sarti, M., Nitrini, R., Ferreira, F.F., Brucki, D.: An assessment of direct and indirect costs of dementia in Brazil. PLoS ONE **13**(3), 1–15 (2018)

Glasby, J., Thomas, S.: Understanding and responding to the needs of the carers of people with dementia in the UK, US and beyond. Birmingham 2018. https://www.birmingham.ac.uk/ Documents/college-social-sciences/social-policy/carers-of. Last Accessed 17 May 2019

Grey, T., Pierce, M., Cahill, S., Dyer, M.: Universal Design Guidelines. Dementia Friendly Dwellings for People with Dementia, their Families and Carers. National Disability Authority. Centre for Excellence in Universal Design, 3–178 (2015)

Henaff, M., Strong, T.B.: Public Space and Democracy. University of Minnesota Press, Minneapolis (2001)

Hendriks, N., Wilkinson, A., Schoenaers, D.: Dementia Lab: The Role of Design (2017). http://www.dementialabconference.com/Publications/Dementialab_Publication_2016_EN.pdf. Last accessed 10 Apr 2018

Jais, C., Hignett, S., Estupinan, Z.G., Hogervorst, E.: Evidence based dementia personas: human factors design for people living with dementia. Ergonomics For People With Disabilities, pp. 215–226. Sciendo, Warsaw, Poland (2018)

Jais, C., Hignett, S., Hogervorst, E.: Developing personas for ISE in the design of dementia care environments. In: Proceedings of Healthcare Ergonomics & Patient Safety (HEPS) Conference, pp. 210–216 (2016)

Jordaan, J.: Constructing Place; Towards a Twenty-First Century Phenomenological Architectural Framework. Unpublished PhD dissertation, University of Pretoria, Pretoria (2015)

Khonje, V., Milligan, V.C., Yako, Y., Mabelane, M., Borochowitz, K.E., de Jager, C.A.: Knowledge, attitudes and beliefs about dementia in an urban Xhosa-Speaking community in South Africa. Adv. Alzheimer's Dis. **4**, 21–36 (2015)

La Fontaine, J., Jutlla, K., Read, K., Brooker, D., Evans, S.: The experiences, needs and outcomes for carers of people with dementia: literature review. Report published by the Association for Dementia Studies, Worcester University, UK (2016)

Manthorpe, J., Iliffe, S.: The Dialectics of dememntia, London (2016). https://www.researchgate.net/publication/311536791_The_dialectics_of_dementia. Last accessed 9 Apr 2018

Marquardt, G., Beuter, K., Motzek, T.: Impact of the Design of the Built Environment on People with Dementia: An Evidence-Based Review. 8(1), pp. 121–157 (2014). Last accessed 1 Feb 2017

Prince, M., Comas-Herrera, M.A., Knapp, M., Guerchet, M., Karagiannidou, M.M.: World Alzheimer Report 2016 Improving healthcare for people living with dementia coverage, Quality and costs now and In the future (2016). https://www.alz.co.uk/research/WorldAlzheimerReport2016.pdf. Last accessed 22 Oct 2017

Seamon, D.: Lived bodies, place, and phenomenology; implications for human rights and environmental justice. J. Hum. Rights Environ. **4**(2), 143–166 (2013)

Van Steenwinkel, I.: Offering architects insights into living with dementia Three case studies on orientation in space-time-identity (2015). https://www.kuleuven.be/lucas/pub/publi_upload/2015_full_phd_IrisVanSteenwinkel.pdf. Last accessed 16 Feb 2017

Walker, R., Paddick, S.: Dementia prevention in low-income and middle-income countries: a cautious step forward. The Lancet Global Health, 7 May 2019, pp. 1–2 (2019)

Wiersma, E.C., Sameshima, P., Dupuis, S., Caffery, P., Harvey, D.: Mapping the Dementia Journey (2014). https://www.alz.co.uk/sites/defaukt/files/conf2014/OC105.pdf. Last accessed 9 Apr 2018

Wong, C., Leland, N.E.: Applying the Person-Environment-Occupation Model to Improve Dementia Care. OT Practice: CE-1-CE-7 (2018). https://www.aota.org/~/media/Corporate/Files/Publications/CE-Articles/CE-Article-May18.pdf. Last accessed 17 May 2019

Swaffer, K.: Dementia: stigma, language, and dementia-friendly. Dementia **13**(6), 709–716 (2014)

Emily Carr University Zeitgeist Program

Bringing Together Student Designers and Care Home Residents to Co-design Publications — a Social Innovation Project

Caylee Raber[1]([⊠]), Jon Hannan[1], Mariko Sakamoto[2]⬤,
Srushti Kulkarni[1], Nadia Beyzaei[1]⬤, Amen Salami[1], Donna Levi[3],
and Alison Phinney[2]⬤

[1] Health Design Lab, Emily Carr University of Art + Design,
Vancouver, Canada
raber@ecuad.ca
[2] School of Nursing, University of British Columbia, Vancouver, Canada
[3] UBC Hospital – Purdy Pavilion Care Home, Vancouver Coastal Health,
Vancouver, Canada

Abstract. The Emily Carr University (ECU) Zeitgeist Project is a unique design-based project concept where communication design students and residents in care homes engage in a variety of activities over six sessions together, with the goal of co-creating mini-publications featuring the residents' stories. While the project's overarching purpose is to provide social interaction and inter-generational exchange for the residents and students, it also provides an opportunity for the residents, including those living with dementia, to showcase their stories and to actively participate in a design project. The students in turn, not only have the opportunity to develop their design skills, but also learn to connect as young adults with older individuals, who have meaningful stories and experiences to share with them. Overall, this paper discusses the relationship building that occurs between the students and the residents, specifically the storytelling and co-designing relationships, that are key to the ECU Zeitgeist Project's success as a reciprocal and inclusive program engaging older adults, particularly those with dementia, in collaborative and participatory design processes.

Keywords: Storytelling · Intergenerational exchange · Dementia · Co-design · Participatory design research · Communication design · Ageing · Printmaking

1 Introduction

The Emily Carr University (ECU) Zeitgeist Program—inspired by a Swiss project known as the Zeitgeist Kollektiv [1, 2]—began in the Spring of 2018 as a collaboration between a Western Canadian art + design university and a long-term care home. As a social innovation initiative, this program is designed to connect post-secondary level students with residents living in care homes.

© Springer Nature Switzerland AG 2019
R. Brankaert and W. IJsselsteijn (Eds.): D-Lab 2019, CCIS 1117, pp. 62–70, 2019.
https://doi.org/10.1007/978-3-030-33540-3_6

The ECU Zeitgeist Program runs over the course of a post-secondary school term, and includes six one-hour sessions at a care home. At the first session, groups comprised of 3–4 students and 2–3 residents are assigned, and continue to work together over the remaining five sessions to co-create mini-publications featuring the residents' stories:

- Session 1: Getting to know you exercise (organized by the care home)
- Session 2: Getting to know you activity (designed by students)
- Session 3 & 4: Content generation utilizing participatory design-based activities
- Session 5: Review of drafted content
- Session 6: Sharing of final printed publications.

The Vancouver (British Columbia, Canada) iteration of the ECU Zeitgeist Program engages students in a third-year communication design course (n = 18), with residents living in long-term care homes (n = 15); within this context, students are involved in this program as part of their course curriculum, while residents are invited to participate in this program by their care home recreation therapist as part of their recreational therapy care plan.

While the overarching purpose of the program is to provide meaningful social interaction and intergenerational exchange for the residents and students, the project also provides a unique opportunity for residents to showcase their stories and to actively participate in a design project. This paper is centered on the relationship building that occurs between the students and residents as they engage in storytelling together; This is core to Zeitgeist's success in engaging older adults, particularly those with dementia, in collaborative and participatory design processes.

2 Storytelling and the Zeitgeist Program

As human beings, we all have our own narrative identity, in terms of the stories we construct about ourselves, defining who we are, not only to others but also to ourselves [3]. Identity scholars have long proclaimed the importance of being able to situate the self within a life narrative, where the disparate aspects of a person's sense of self, one's different stories, can be unified into an enduring account of our lives [3, 4]. The development of one's narrative identity is a lifelong process and should continue as part of ageing [5]. Unfortunately, this is not always the case and older people's life stories can become co-opted and overtaken by generalized and negative perceptions of old age, particularly when there is a dementia diagnosis involved and when living in environments such as residential care [6, 7].

Narrative storytelling can help us to understand ourselves by integrating the different aspects of self, effectively our past, present and future selves [8]. Storytelling is not only a therapeutic undertaking but also a useful way of exploring and better understanding people's experiences of health and illness [8, 9]. In addition, research in storytelling in health contexts such as dementia care has demonstrated that having one's story heard and acknowledged can be affirming to a person's sense of identity, as well as their feelings of self-worth [10]. As such, the Zeitgeist program, as an exercise in storytelling and inter-generational exchange, is a unique opportunity for older people, including those living with dementia, to engage with much younger design students. It is an opportunity to share their personal narratives, and to continue to add to their sense of who they are. In addition, the students as communication designers are bringing specialized and particular knowledge to their interactions with the residents. In fact, storytelling is a narrative technique used by many designers, particularly in communication design where the basic objective is to create a unique and visual product based on clients' ideas and experiences [11, 12].

3   Zeitgeist's Relational Process

The storytelling that occurs in the Zeitgeist sessions comes to fruition by virtue of the relationship building that occurs throughout all of the resident-student interactions. The residents who participate in Zeitgeist have all experienced different aspects of the ageing process. For instance, some of the residents live with mild to moderate dementia, others with profound physical challenges, while some live with both. All of the residents share a need to be living in residential care, in order for their daily care needs to be met. The students are all third-year undergraduate design students—and for the most part—in their early twenties. In general, there is a wide age gap between most of the residents and students, which translates to many social, cultural and generational differences amongst the two groups of participants. For instance, the students have had limited exposure to care homes, and do not have much experience with some of the challenges older adults face, such as living with dementia, particularly in its less severe stages. On the other hand, the residents do not get to spend a lot of time with younger people, such as university students, especially those of design background. Bridging these differences is important, and connecting relationally is a crucial aspect of the six sessions that occur in Zeitgeist, in order for the residents' stories to come to the fore, and for the collaborative and co-designing aspect of the project to successfully occur. The following paragraphs will describe how the students and residents engage with one another and build the relationships that have come to characterize the process of engagement and design that is the Zeitgeist project.

3.1   Forming the Storytelling Relationship

"It could be dangerous getting to know me." a resident jokingly said to the students when they had said they want to get to know him.

As the design students and residents meet and get to know one another over 2.5 months, during the six one-hour sessions, they engage in a variety of activities that help to stimulate storytelling, such as looking at pictures, working on collages together or participating in games. The activities are non-hierarchical in nature, as the students also participate, and in this way, relationships are built on a level playing field. For instance, during one particular encounter, a student and resident came together for a nail polish session that was thoroughly enjoyed by all. Overall, these informal activities help to foster a connection between the residents and students, allowing them to get to know one another and provide a comfortable basis from which stories can begin to be shared. Despite many of the differences that exist between them, both the students and residents are able to find commonalities such as similar place of origin, comparable travelling experiences, or share personal interests. For instance, one particular student discovered that his mother had lived in the same neighbourhood in Hong Kong as the resident he was getting to know. This provided a common bond between them that helped to build their particular storytelling and design relationship.

Overall, as levels of comfort among one another build, students prompt the residents to engage in life review and to share experiences and stories from their pasts. For residents living with dementia, sharing their stories with the students can be more challenging. In some cases, it is not always possible for students to ask for or receive a chronological account of the resident's past experiences. Prior to the beginning of the session, the students participate in a session led by a nursing professor, where they are provided with information on how to communicate respectfully and effectively with people living with dementia. This helps to dispel any negative perceptions to students may have, as well as reassures them. In this way, the students are prepared to follow the residents' stories wherever they are apt to go, whether or not they "make sense" or follow a specific and recognizable timeline.

3.2   Building the Co-designing Relationship

As one resident explained, "I really enjoyed working together on it and putting it together. I think we all got a lot out of it". The students are quick to adapt to what is comfortable for the residents, and as the sessions progress, there is a sustained focus on the co-construction of the stories that are ultimately included in the final mini-publications. These publications take the form of colourful booklets, which are created using a Risograph printer, which is often described to the residents as similar to a Gestetner printer. A Gestetner is an old-fashioned stencil printer that used a similar process to the Risograph and often allows residents to better understand the production process. As a digital stencil duplicator where a master sheet is created from which many copies can be made, Risograph printing is inexpensive and allows for mass dissemination. This printing technique also results in a distinctive printed product, brightly coloured with a rustic look and grainy texture, which is quite different from the more typical printed materials the residents might be used to. In general, the residents have enjoyed the look of the final publications, although one resident did not like the style of the Risograph printing, calling it "lousy print job!" In the end, the mini-publications become a physical manifestation of the stories themselves and are often illustrated with thoughtful drawings and pictures created by the students. Importantly, the process is collaborative, in that the students bring forth their initial designs to the residents to receive feedback and to make changes as necessary. This is an enjoyable and meaningful process for the residents.

In the end, the particular design-based relationship between the students as designers and the residents, as their clients, is crucial to the co-designing process. In all designer-client relationships, the designer needs to understand what the client wants, ensuring that the final work presented is meaningful to the client and meets the requirements at hand. Thus, as designers, the students need to acknowledge any physical or cognitive challenges of the residents. For instance, they must consider that the text is readable to all the residents, in some cases ensuring that the font choice is legible and large enough, and with a pleasing but subtle visual contrast that is not too distracting. In addition, while the final publications are definitely co-created, there is a certain amount of creative license that the students take upon themselves, in terms of how they interpret the final stories. This is particularly the case when there are residents involved who may have some challenges communicating or who live with dementia, where the students must creatively piece the story together according to their own interpretations. This has resulted in some compelling and creative publications, where students and residents have generated new narratives that are totally unrelated to their pasts. For example, one student showed the residents an example of a contemporary Japanese comic book style. This inspired the group to create a comic book based on shared discussions about superheroes and cats, creating a different type of narrative and mini-publication altogether. In another instance, a student created a booklet printed on pink sheets of paper, sensitively and beautifully representing a resident's love of pink nail polish, lipstick and rouge, who had some challenges telling her story because of her dementia, but who was still demonstrably able to share aspects of herself with the student. Overall, understanding the way in which the residents are comfortable in expressing themselves and then adapting that method of communication to encourage conversations with residents who have dementia is an essential lesson for the students, both as designers needing to identify their clients' stories and esthetics, and as young adults learning to connect to older individuals who have aspects of themselves to share with others.

3.3 Creating Lasting Storytelling Relationships and Opportunities

"Is it over already? My memories are just getting warmed up." – a 95-year-old resident.

By the sixth and final session, the students have completed their mini-publications and share and enjoy them with the residents at their last get-together. Overall, 40 copies of each publication are printed, so that the residents can keep as many as they want, as well as pass on copies to friends, family members, staff members at their care facilities, or whomever they choose to. In this way, the ability to share the publications with others begins the storytelling cycle anew, as the stories can be "told" again, whenever the publications are shared and read by others. Apart from the opportunity, the completed publications represent as a story that can be shared and passed along to others, there is also a fair amount of story-sharing that occurs in the final session together, as time is set aside so that the residents can read the final publications with the students they created them with. Time is also spent in a group-sharing session where both the residents and students share, with the other participants in the project, their experiences working and storytelling together.

For residents living with dementia, the Zeitgeist process has unfolded in particularly meaningful ways. For instance, one resident living with dementia was asked how she felt about the publication that a student had created for her. She was unsure how to answer and seemed hesitant about the publication she was holding in her hand, perhaps having already forgotten about it. The student sitting next to her responded by saying "that's okay, we can read it again", signifying that "her story" was easily accessible and could be read again whenever needed. While this was happening, it was observed that several of the other residents in the room, as well as some of the care facility's staff, were reading a few of the extra copies of this resident's publications. Effectively, her story was being shared with, and told to others, despite this resident not being able to share it herself within that moment. This is significant as care home staff have shared with the Zeitgeist team that they have learned new aspects about the residents that they routinely care for, that they were not previously aware of.

4 Discussion

Overall, the impact of the relational aspects of the program, both for the residents and the students is quite clear, for it has been noted in the three Zeitgeist programs that have run thus far, that the residents and students have both learned a lot from one another. The residents enjoy spending time with younger people and for many, participating in the project and co-creating the publication is an opportunity to keep their narratives open in the long term as their stories now exist in a format that can be kept and shared with others. In terms of the students, who have not only been able to learn from an older generation and to spend time at a residential care home, there is a growing realization of the lives they have yet to lead and the stories they too have yet to create. As one of the students acknowledged, "just having the chance to see how these people have lived, is very inspiring in ways, and makes me want to do things to make sure that one day, I have a story to tell too. I learned not only about them, but also about me – my skills, my life, and where I can go next". In this regard, there is a relational aspect to the resident and student interactions that is dialogical in nature, where all of the participants' selves come to the fore, a process that is fostered within the relationship building that is specific to the Zeitgeist project [13]. The dialogical relationality is apparent as the students and residents are able to learn about one other, despite great differences in age, social location and cultural experiences, and in doing so learn a bit more about themselves.

Zeitgeist, as an inter-generational project of engagement and social interaction, also reveals how closely all of our stories are connected and bound to those of others', despite some of the great differences that can exist between people [14]. It is important to note that the relationship building that occurs in Zeitgeist is fostered within the design process. The design process begins from the first day of the sessions and continues to the very end. Right from introducing themselves, making the residents comfortable and putting them in the spotlight for the Q and A sessions, students use their design skills to develop innovative activities to enhance the engagement of the residents. From designing creative and visual methods and games to engage the residents, to collecting information, gathering the accurate intel and interpreting it into draft layouts, and making revisions based on feedback from residents, students are employing their design skills. As stories are collected, students work through an iterative design process to explore different communication design strategies to pull what may initially feel like disparate bits of information together into a cohesive and rich story. As one student explained: "I learnt how to take important or catchy bits from the conversations with the resident and turn that into an interesting story. Then design something that would encapsulate those stories". In many cases, brief segments of conversations are brought to life through the intentional use of type, colour and illustrations; there are key skills for communication designers that are fostered through this project.

Finally, the Zeitgeist project demonstrates that there is a valuable role for storytelling in connecting people, particularly for those living with dementia. It is increasingly being recognized that those who live with dementia have in fact not been robbed of their identity and sense of self, as it may have been commonly considered in the past [15]. In accordance with this view, it can be argued that storytelling, and the relationships that are built as part of this process, can not only work towards interrupting the more damaging social discourses that surround ageing but persistent and negative views about dementia as well. This could be particularly important when considering the demographic changes in population ageing that are occurring at this time, as well as existing social understandings that affect perspectives and understandings of ageing and later life. It is also helpful to remember that while people living with dementia may have difficulties with their memories, or have challenges in communicating effectively with others, they are still individuals with stories that define them, and as such are "still part of social worlds where stories and storytelling are important" [15]. In this way, the Zeitgeist project is particularly effective at demonstrating that people living with dementia still have a sense of self and identity to share and as such, their own stories to tell. It is also important to highlight the value of each session, in the moment, for providing the opportunity for meaningful engagement of residents in relationship building and storytelling, independent of their recollection of the session at a later date. Further we learned that residents appreciated the opportunity to contribute to something beyond the care home. The Zeitgeist project gave them a sense of purpose and a meaningful way to contribute to the students' learning and the community.

5   Conclusion

"I was uncertain what the benefits for the residents would be when we started this project. After hearing their closing words at our last session, I finally understood it from their perspective. The smallest things, as recalling a story from when they were young brought them so much joy and gratefulness. It is always an enjoyable experience to exchange stories, but to take it to the next level and create a publication about them, validates that their stories are important, valuable, and remembered."—design student.

The most significant part of the ECU Zeitgeist Program has been the connections being formed between residents and students, through mutual opportunities for not only being listeners, but learners and teachers of different disciplines. What started as a class assignment, soon turned into a social innovation project with deeper meaning and lasting value.

Storytelling has often been a way of passing on priceless experiences from the lives of the elderly of some communities; some would even consider these methods to be sacred [16]. In this way, storytelling has been used as an escape from the generic 'question and answer' format, to a focus towards relationship building between students and residents. This project gives residents the opportunity to not only be the client but the designer, as the they are involved in the ongoing design process in a meaningful way—ingredients for social innovation based on the premise of "recombining existing resources and capabilities to create new functions and new meanings". Through this, it is important to not only consider older adults for what they need but also for what they are able to contribute [17]. Within this context, the designer's role has been to foster interactions and facilitate activities that are accessible to seniors, including those with varying levels of dementia—something that goes beyond typical design curriculum at the undergraduate level. Had this project been integrated in a course other than communication design, the outcome would inherently be different in both method and outcome, which poses a unique opportunity for further exploration to other disciplines in academia. This is currently being explored by the ECU team, in the context of creating a 'How-to-Guide' for other local and international academic institutions to implement the ECU Zeitgeist Program in their own settings and build partnerships within their own communities.—How might other academic organizations use the ECU Zeitgeist Program as a mode of social innovation that provides a starting point for building connections with care homes, in a meaningful way, with mutual benefits?

"I learned that stories are a powerful tool to bring people together, no matter what age, culture, or status."—design student.

References

1. Kerchof, C.: Senior media collective: turning nursing homes into media houses. Master of Arts in Design. Zurich University of the Arts (2015)
2. Kerchof, C.: The Zeitgeist project: Creating a magazine for storytelling and universal editorial design (Das Zeitgeist-Projekt). In: Müller, F. (ed.) Designethnogafie. Springer, Berlin (2018)
3. McAdams, D., Josselson, R., Lieblich, A.: Introduction. In: McAdams, D., Josselson, R., Lieblich, A. (eds.) Identity and Story: Creating Self in Narrative, pp. 3–11. American Psychological Association, Washington (2006)
4. McLean, K., Pasupathi, M.: Old, new, borrowed, blue? The emergence and retention of personal meaning in autobiographical storytelling. J. Pers. **79**(1), 135–163 (2011). https://doi.org/10.1111/j.1467-6494.2010.0067
5. Randall, W., Balwin, C., McKenzie-Mohr, S., McKim, E., Furlong, D.: Narrative and resilience: a comparative analysis of how older adults story their lives. J. Aging Stud. **34**, 155–161 (2015). https://doi.org/10.1016/j.jaging.2015.02.010
6. Bohlmeijer, E., Westerhof, G., Randall, W., Tromp, T., Kenyon, G.: Narrative foreclosure in later life: preliminary considerations for a new sensitizing concept. J. Aging Stud. **25**, 364–370 (2011). https://doi.org/10.1016/j.jaging.2011.01.003
7. McParland, P., Kelly, F., Innes, A.: Dichotomising dementia: is there another way? Sociol. Health Illn. **39**(2), 258–269 (2017). https://doi.org/10.1111/1467-9566.12438
8. D'Cruz, K., Douglas, J., Serry, T.: Narrative storytelling as both an advocacy tool and therapeutic process: perspectives of adult storytellers with acquired brain injury. Neuropsychol. Rehabil., 1–21 (2019). https://doi.org/10.1080/09602100.2019.1586733
9. Scott, S., Brett-MacLean, P., Archibald, M., Hartling, L.: Protocol for systematic review of the use of narrative storytelling and visual-arts-based approaches as knowledge translation tools in healthcare. Syst. Rev. **2**(19), 1–7 (2013). http://www.systematicreviewsjournal.com/content/2/1/19

10. Heggestad, A., Slettebo, A.: How individuals with dementia in nursing homes maintain their dignity through life's storytelling – a case study. J. Clin. Nurs. **24**, 2323–2330 (2015). https://doi.org/10.1111/jocn.12837
11. Cezzar, J.: What Is Graphic Design? AIGA (2017). www.aiga.org/guide-whatisgraphicdesign
12. Gausepohl, K., Winchester, W., Smith-Jackson, T., Kleiner, B., & Arthur, J.D.: A conceptual model for the role of storytelling in design: leveraging narrative inquiry in user-centred design (UCD). Health Technol. **6** (2016). https://doi.org/10.1007/s12553-015-0123-1
13. Hannan, J., et al.: Zeitgeist publication: a storytelling project with residents and design students. Des. Health (2019). https://doi.org/10.1080/24735132.2019.1596210
14. Freeman, M.: Why narrative matters: philosophy, method, theory. Storyworlds J. Narrat. Stud. **18**(1), 137–152 (2016). https://www.jstor.org/stable/10.5250/storyworlds.8.1.0137
15. Hyden, L.: Entangled Narratives: Collaborative Storytelling and the Re-Imagining of Dementia. Oxford Scholarship Online (2018). https://doi.org/10.1093/oso/9780199391578.001.0001
16. Corntassel, J.: Indigenous storytelling, truth-telling, and community approaches to reconciliation. Engl. Stud. Can. **35**(1), 137–159 (2009)
17. Manzini, E.: Design When Everybody Designs: An Introduction to Design for Social Innovation (2015)

Technology and Experience

Sentimental Audio Memories: Exploring the Emotion and Meaning of Everyday Sounds

Sarah Campbell[1]([⊠])(iD), David Frohlich[1], Norman Alm[2],
and Adam Vaughan[3]

[1] Digital World Research Centre, Department of Music and Media,
University of Surrey, Guildford, UK
sarah.campbell@surrey.ac.uk
[2] Department of Music and Media, University of Surrey, Guildford, UK
[3] Unforgettable, London, UK

Abstract. Numerous studies have shown the beneficial effect of music for people with dementia, particularly within reminiscence therapy. In this project we explored the potential role of everyday sound recordings which evoke an emotional response for producing similar benefits. To first explore what we call 'sentimental' sounds we conducted an online survey in partnership with a dementia organisation, using a co-design approach with carers and family members of people with dementia. Sounds and memories for each of the four quadrants of a circumplex emotion space were captured as free text narratives. The survey demonstrated what sounds are sentimental, and the memories and emotions associated with these sounds. Sounds eliciting positively valenced emotions and memories comprised natural, familiar soundscapes. In contrast, sounds evoking negatively valenced emotions and memories were manmade and intrusive. Results showed consistency across people as to the types of sounds eliciting the same emotions, although the meanings of these sounds were highly idiosyncratic. Further, some sounds were associated with both positive and negative emotions through poignant memories, depending upon the context and nature of the particular sound. Results also indicated the value of narratives for structuring the presentation of sounds themselves.

Keywords: Sound · Emotion · Reminiscence · Dementia

1 Introduction

Numerous studies have shown the beneficial effect of music therapy for people with dementia, in reducing anxiety, increasing wellbeing and stimulating memories, particularly during reminiscence therapy. Reminiscence therapy (RT) is an established intervention used with people with dementia [1], where memories that are personally significant are stimulated to be recalled or told to others [2]. However, currently reminiscence therapy is mainly conducted either with a group of people with dementia, or with a person with dementia and their paid carer in a residential care home [3]. The potential of facilitating reminiscence activities within the home environment between people with dementia and their family and friends, and the benefit this could serve for

© Springer Nature Switzerland AG 2019
R. Brankaert and W. IJsselsteijn (Eds.): D-Lab 2019, CCIS 1117, pp. 73–81, 2019.
https://doi.org/10.1007/978-3-030-33540-3_7

not only the person with dementia but also the family member carers, has not been fully explored. The potential of everyday sounds for reminiscence in dementia care is a relatively new area. Therefore, it was decided in order to successfully co-design reminiscence activities for use at home, it was first necessary to explore with carers the relevance of sounds, and which sounds in particular, associated with emotional memories. Further, it was deemed important to pilot various question approaches to ascertain which types of questions best elicited rich descriptions of memories and associated sounds, before the co-design stage with people with dementia. These were the aims of the current study, which is the first stage of a larger project called 'Sentimental Audio Memories in dementia care'. The current study will inform the second stage of the project, where people with dementia and their family members will be involved in co-designing personalised sentimental soundscape playlists. The project will examine the benefits of 'sentimental sounds', which we define as those associated with a precious memory.

Various media have been used and shown to be beneficial for RT for people with dementia [4, 5]. Music, in particular, is a popular tool to facilitate reminiscing [6, 7]. However, research has not explored whether everyday recorded sounds can also be beneficial for people with dementia, in a similar way to music. This is despite evidence showing individual sounds are as evocative for autobiographical memory as photographs [8–10]. Research shows people have preferences for types of everyday sounds [11] and the value of soundscapes in evoking memory. However, the relationship between everyday soundscapes and the emotions and memories they evoke requires more research. Previous research has focussed on the psychoacoustics of sounds and perception of these sounds [12], preferences rather than evoked emotions [11], and has tended to focus on the value of sounds [13] at the point of memory encoding [10] rather than memory recall. The aim of the current study was to explore what sounds are useful in evoking emotional memories for carers of people with dementia, and how to elicit these data, as a first step to creating evocative soundscapes that could be beneficial for people with dementia and their informal carers in the home environment. This builds on work by Houben et al. [14], which used generic soundscapes of everyday sounds as a tool for reminiscing with people in dementia.

2 Method

Twenty-two carers of people with dementia completed an online survey (male = 1, female = 21). Participants were accessed from the industry partner's database. Participants were from a range of age ranges (40–49 years = 2; 50–59 years = 7; 60–69 years = 8; 70–79 years = 5). Participants fulfilled a variety of carer roles, including having a parent with dementia (N = 13), a spouse with dementia (N = 3), a relative with dementia (N = 2) and caring for someone with dementia through a professional relationship (N = 4).

Participants were asked two types of questions: firstly, to recall their specific emotional memories, and then to describe the everyday sounds associated with these memories. For example, one question was to describe a happy memory and then describe the sounds associated with it. Secondly, participants were asked to detail sounds associated with particular emotions, then to explain why these sounds were emotionally evocative. For example, another question was to describe sounds that made you feel sad and explain why. Questions were designed to represent the four emotion quadrants of the circumplex emotion space [15] with Fig. 1 showing the four key emotions from which the questions were derived. This was done to address a short-coming in the literature which tends to focus only on the positive emotion space. Participants were instructed to focus on everyday sounds, rather than music. Qualitative data was captured in the form of free text comments and analysed using content analysis [16], focussing on type of emotion, type of sound and narrative content. Data were then explored using themes derived from the narrative content and through application of the circumplex model of emotion as a framework.

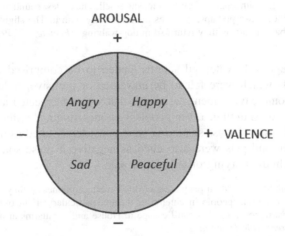

Fig. 1. Emotion topics determining questions about sound representing four quadrants in the circumplex model of emotion (after [15]).

3   Results and Discussion

Results showed similar patterns of the types of memories evoked as in other memory studies, with memories largely capturing childhood and early adulthood, evidencing a reminiscence bump [17]. The analysis showed that sounds differed more by positive or negative valence than by level of arousal or by specific emotion. Positive sounds tended to be comprised of predominantly natural sounds or soundscapes reflecting intimate, family environments, along with sounds of joy, such as children laughing or contented pet sounds.

"Laughter, this was a theme when all these people got together and the sound of the sea, also cosy in the caravan with the sound of rain on the metal roof". *Female, 60–69, with a parent with dementia.*

"Walking along a beach in the autumn, with the wind blowing. Waves crashing, seabirds calling, the sound of wind blowing". *Female, 60–69, with a parent with dementia.*

"My mobile phone - it's ring tone is a special song from 1973! Birdsong, the murmur of childrens' voices from nearby school playground…Little snorty noises from our dog and the sound of the front door when my husband gets in in the evenings, followed by the theme tune to the BBC Six O'clock News". *Female, 50–59, with a relative with dementia.*

Familiar sounds were cited as positive, which is common within the music literature. Birdsong, sounds of water, wind rustling in the trees, cat purrs, and background sounds of families in close quarters were consistently cited as being associated to positive emotions and memories.

"Gentle buzzing of insects. Bird sounds, not lots of song, just single occasional calls from multiple directions. Rustling in the long grass. A distant dog bark. The tractor sounds are very evocative as they rumble along well into the night and for some reason remind me of being a child and going to bed whilst it was still light outside, and finding my bedcovers were warm from the days sunlight with a particularly comforting smell. The curlew sound brings something bigger than happiness, awe perhaps, it makes me long to fly with it. The slight squeak of my neighbours' five-barred gate as they return from dog-walking". *Female, 50–59, with a parent with dementia.*

In contrast, negatively valenced sounds tended to be comprised of manmade or mechanical sounds which were felt to be unwanted or intrusive, reflecting a lack of control over the sonic environment, or sounds that were unexpected and loud. People talking too loudly or shouting, other people's phones ringing, traffic sounds, plates smashing, door slams, and glass shattering were consistently cited as negative sounds. Sounds of children and pets were also cited as negative if these sounds represented distress, such as children crying or animals in pain.

"Noise from mobile devices when people either don't wear earphones or they do but can still hear. Noisy children. Loud people in cinema or theatre, particularly if inconsiderate during performance. Construction noise if I can't escape it. House and car alarms at night". *Female, 40–49, with a parent with dementia.*

"Chalk scraping on board. School days…Horns blaring. Stress and fear…Child crying. Despair. Being parent under stress… People laughing at the vulnerable…Plate or glass falling onto the floor and smashing…Dogs barking repeatedly…Blaring music…infringement of peace". *Female, 70–79, with a parent with dementia.*

Happy soundscapes tended to be busy, featuring human voices and personal activities. Peaceful soundscapes were similar, although conveyed more space and were comprised of primarily natural sounds. The following quotes are taken from one male participant (aged 50–59, with a parent with dementia), first showing his happy memory sounds, followed by peaceful memory sounds:

"The hiss turning on the gas and the whoosh sound as the gas mantle was lit with a match for the lights inside the caravan. Seagulls making noises. The waves on the beach. The sounds we made trampolining and roller skating. The sound of the rain on the caravan roof and windows in a gale. The fisherman's boat chugging along when we went line fishing. The Bingo caller. Sounds of the slot machines. Playing card games shouting out "Snap!". Listening to the radio for hours as we had no television in the caravan in the 1970s. The sound of the caravan door opening and closing. The sound of opening the windows and slamming them shut. The clanking of the gas cylinder when it had to be changed over. The different acoustics of being inside a confined space all together rather than in a big house. Laughing and joking together". *Sounds associated with a happy memory.*

"Few sounds. Peace and quiet. Cars on the road driving slowly through the park. Birds. People playing football. Children playing. Sound of walking on a gravel path. Sound of wind rustling leaves in the many trees. Many airplanes overhead as they are on the flight path to Heathrow airport nearby. Dogs barking. Ducks quacking". *Sounds associated with a peaceful memory.*

One unexpected finding was that some man-made digital sounds, such as mobile phone ringtones, were judged positive due to associations with social connection and personal relationships.

"Sounds I love...phone ringing-friends or family calling. FaceTime sound on my mobile phone-seeing friends and family keeping in touch". *Male, 50–59, with a parent with dementia.*

This demonstrates another finding across the data. Some sounds were associated with both positive and negative emotions, depending upon the specific acoustic properties of the sound, what it represented and the associations it had with different contexts. For example, the sound of children could be either positive or negative, depending upon whether the child was "giggling" or "chortling", eliciting positive emotions, or whether the child was "crying" or "screaming", associated with distress. This shows the context in which the sound is embedded is critical for determining the emotions and memories that are elicited. In another example, the sound of a pet donkey braying was said to be positive in one comment, but also negative in another as the donkey died long ago. She says "I love the sound of a donkey braying -reminds me of our childhood pet Charlie". Then later she says "the donkey braying reminds me of my favourite pet and my childhood so makes me sad that it has long gone". *(Female, 60–69, with a parent with dementia).* This can be seen as a poignant or nostalgic memory for something happy that was lost.

The results also showed that whilst the sounds may be consistent across participants, the reasons for these sounds being loved or hated were idiosyncratic. For example, whilst waves were widely cited as positive sounds, these waves represented different beaches that were associated with different memories, such as favourite holiday spots or reminders of family holidays.

"Being on holiday in a quiet resort. The waves gently lapping. The wind gently blowing. The warmth seeping into my body. Nothing to do. Nowhere to go. Just pure relaxation. The odd bird calling. People walking by chatting as they go... The waves gently lapping. The wind gently blowing. Occasional bird calls". *Female, 70–79, with a spouse with dementia, peaceful memory and associated sounds.*

"I lived in the Bahamas for a while and before it was built up we would take a picnic to the end of Paradise Island and sit on the beach. White sand, blue, blue water, and whilst sitting there we saw a Ray go along the shallows. We were both happy and contented although life was not easy on the island small snippets gave so much back. The sounds associated are quiet, and gentle lapping water". *Female, 60–69, with a parent with dementia, recalling their peaceful memory and associated sounds.*

"Watching the sun set along the North Wales coast from Deganwy. Felt totally at peace and in the moment. No worries or things to sort, very mindful! Listening to the sea and the birds, no one else around. The associated sounds were the sea and the birds". *Female, 40–49, with a parent with dementia, recalling a happy memory and associated sounds.*

Further, whilst birdsong was widely cited as a positive sound, the type of birdsong was different across participants. For example, one participant cited the sound of "woodpigeons", whereas another cited "seagulls", one cited "blackbirds" and another cited "skylark".

Together, these results demonstrate the importance of eliciting narratives about sounds, for understanding their meaning and why they have their effect by association. Many narratives described a kind of journey through sounds associated with particular places, contexts or memories, such as caravan holidays or family rituals. These point to the importance of memories as an organising construct for sound collections, and memory narratives as a technique for their presentation and interpretation.

"Waking up as a child in my bedroom on summer mornings. In the school holidays the days were always full of promise - no particular place to be or things to do just freedom. There was always a dawn chorus and that was supplemented by the neighbour's chickens - the cockerel and then general cluckings. I also like to remember the general background noises of my parents getting up, moving about downstairs - the kettle whistling, the paper being delivered, etc." *Female, 50–59, with a relative with dementia.*

"Warm, still, summer evening. Sky darkening blue and clear. A crescent moon glowing pale in the early evening light. Insects flying drowsily in groups visible just above the top-stones of a dry-stone wall. A curlew passing rapidly somewhere above; the volume of its haunting cry increasing rapidly and then lost in the contours of high moorland visible all around. The mountain in front of me brooding and dark. No particular thoughts, just a sense of the largely unknown and unseen busy things happening in the non-human realm around me. Other bird sounds; occasional and from random directions. I'm standing on a patch of grass with senses awake to the purity of the colours of the light and to the purity of the sounds that paradoxically elicit a sense of peace. I feel as though my awareness is hovering a little above ground and being drawn into fathomlessness. And a distant tractor gently rumbling on into the night as the work goes on to get the hay inside before it rains. The people I love the most are all nearby and are doing OK. I feel safe". *Female, 50–59, with a parent with dementia.*

Finally, we want to report a personal observation as analysts of these kinds of narratives, as the previous quote illustrates. We felt quite privileged to be reading them as powerful insights into the personalities and lives of the authors. This is despite the anonymous and impersonal method of collection via an online form. Many narratives revealed special, intimate and private moments that are rarely shared in ordinary conversation, such the memory of a sister and brother making Sunday breakfast in bed for their parents and its associated sounds.

"There are many - but a very happy memory is Sunday breakfast with my parents as a child. My brother and I thought we were so subtle getting out of bed and tip toeing downstairs to make breakfast for our parents. The clanking and banging of plates clearly couldn't be heard upstairs as we spoke in hushed voices. The sound of the chair scraping across the floor so I could stand on it to stir the scrambled eggs and turn the bacon under the grill... nor the aroma of the cooking bacon were discernible upstairs in the small 3 bedroom house we lived in. We were always so happy when we put our feast on the tray and carried it upstairs and devastated when our parents insisted on eating at the table rather than in bed. And then we would talk...talk about everything that has happened during the week - and laugh endlessly...normally at our parents' expense! The sounds associated are the clanking of the pan on the job and the wooden spoon slowly bashing the sides of the pan whilst stirring the scrambled eggs (the way my dad taught me and before microwaves). Then of course is the scraping of the grill pan as first we grilled the bacon and then the bread. The kettle whistling on the job before the invention of the electric kettle (or at least before we ever had one!). I also remember the sound of our heavy plates (Poole pottery seconds - when nobody wanted them!) clanking together and against the cups. I also remember the hushed voices as my brother and I went about our respective tasks - proud of our achievements and convinced as ever around the stealth of our plan". *Female, 50–59, with a parent with dementia.*

This demonstrates the potential value of using everyday sounds, or questions about sounds, as stimuli for personal recollections that may not be triggered or discussed through visual stimuli, such as photos. Photos tend to capture important moments that are publicly experienced, whereas sounds appear to evoke very ordinary everyday experiences of life that are intimate by nature. Hence, using everyday sounds for RT has the potential to open up a different aspect of the participant's world, perhaps forgotten, and connect them to recollections of their past daily lives.

"It's the little things - I like hearing our neighbour's car doors opening and closing and I listen out for little Emily – she's such a joy. I love the sound of the squirrels taking nuts out of their feeder and the bang as the lid drops down. I once watched and counted 23 bangs as the fattest squirrel in the world tucked in to his breakfast. I love the sound of lapping water - which always reminds me of playing with my children at bath time when they were young. I used to soap them and they always thought it would be really helpful to soap my arms too - so I would sit there elbow deep in water being soaped and splashed. Which reminds me there is nothing better than the sound of a little girl laughing and giggling - it always reminds me of taking my girls to the park and pushing them on the swings - and the whispers of little girls always reminds me of the devastation in the playroom as they lined up every toy they had to attend yet another teddy wedding (at one point I think these were a weekly affair in our house!)" *Female, 50–59, with a parent with dementia.*

4   Conclusion

Results showed consistency across individuals as to the types of everyday sounds that are associated with positive and negative emotions. These sounds align with findings from the music literature, such as familiar sounds being positive and unexpected sounds being negative [18]. These similarities justify further exploration of how everyday sounds could be beneficial for RT and for people with dementia to facilitate recall and elicit a variety of emotions. In a second phase of research, we are exploring the notion of Sentimental Audio Memories further with home visits to people with dementia and their carers, involving playback of personal sounds for feedback and discussion.

The current study's approach to explore the four quadrants of the emotion space provided interesting insights into what sounds could be beneficial and why, beyond merely preference or positive emotions. It is clear that complex soundscapes related to specific autobiographical memories and accompanied by a personal narrative may offer more potential than using either generic soundscapes not associated to a narrative, or single sounds.

The use of everyday recorded sounds, as opposed to other media, potentially enables different types of memories to be elicited, specifically those that enable recollection of private and intimate everyday life, rather than specific, one-off important events. Future research should explore what value these everyday recollections may offer that is distinct from the types of recollections evoked by other media. Our discovery of sounds associated with both positive and negative emotions is important here because it suggests that mixed emotions may be evoked by nostalgic sounds for happy times that are now lost. We believe this is a healthy thing, not to be avoided by research or technology for people with dementia. This is similar to findings showing that people enjoy sad music when it evokes past memories [19] and the role of nostalgia as a restorative factor to counter loneliness [20]. There is a tendency inspired by concerns for ethical treatment of vulnerable people to avoid exposure to negative emotions and experiences. However, our data suggests that negative emotions may sometimes be part and parcel of positive ones, and may even be the most life affirming. The ability for a film to make someone cry is not normally considered a bad thing and we think the same should apply to sounds and other stimuli for reminiscing and reflecting on life.

"The sound of my dad singing makes me smile. My dad has dementia, and when he's singing he expresses himself more clearly, seems to be more in control of his world and I believe he has a level of contentment". *Female, 50–59, with a parent with dementia.*

"I love a steam train sound, reminds me so much of my dad whose passion was steam trains (his interest now diminished due to dementia)". *Female, 60–69, with a parent with dementia.*

In this first stage of a larger project, we have established everyday sounds have great potential for reminiscence activities, offering the potential to stimulate different types of memories to other media. Results showed asking about memories and extrapolating sounds from these was more effective that asking about sounds initially, then associated memories. It is emerged the importance of personal narrative and therefore personalised soundscapes. In the second stage of the project, where we will co-design reminiscence with sentimental sounds with people with dementia and their family member carers in their home, the current study will inform our approach. Namely, we will first ask people with dementia and their carers about their memories, then extrapolate the sounds from these data. Secondly, we will explore the role of nostalgic and negative memory reminiscence, rather than focusing only on positive memories. Thirdly, the soundscapes we create will be personalised for the person with dementia, rather than generic. The second co-design stage will compare single sounds, complex soundscapes generated from narrative content and generic soundscapes with people with dementia and their carers, to further explore results from the current study. Finally, the current study has demonstrated the value of reminiscing for carers of people with dementia, facilitated through everyday sounds, and thus justifies the second stage of the project exploring a collaborative reminiscent activity between people with dementia and their family member carers in the home environment.

Acknowledgements. This work was supported by EPSRC grant Making Sense of Sounds and EPSRC IAA grant Sentimental Audio Memories for dementia Care, grant number EP/N014111/1.

References

1. Dempsey, L., et al.: Reminiscence in dementia: a concept analysis. Dementia **13**(2), 176–192 (2014)
2. Pinquart, M., Forstmeier, S.: Effects of reminiscence interventions on psychosocial outcomes: a meta-analysis. Aging Ment. Health **16**(5), 541–558 (2012)
3. Beard, R.L.: Art therapies and dementia care: a systematic review. Dementia **11**(5), 633–656 (2012)
4. Alm, N., Dye, R., Gowans, G., Campbell, J., Astell, A., Ellis, M.: A communication support system for older people with dementia. Computer **40**(5), 35–41 (2007)
5. Yasuda, K., Kuwabara, K., Kuwahara, N., Abe, S., Tetsutani, N.: Effectiveness of personalised reminiscence photo videos for individuals with dementia. Neuropsychol. Rehabil. **19**(4), 603–619 (2009)
6. Istvandity, L.: Combining music and reminiscence therapy interventions for wellbeing in elderly populations: a systematic review. Complement. Ther. Clin. Pract. **28**, 18–25 (2017)
7. Elliott, M., Gardner, P.: The role of music in the lives of older adults with dementia ageing in place: a scoping review. Dementia **17**(2), 199–213 (2018)
8. Bijsterveld, K., Van Dijck, J.: Sound Souvenirs: Audio Technologies, Memory and Cultural Practices. University Press, Amsterdam (2009)
9. Frohlich, D.M.: Audiophotography: Bringing Photos to Life with Sounds. Springer, Berlin (2004). https://doi.org/10.1007/978-1-4020-2210-4
10. Frohlich, D.M.: Fast Design, Slow Innovation: Audiophotography Ten Years On. Springer, Cham (2015). https://doi.org/10.1007/978-3-319-21939-4
11. Schafer, R.M.: The Soundscape: Our Sonic Environment and the Tuning of the World. Destiny Books, Rochester (1994)
12. Bones, O., Cox, T.J., Davies, W.J.: Sound categories: category formation and evidence-based taxonomies. Front. Psychol. **9**, 1277 (2018)
13. Oleksik, G., Frohlich, D., Brown, L.M., Sellen, A.: Sonic interventions: understanding and extending the domestic soundscape. In: Proceedings of the SIGCHI Conference on Human Factors in Computing Systems, pp. 1419–1428. ACM, April 2008
14. Houben, M., Brankaert, R., Bakker, S., Kenning, G., Bongers, I., Eggen B.: Foregrounding everyday sounds in dementia. In: Proceedings of the DIS 2019 Conference on Designing Interactive Systems, June 2019
15. Russell, J.A.: A circumplex model of affect. J. Pers. Soc. Psychol. **39**(6), 1161–1178 (1980)
16. Elo, S., Kyngäs, H.: The qualitative content analysis process. J. Adv. Nurs. **62**(1), 107–115 (2008)
17. Rathbone, C.J., Moulin, C.J., Conway, M.A.: Self-centered memories: the reminiscence bump and the self. Mem. Cogn. **36**(8), 1403–1414 (2008)
18. Ali, S.O., Peynircioğğlu, Z.F.: Intensity of emotions conveyed and elicited by familiar and unfamiliar music. Music. Percept. Interdiscip. J. **27**(3), 177–182 (2010)
19. Sachs, M.E., Damasio, A., Habibi, A.: The pleasures of sad music: a systematic review. Front. Hum. Neurosci. **9**, 404 (2015)
20. Zhou, X., Sedikides, C., Wildschut, T., Gao, D.G.: Counteracting loneliness: on the restorative function of nostalgia. Psychol. Sci. **19**(10), 1023–1029 (2008)

Improvisation and Reciprocal Design: Soundplay for Dementia

Gail Kenning[1,4](✉) ⓘ, Alon Ilsar[2] ⓘ, Rens Brankaert[3,5] ⓘ,
and Mark Evans[1] ⓘ

[1] Faculty of Arts and Social Sciences, University of Technology Sydney,
Sydney, Australia
Gail.kenning@uts.edu.au
[2] Faculty of IT, Monash University, Melbourne, Australia
[3] Industrial Design, Systemic Change Group, Eindhoven University of
Technology, Eindhoven, The Netherlands
[4] Ageing Futures Institute University of New South Wales, Sydney, Australia
[5] Institute of Allied Health Professions, Fontys University of Applied Sciences,
Eindhoven, The Netherlands

Abstract. Design and research studies regarding the impact of music on the wellbeing of people living with advanced dementia are ongoing. Many of these focus on reminiscence and the use of familiar songs, music and instruments. However, fewer studies have explored the creative and improvisational aspects of music making with people living with advanced dementia. This project explored the response of people from this group to an innovative gestural electronic instrument—The AirSticks™. The engagement promoted creative musical improvisation and resulted in a highly emotive response from one particular participant, suggesting the creative impulse can be retained.

Keywords: Dementia · Design · Improvisation · Music · Creativity

1   Introduction

Everyday acts of creativity have been shown to impact flourishing and improve individual's wellbeing (Conner et al. 2017). The impact of art, design and music programs have been theoretically and empirically explored and show both individual and social benefits for people in general and more specifically people living with dementia. However, people living with dementia, especially in the advanced stages, have less opportunity for self-directed open-ended creativity or improvisation, and as a result their creative engagements are therefore limited. This paper discusses a project to explore the creative and improvisational aspects of musical engagement directly with people living with dementia.

Research has shown that people in advanced stages of dementia positively respond to familiar music and may recall or affectively 'remember' songs, music and lyrics when exposed to them. Creative group therapy sessions in this context often explore music making with people living with dementia by, for example, playing commonplace percussion instruments such as drums or tambourine, which may or may not be familiar

R. Brankaert and W. IJsselsteijn (Eds.): D-Lab 2019, CCIS 1117, pp. 82–91, 2019.
https://doi.org/10.1007/978-3-030-33540-3_8

to individual participants. But, the open-ended possibilities for creative sound improvisation in relation to people living with dementia remains under explored and is often not part of music therapy programs. During a pilot project, called *Soundplay for wellbeing* people living with dementia were introduced to new technologies; new ways to explore sound, by working spatially with sound; and new types of electronically generated sounds. All of these approaches were unfamiliar to them. Workshops were held with people living with advanced dementia to expose them to these different ways of exploring sound. During these workshops we examined their response to an innovative gestural electronic musical instrument—The AirSticks[TM]— which had been developed for use by professional electronic musicians. The aim was to understand whether people living with advanced dementia could engage with The AirSticks[TM], to what extent they would be interested in engaging creatively and using the system for improvisation with sound, and what changes needed to be made to the hardware and software of The AirSticks[TM] to make them accessible and available to people living with dementia. Alongside The AirStick[TM], participants were introduced to Makey Makey[TM] technology in the form of an easy access 'drum kit' and 'piano'. The participants in the workshops responded with varying degrees of interest to these technologies. However, one participant showed an intense curiosity which eventuated in a deep affective response when she engaged in a spontaneous improvisation with a professional musician engaged as a researcher on the pilot project. This study showed that improvisation and creativity with sound can be activated by modern technology and opens an exciting field of research to pursue further.

2 Background

Research has increasingly shown how music can positively impact people living with mild cognitive impairment, limited cognitive functions, and advanced dementia (Baird and Samson, 2015; Gold, 2013). For example, personalised playlists and soundscapes are increasingly being assembled by family members and care givers to enable people living with advanced dementia to listen to favourite or familiar songs and sounds as an activity in itself, and to be used in music players embedded in tangible objects (Kenning 2018; Treadaway and Kenning 2015). These sound fragments and music selected by family members and care givers are used to stimulate, excite, calm and relax, to prompt memory recall, or to elicit affective responses from people living with advanced dementia in aged and dementia care settings. An exemplar of this type of approach is the *Music and Memory program* developed in Canada, and now operating worldwide, which attests to the impact that music has in improving the wellbeing of people living with dementia (http://www.MusicandMemory.org 2011). In the context of listening to music and soundscapes, the tunes, lyrics, and songs are usually familiar to the person living with dementia, and even if they are not able to recall the music specifically, they may have an affective or implicit memory response to what they hear (Sabat, 2006).

Similarly when people living with advanced dementia engage in music making, they often engage with commonplace musical instruments, (or objects that act as substitutes), although, all participants may not have used them before ("Drumming workshops" 2019). Often, in these types of activities there is no intent to extend the use of the musical instruments beyond its conventional use, to explore individual creative responses to music making or to promote improvisation. However, recent research studies and design projects have begun to explore the impact of both familiar and unfamiliar music, ambient sounds and soundscapes on people living with dementia (Houben et al. 2019; Kenning et al. 2018). For example, the *Everyday Sounds Of Dementia* project explores sounds and soundscapes with people living with dementia and shows that technology can be used to support the associative capacity of people with dementia and provide a pleasant and creative moment together instigated by sounds (Houben et al. 2019; Kenning et al. 2018).

The aims of the *Soundplay for Wellbeing* project were to explore the extent to which people living with advanced dementia could engage creatively with The Air-Sticks™ and to what extent they could musically improvise. Musical improvisation is a complex concept and definitions of what constitutes improvisation vary. They include, for example the extent to which the performer can perform impromptu music in a creative and spontaneous way (Azzara 2002) and where "…an individual has internalized a music vocabulary and is able to understand and to express musical ideas spontaneously, in the moment of performance" (Hickey 2002). Improvisation is therefore about taking and relinquishing initiative (when playing along with someone else) and is an 'in the moment' experience.

In design for people with dementia co-design approaches have been adapted to enable people living with dementia, even in advanced stages of the disease, to engage and contribute to the development of services, products and activities that can support their general health and wellbeing and increase their quality of life (Hendriks et al. 2014; Kenning 2017; Maldonado Branco et al. 2017; Treadaway and Kenning 2015). Such approaches often use visual and tactile probes in workshop environments to elicit verbal and non-verbal responses to influence design decisions and so contribute to ongoing development of new ideas. The aim of the *Soundplay for Wellbeing* project was to use a well-developed prototype, the AirSticks™, which was close to being a finished product designed for use by professional musicians——and explore whether it would transfer into the domain of dementia care. We wanted to find out whether there was any interest in engaging with the instrument, whether it would be a tool for creativity and improvisation and how it could be further adapted to suit the needs of people living with advanced dementia.

3   Methodology

We set up two workshops in two residential care facilities in Sydney, Australia and used these to explore the extent to which people living with advanced dementia would be motivated to engage creatively in musical improvisation with electronically generated music using an unfamiliar musical instrument—The AirSticks™. A total of eleven participants took part in the workshops each with a diagnosis of dementia, as advised by the care organisation with the duty of care for them. The project used a research through design approach by using developed design prototypes, in varying degrees of finish, to assess the interest and impact by and on people living with advanced dementia (Zimmerman and Forlizzi 2014). During the session the researchers made observations and notes of how people with dementia engaged with the various technologies present.

3.1 The Prototypes

The main aim of the *Soundplay for Wellbeing* project was to investigate the responses of participants in the use of and creative engagement with the technology. The main focus of the workshops were the AirSticks™ and therefore we set up two 'stations' where people could explore them. Next to these, we also created two Makey Makey™ prototypes, these were used to engage participants when the AirSticks™ were in use by other participants and provide insights concerning engagement in their own right. Makey Makey™ is an 'off the shelf' simple circuit board acclaimed as an 'invention kit for everyone'. The Makey Makey™ prototypes were chosen because they used electronic technology to support music making and had been used successfully in a previous separate study which had explored reciprocal design approaches (Kenning 2018). When used in the earlier project the Makey Makey™ 'piano' and 'drums' prototypes gave researchers insights into the level of interest and ability of participants living with advanced dementia had in engaging in creative sound play. The findings from that study showed that the Makey Makey™ musical instrument prototypes had generated sustained interest with people living with advanced dementia (Kenning 2017). In this *Soundplay for Wellbeing* pilot study, the Makey Makey™ hardware and software kits were used to make a representation of a piano, and a combined piano/drumkit with conductive foil.

The primary prototype to be explored was The AirSticks™, a gestural musical instrument developed for professional electronic percussionists. It was designed by drummer and electronic producer Dr Alon Ilsar (second author) and computer programmer and composer Mark Havryliv. The AirSticks™ system uses off the shelf gestural game controllers to generate a MIDI output. By moving the controllers in space, tracked by a central hub, different sound mappings could be added. The designers explored many different ways that the movement of the controllers could be mapped to sound. They investigated a range of approaches working within diverse collaborative musical performers in a range of situations to overcome 'creative paralysis'. This resulted in custom software allows sound to be mapped spatially to the motion capture technology of the controllers. The result is a 'gestural instrument' that converts the physical movement of the user, through a mapping process using computer software, into data and sound. The software provides access to a wide range of instrument sounds (drums, harp, bells, etc), it can be programmed to recreate ambient sounds such as church bells, wind, water, or birds, or play a personalised musical playlist of songs. The range of sounds available through The AirSticks™ is vast, and at the discretion of the composer. All of the sound elements can be 'positioned' in space and 'found' by moving the hardware controller in different directions with up to six degrees of freedom.

3.2 Method

Before attendees arrived at the workshop tables and chairs were located at each corner of the room to create 'sound stations'. On two tables there were a set of AirSticks™, two controllers and a central hub, linked to a computer with The AirSticks™ custom designed spatial sound software installed, and a speaker. On the other two tables was a Makey Makey™ 'piano' and a Makey Makey™ 'piano/drum kit' available for interaction (Fig. 1). These consisted of conductive metal tape, to indicate piano keys and drums, placed on a sheet of acrylic. The metal tape was then connected to the Makey Makey™ circuit board connected to a computer and speaker, loaded with the Makey Makey™ music software.

Researchers worked together one-on-one with participants as they engaged with each of the systems present at the sound stations. During these sessions the researchers made recordings and notes of the engagements, aiming to stimulate the people living with dementia positively as much as possible. If a person was not interested or no longer engaged with the system the researcher would retreat and facilitate a safe environment. We will refer to both systems used during the study as "musical instruments".

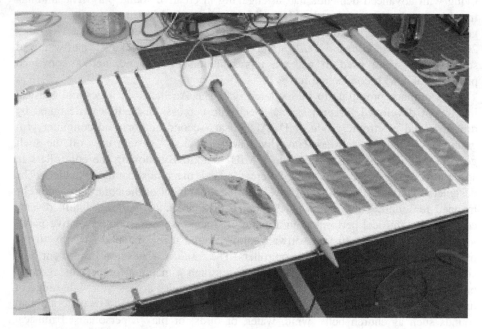

Fig. 1. The Makey Makey™ 'piano/drum kit' prototype in production

4 Findings

A total of eleven participants took part in the study across two residential care facilities. The responses to the AirSticks™ and the Makey Makey™ prototypes varied greatly. One woman refused to engage in any way with any of the instruments stating that her husband *"was the musical one, he was so musical"*. Another woman, 'Paula' engaged for a short period of time, but her responses appeared to be complicit rather than curious, as she did what was suggested to her and no more. It became apparent that she was more focussed on going outside for a cigarette, and she left the workshop early. 'Neela' had reduced mobility and physical limitations in her arms and hand movements. She was not able to engage fully with the musical instruments. But she stayed throughout the workshop and engaged as far as possible with curiosity. While a range of responses were observed this paper will primarily focus on the response of one participant, 'Violet', because of the intensity of her engagement and because she provided insights to how the AirSticks™ could impact on emotion and wellbeing.

'Violet' was a participant in the second workshop, in the second aged care facility visited for this study. She was brought into the workshop room by a carer who introduced her to the researchers, along with another participant, introduced as her best friend who she had known since early childhood. She was small and looked frail and was not able to speak. She smiled constantly and laughed often when she was spoken to. She was taken to one of the sound stations with the AirSticks™. The software had been programmed to play a range of musical instrument that were clearly distinguishable (harp, drums, and bells). A games controller was placed in her hand and she was shown how if she moved the controller the sounds, playing through the speaker via the computer, changed. 'Violet' engaged immediately holding on to the game controller and moving it in the way she had been shown. She was accompanied by one of the researchers who sat alongside her. As she engaged with the sounds of a harp she began to sing. The words of the song, or the tune being sung were not clear or coherent, but she put a great deal of energy into the process moving her hand holding the games controller from side to side. The researcher alongside copied her responses and also began to sing and hum. They continued in this way for a sustained period of time. 'Violet' showed no sign of tiring and laughed frequently. Subsequently, 'Violet' was introduced to the other two sound stations where the Makey Makey™ equipment was located. Again, she engaged with great gusto, laughing, smiling, and playing the 'piano' and the 'piano/drums', to such an extent that wear and tear was beginning to show on both of the Makey Makey™ prototypes as the metallic tape began to wear thin.

Towards the end of the workshop 'Violet' was taken to the 'sound station' where the second AirSticks™ were located. The software at this station had been set up to play excerpts of music in the form of a spatialised playlist. By pointing the AirSticks™ up and to the right rock n roll music played, pointing down to the left played Bach. Other accessible music included the Beatles, and Country music, all curated to match the possible interest and age category of the participants. As 'Violet' sat down to engage with the AirSticks™, she understood how to use the games controller because of her previous experience of The AirSticks™ at the first 'sound station'. But because she engaged with such a flourish and moved her arms and the controller around often and quickly, only small fragments of the programmed songs could be heard. Songs could not be differentiated one from another and sounds became indistinguishable. It was also difficult to relate the sounds being played to the movement of her body. While this version of the software that operated as a spatially located playlist of songs, had worked particularly well for another participant whose movement was slower and physical dexterity more limited, it became apparent that this version of the software and sounds selected, did not activate or stimulate 'Violet'.

At this point 'Violet' was accompanied by a researcher who was a professional musician and the inventor of The AirSticks™. Recognising the inappropriateness of this soundtrack for 'Violet', he loaded a soundscape that had been created for a professional music audience to show the range of possibilities offered by the AirSticks™. The soundscape provided access to a range of instruments such as gamelan, xylophone, drums, and harp, which could all be accessed spontaneously through specific movements or combination of movements. The researcher sat alongside her, placed a controller in her hand, picked up the second controller and began to make broad strokes in space, with it. 'Violet' copied. As they sat together she continued copying his movements and appeared to recognise how the sounds changed with different movements. This process continued for more than fifteen minutes. Their movement were both synchronous and asynchronous as they engaged together. Throughout the experience 'Violet' was singing loudly. Her words were not coherent and the singing was akin to an intense wailing (but did not signal any distress).

During the shared experience, after a sustained period the researcher began to slowly place the controller down seemingly signalling the end of the session. 'Violet' began to follow suit and then stopped. She then lifted the controller and began to explore the soundscape alone. The wailing continued and became more emotive. The sound coming from her had turned more melancholic. 'Violet' was no longer smiling or laughing as she had been. But neither did she appear distressed as she wiped a tear from her eye and continued to make electronic musical sounds. The researcher, who had led the initial engagement now joined in again, but this time he followed her movements as they took turns to lead the activity. They improvised together for in excess of 25 min exploring the range of instruments and ways to play them.

As the improvisation came to an end there was a short silence when all three researchers, the carers in the room and 'Violet' stopped. She appeared happy and tired. The carer suggested that it was time for her to go. Her friend, who had come into the room with her began to talk to her and comment on her playing. 'Violet' seemed to respond, but her words remained incoherent. She was laughing as she left. 'Violet' had engaged in an exuberant improvisation with the researcher in the workshop and had exhibited signs of, in Hickey's terms, 'internalising a music vocabulary' of how to create sounds using The AirSticks™. During the engagement with the Airsticks™, 'Violet' showed a surprisingly authentic and in-control engagement with technology that she was unfamiliar with. During the improvisation phase (Fig. 2), her emotional expressiveness increased as well as signs of taking initiative and a better understanding of place and time.

Fig. 2. 'Violet' engages in musical improvisation with a researcher and musician

5 Discussion

In this study we showed how newly appropriated technology could lead to surprisingly creative engagements with sound including aspects of improvisation. The AirSticks™ had not been designed specifically for people living with dementia. Instead, the instrument had been developed to support musical creativity for professional musicians. Post-development the AirSticks™ had been introduced to a range of people including musicians and choreographers, and people with access needs including people with autism and paraplegia, to explore inclusive creative engagement possibilities. The decision to engage with people living with dementia came about due to the recognition of the creative possibilities that The AirSticks™ offered. This provided opportunity for creative sound researchers, design for dementia researchers and dementia care staff to collaborate and explore the potential in this area. It was important that the engagement with people living with dementia began while The AirSticks™ was still in a development stage (with no market product yet available). This allowed for changes to be made to the hardware and software and for improved versions of the hardware to be produced specifically for this population and scenarios as described in the findings. In addition, it was important to examine the response of people living with dementia to The AirSticks™ in context, and to establish a framework for the types of soundscapes designed in the software that would have most impact. This sketches the beginning of a new type of research where the value of creative engagement and the lasting characteristics of the active engagement with sound should be investigated further.

In working with people living with advanced dementia in a workshop environment to understand how The AirSticks™ could be developed to support creativity and improvisation in this space, it was important that the workshops employed a reciprocal design approach. This meant ensuring that while researchers and designers gained knowledge about the potential for musical improvisation in this space, the participants had a positive, enjoyable experience (Kenning, 2018). This proved to be the case, not only for 'Violet', but also for participants whose responses to The AirSticks™ were not always as enthusiastic as 'Violet's', but they were observed enjoying the opportunity for social connection and engagement.

6   Conclusion

The AirSticks™ had not been designed for creative engagements by people living with advanced dementia. But the potential for this technology to contribute in this space became apparent when researchers were able to engage and explore the cross-disciplinary possibilities of the creative systems, processes and objects. While engaging with the developed prototypes for creative sound improvisation in the aged and dementia care environment directly with people living with advanced dementia, it became apparent that the creative impulse can be retained into the advanced stages of the condition. It was also apparent that technology and lack of familiarity with sounds or instruments was not necessarily off putting to people living with dementia. The AirSticks™ revealed the creative potential and drive of people living with dementia through 'Violet' and her personal and exuberant engagement. The use of the AirSticks™ in this environment showed what can be achieved through the collaborative engagement of researchers, designers, and care workers working across disciplines.

References

"Drumming workshops": 'Drumming workshops music to residents' ears. Aged Care Guide (2019). https://www.agedcareguide.com.au/talking-aged-care/drumming-workshops-music-to-residents-ears. Accessed Sept 2019

Azzara, C.D.: Improvisation. In: Colwell, R., Richardson, C. (eds.) New Handbook of Research in Music Teaching and Learning, pp. 171–187. Oxford University Press, Oxford (2002)

Conner, T.S., DeYoung, C.G., Silvia, P.J.: Everyday creative activity as a path to flourishing. J. Positive Psychol. 13(2) (2017). https://doi.org/10.1080/17439760.2016.1257049

Hendriks, N., Huybrechts, L., Wilkinson, A., Slegers, K.: Challenges in doing participatory design with people with dementia. In: Proceedings of the 13th Participatory Design Conference on Short Papers, Industry Cases, Workshop Descriptions, Doctoral Consortium papers, and Keynote abstracts - PDC 2014, vol. 2, pp. 33–36 (2014). Accessed http://dl.acm.org/citation.cfm?doid=2662155.2662196

Hickey, M.: Creativity research in music, visual art, theatre and dance. In: Colwell, R., Richardson, C. (eds.) New Handbook of Research in Music Teaching and Learning, pp. 398–415. Oxford University Press, Oxford (2002)

Houben, M., Brankaert, R., Bakker, S., Kenning, G., Bongers, I., Eggen, B.: Foregrounding Everyday Sounds in Dementia. Paper presented at the DIS 2019, San Diego (2019)

http://www.MusicandMemory.org (Producer). (2011). Alive Inside Film of Music and Memory Project - Henry's Story. [Video]. https://www.youtube.com/watch?v=5FWn4JB2YLU

Kenning, G.: Making It Together: Reciprocal design to promote positive wellbeing for people living with dementia. University of Technology Sydney (2017)

Kenning, G.: Reciprocal design: inclusive design approaches for people with late stage dementia. Des. Health 2(1), 1–21 (2018). https://doi.org/10.1080/24735132.2018.1453638

Kenning, G., Brankaert, R., Houben, M.: Exploring your soundscape. In: Paper presented at the Dementia Lab, Newcastle, UK (2018)

Maldonado Branco, R., Quental, J., Ribeiro, Ó.: Personalised participation: an approach to involve people with dementia and their families in a participatory design project. CoDesign 13(2), 127–143 (2017). https://doi.org/10.1080/15710882.2017.1310903

Sabat, S.R.: Implicit memory and people with Alzheimer's disease: implications for caregiving. Am. J. Alzheimer's Dis. Dementias 21(1), 11–14 (2006). https://doi.org/10.1177/153331750602100113

Treadaway, C., Kenning, G.: Sensor e-Textiles: person centred co-design for people with later stage dementia. Working Older People 20(2), 76–85 (2015)

Zimmerman, J., Forlizzi, J.: Research through design in HCI. In: Olson, J.S., Kellogg, W.A. (eds.) Ways of Knowing in HCI, pp. 167–189. Springer, New York (2014). https://doi.org/10.1007/978-1-4939-0378-8_8

Exploring How an Interactive Placemat Can Influence Eating Activities for People with Dementia

Ward de Groot, Maarten Houben[(✉)], and Bart Hengeveld

Department of Industrial Design, University of Technology Eindhoven,
Groene Loper 3, 5612 AE Eindhoven, The Netherlands
m.houben1@tue.nl

Abstract. People with dementia often face problems during eating activities, due to the loss of physical and cognitive functioning. With an increasing amount of research suggesting how everyday sounds can have beneficial effects for people with dementia, we raise the question whether everyday sounds related to eating can improve dining experiences in care facilities. To explore this, we deployed an interactive placemat during the eating activities of people with dementia. Observations and interviews gave insight into the interactions with the placemat, how these interactions offered distractions and the general atmosphere during eating activities. We encourage design-researchers to explore how sound-based interventions promote good eating behaviors, but an understanding of how people with dementia engage with sound and other sensory stimuli is needed in order for these interventions to be successful.

Keywords: Dementia · Care homes · Everyday sounds · Eating experience · Research through design

1 Introduction

As there is no cure for dementia to this day, alternative non-pharmacological approaches are needed to attend to the needs of people with dementia. Herein, technology plays a role by assisting people with dementia and enriching their daily activities [1]. Assistive technologies such as Qwiek.up [2] offer possibilities for caregivers to provide multi-sensorial stimuli to people with dementia by letting them engage with a combination of visual projections and sounds. The Tovertafel [3] is a playful intervention which lets people with late stage dementia interact with a diverse set of games which are projected on the dining table. Both of these designs demonstrate how technology can offer meaningful interactions that reduce agitated behavior and boredom during day-to-day activities and care routines.

Dementia induces problems on the daily activity of eating, as people lose physical and cognitive functioning [4]. However, the eating activity is considered to be important as people with dementia tend to be prone to malnutrition [5]. Stone [4] also mentions that improving the dining environment in care homes is a strategy in minimizing these difficulties to improve the eating behaviors of people with dementia.

© Springer Nature Switzerland AG 2019
R. Brankaert and W. IJsselsteijn (Eds.): D-Lab 2019, CCIS 1117, pp. 92–100, 2019.
https://doi.org/10.1007/978-3-030-33540-3_9

For instance, by prompting recognition that it is time for a meal by using placemats and cutlery [6]. Timlin and Rysenbry [7] designed tableware which reduced the complexity of handling cutlery and improved the eating activities of people in different stages of dementia. Additionally, playing relaxing or familiar background music improves the dining experience in care facilities, as it helps to reduce agitation [8, 9].

Similarly, everyday sounds other than music can offer a sense of relief and distraction by triggering meaningful associations and as such providing meaning to activities in the here and now [10]. This raises the question whether everyday sounds related to eating or food can improve the overall eating experience of people with dementia. In this paper we present the design and evaluation of an interactive placemat for improving the experience of eating moments for people with dementia and their caregivers. Furthermore, we offer insights in how interactions with touch and sound offered distraction before and in between eating moments, and present design implications for further research.

2 Interactive Placemat

2.1 Design Description

The design's aim was to let people with dementia engage with everyday sounds prior to their eating activities. The placemat was intended to prompt recognition that it is time for an eating activity through pictures and sounds. Three off-the-shelf placemats were modified to feature four conductive touch pads each (Fig. 1). The touchpads all included a picture related to the corresponding eating activity (breakfast, lunch, dinner). Whenever one of the pads was touched, a sound associated with the picture on the pad (see Table 1) was triggered. Whenever a sound was already playing and another touch input was given, the playing sound was interrupted by the newly initiated sound. The placemat only produced sounds that were initiated by the person with dementia by interacting with the touchpads. The sounds were designed to be equally loud, but varied in length (see Table 1).

2.2 Design Rationale

Working with contrast is common practice in the field of dementia, since the acuity of the human eye deteriorates as it ages [11]. For this reason, we modified the pictures on the placemat so that the food related object is isolated from its background. The background of each picture is made green, as the human eye is most sensitive to this color [12].

The design tries to promote a positive influence before each meal, whilst not interfering during the eating activity. Therefore, the sounds can be triggered easily by touching a capacitive sensor, rather than e.g. a pressure sensor. This makes triggering the sounds easy before the residents get their food, and will minimize interaction during eating, as the plates and cutlery used during the eating activity itself will not trigger any sounds without physically touching the capacitive sensors.

Fig. 1. Each of the four pads triggers a sound which corresponds with the picture on the pad.

Table 1. The pictures and corresponding sounds depicted various forms of food or actions related to eating.

Picture description	Sound description	Duration (s)
Cup of tomato soup	Pouring liquid in a bowl, blowing, slurping	18
Cup of vegetable soup	Pouring liquid in a bowl, blowing, slurping	18
Cup of coffee	Fetching a ceramic cup, grinding coffee beans, pouring liquid in a cup, stirring with a metal spoon, blowing, slurping	33
Bowl of yogurt	Metal spoon in a bowl, softly slurping	21
Someone cutting bread	Cutting bread, spreading bread, crunchy chewing	21
Plate with potatoes, vegetables and meat	Sizzling meat in a pan, fetching a ceramic plate, scraping a metal spatula in a pan, closing a metal pan's lid	17
Cutlery in a drawer	Rumbling with metal cutlery	8

The sounds incorporated in the design relate to the objects depicted on the place-mat, as shown in Table 1. Rather than utilizing social ques in the sound design, directive ques have been used to make the correlation between sound and picture as clear as possible. Additionally, there was an ethical concern that sounds of more complex or social nature could possibly confuse the participants or other residents present in the environment.

3 Field Study

3.1 Study Setup

Proxy consent was sought from the participants' informal caregivers and relatives after they were extensively briefed about the aim and setup of the study. This was done by a consent form, accompanied with an information letter. Furthermore, consent was not seen as a one-time measure, but as a continuous process [13] where participants were asked multiple times throughout the study period if they still wanted to participate. Moreover, the participants were observed continuously, and caregivers were present to determine whether the eating activity was disturbed in any way due to the deployment. Relatives of residents who did not actively take part in this study were informed by e-mail as well.

The designs were deployed in a local residential care facility for three eating activities per participant. In total, four people with dementia were observed individually (Table 2). The interactive placemat was deployed once for each eating activity, namely breakfast (B), lunch (L), and dinner (D). The residents were observed starting from moments before the placement of the interactive placemat, until they finished the eating activity. After three observations, semi-structured interviews [14] were held with the caregivers and resident assistants (Table 3). A caregiver who was present during each eating activity was asked if he/she had observed differences in behavior or mood of the participants to compare or contrast with the researcher's observations.

The observations of the residents and the semi-structured interviews with the caregivers and assistants were transcribed, and a thematic analysis [15] was conducted using an inductive approach. By analysing the transcribed data, the following themes came into view: (1) Eating behaviors, (2) Residents' and caregivers' interactions with interactive placemat, (3) Distraction, and (4) Atmosphere.

Table 2. Demographical data of participants.

Participant	Male/Female	Age	Stage of dementia
P1	Female	79	Severe
P2	Female	91	Moderate
P3	Female	93	Moderate
P4	Male	93	Moderate

Table 3. Interviewed caregivers with their function.

Interviewee	Male/Female	Caregiver function
Q1	Male	Resident assistant
Q2	Male	Regular caregiver
Q3	Female	Resident assistant

3.2   Eating Behaviors

Observations prior to the deployment of the interactive placemat in the shared living room of the residents revealed notable differences in eating behaviors among the residents. All the participants of the field study could eat independently. However, struggles were encountered occasionally. For instance, P4 spilled some soup during lunch: *"he drips soup while directing his spoon towards his mouth"* [P4 – L]. Furthermore, P1 is diagnosed with dysphagia and struggled to direct food from the plate to her mouth: *"when she dropped food on her lap, she tried to scoop up the food, which seemed to require her much effort"* [P1 – D]. Moreover, during the observed lunch of P1, it was necessary for the caregiver to feed her. This is in contrast with the other participants, who showed independent eating behavior during the observed eating activities (Fig. 2).

Fig. 2. Participant eating her breakfast.

3.3   Interactions with Interactive Placemat

None of the participants appeared to deliberately interact with the pads on the placemat. It is sometimes hard to judge whether a pad is touched, thus triggering a sound, on purpose or by accident. If a sound was triggered however, the participants did not explicitly react to the sound for the majority of times. P3 triggered a sound during the dinner observation, to which she reacted the following: *"What do I hear, behind my left ear? Behind this ear I hear something, at that side"*.

The pictures presented on the interactive placemat seemed to trigger some interactions for the participants as well [P2 – L; P3 – D; P4 – L]. As P2 finished her soup during lunch, she held her mug in her hands while looking at all the pictures, after which she placed her mug on the soup picture. P4 put his drink back on the pad with coffee for three times. During dinner, P3 spoke up after looking at the placemat's pictures: *"Oh, now I see what I have. I have way other food than you all. You could swap it with me. I also have very beautiful knives and forks, and here for example are carrots, and cauliflower, meat, and uhm, baked potatoes".*

At times, a caregiver or resident assistant would interact with the participant through the interactive placemat and ask questions such as: *"Do you hear this?"* [Q1] or *"Do you know what it is?"* [Q1]. P1 did not respond to this question, while P2 noted that she would *"[...] hear sounds all the time."* One caregiver, who was not interviewed, asked P4 if he wanted something to drink while simultaneously touching the pad with soup, triggering the corresponding sound of a pouring liquid, blowing, and slurping. However, P4 did not seem to respond to the sound. After his drink is placed on the placemat, the caregiver again pressed the pad with soup, to which P4 reacts by pointing to the drink and picking it up as the sound is playing.

All participants showed fiddling or fidgeting behavior with the interactive placemat. This was done for example by P1 during breakfast, when she tore off one of the pads completely. P1 also showed fidgeting behavior multiple times during lunch, as she again tried to peel off the pads. P2 and P4 were also observed to be fiddling with the pads [P2 – L; P4 – L, D]. The box in which the electronics and speaker are located was also fidgeted with, sometimes multiple times per session [P2 – D; P3 – B, L, D; P4 – B, L, D]. When the lid of the box was removed by the participant, the researcher would step in and place the lid back over the electronics. For example, when P3 reached out for the box to open it up, she said the following: *"What is this weird thing that has to be placed here? [...] Oh well, ok then"*. Moreover, participants tended to stroke the texture of the placemat multiple times during the observations [P1 – L; P2 – B, D; P3 – L; P4 – L, D] (see Fig. 3).

The caregivers and resident assistants mentioned that they would not use an interactive placemat for every resident. For example, Q2 mentioned that he would use it for *"[...] someone who is in the first stages [of dementia], but not when they are in the advanced stages"*.

Fig. 3. Participant stroking the placemat after finishing lunch

3.4   Distraction

Prior to the observations, Q1 was interviewed to get an impression of how he normally experienced the eating activities. In this interview, the initial idea of the interactive placemat raised concerns regarding distraction: *"Maybe it will make sure that they will be less agitated, but it might also distract them"*. During the observations, none of the participants seemed to have changed their eating behavior due to the deployment of the placemat, which was confirmed by a caregiver each session. Q2 mentioned that P4 *"would find [the interactive placemat] interesting. Otherwise he would maybe stand up and leave, because he has got something to do"*. Q2 said that sometimes P4 would *"stand up and leave because he would not be aware of the fact that he would still get a dessert"*. In cases as Q2 depicts, a distraction before or between receiving a meal could be considered positive. Furthermore, Q3 stated that she thought that the placemat would only distract from the eating activity *"... if there are very loud sounds coming out of it"*. Moreover, during P4's lunch, the present caregiver explicitly turned off the television prior to the eating activity in order to minimize distracting factors in the room. This measure was not specifically meant for P4, as the caregiver called the other resident's name while doing so.

3.5   Atmosphere

Throughout the field study, a general idea of the atmosphere was gained. Overall, the observed breakfasts were experienced as most peaceful. A logical explanation for this could be that each resident would be brought to the communal living room one at a time. This meant that not every other resident would be present during every observation. During all other observations, the atmosphere in the residential care facility was calm, with an exception of P3's observed dinner. Q3 confirmed that before eating, P3 was very agitated. Q3 also mentioned that *"whenever I give someone something to do, they are all really calm, with a puzzle or whatever"*. Even though both Q3 and the researcher observed a change in P3's behavior after the interactive placemat was placed, this does not immediately prove that it was the sole reason for P3 to calm down. The peaceful atmosphere was also achieved by the interactions by caregivers towards participants. For example, during P2's breakfast, the caregiver placed pudding on the corresponding pad and told P2: *"This goes here"*. P2 answered with: *"Yes, that's okay"*. The caregiver continued by touching the pad, triggering a sound and asking P2: *"Do you hear this?"*, to which P2 responded with: *"Yes, I hear it."*

4   Discussion

Even though there were numerous amounts of interactions with the placemat during the eating activities, this did not appear to influence the eating behavior of the participants. The researcher nor the caregivers were able to spot notable differences in the participants' eating behaviors during deployment.

Considering the eating behaviors and the interactions with the placemat, there were speculations from both caregivers and the researcher whether the design would distract the residents from the eating activity. The design could distract from the eating activity as they would be exposed to a new placemat which produces sounds. Therefore, using sound in eating activities should be carefully considered as eating is essential for getting the right nutrition. However, offering forms of distraction proved to be beneficial, as the residents would be able to interact with the placemat when there was no food in front of them. The observations combined with the semi-structured interviews show no evidence that the participants in this study were distracted in a negative way during their eating activities.

The sounds that were triggered appeared to have little effect on the participants. A possible cause of this may be due to interior or exterior sounds overruling the interactive placemat's sound. Another probable cause may be that the sounds were either unclear or not perceivable at all for the participants. Before the field study, we believed that the sounds would naturally evoke responses of the participants. However, this was evidently not the case. Therefore, more research is needed on how people with dementia can perceive and meaningfully interact with sound in a real-life care context (e.g. type, volume, direction, timing).

Future work on augmenting eating activities with sound or other sensory stimuli should focus on facilitating beneficial, multisensorial distractions. This might be achieved by incorporating sounds, though this should be further researched. During the field study, fiddling and fidgeting behaviors did not appear to distract the participants from their eating activities. Provoking this behavior by designing different forms and textures of the pads and pictures on the design could possibly verify these findings. Currently, the placemat was designed for individual use. However, there were cases in which other residents would react or be engaged within the interaction with the placemat. Therefore, it might be interesting to explore how shared interactivity could improve the experience in care facilities during eating activities. This may perhaps be done by designing an interactive tablecloth or interactive tableware.

The design of the interactive placemat in its current state had several limitations. The pictures on the placemat were modified to be as clear as possible, but there was no proof that people with dementia recognized the content of the picture, let alone linked it to a specific sound. There were cases in which participants would touch the pads, but no sound was triggered. The low conductivity of paper in combination with the conductive sensor settings can be a cause of this. Another cause of this is that the speaker would go on stand-by mode whenever it did not receive an input after approximately twenty minutes. If these issues were foreseen or avoided, the observations could have resulted in more reliable insights regarding the interactivity with the placemat.

As a result of a low sample size and limited time for deployment, no bold conclusions can be drawn whether an interactive placemat influences the experience of eating moments for people with dementia or their caregivers. However, our findings suggested that further exploration is needed on how interactions and distractions during eating moments can be utilized to our advantage to improve the eating activities of people with dementia.

5   Conclusion

This paper has provided explorative insights in how interactions with touch and sound offered distraction during eating activities for people with dementia. The short field study focused on how an interactive placemat could influence eating activities for people with dementia and their caregivers. Before, during and after the eating activity, the interactions with the placemat varied from verbal to physical. This opens up an opportunity to design meaningful interactions which promote good eating behaviors whilst utilizing the positive aspects of distractions. However, for these design interventions to be successful, an understanding is needed of how people with dementia engage with sound and other sensory stimuli in their immediate surroundings. With this work, we aim to inspire future design-research that explores the effects of sound in real-life care settings.

Acknowledgements. We would like to thank the care staff and participants at Archipel for facilitating this study and for their cooperation. Moreover, we would like to thank Rens Brankaert, Berry Eggen, Saskia Bakker and Harm van Essen for their feedback and input.

References

1. Cahill, S., Macijauskiene, J., Nygård, A., Faulkner, J., Hagen, I.: Technology in dementia care. Technol. Disabil. **19**(2), 55–60 (2007)
2. Qwiek.up (2016). https://qwiek.eu/up
3. Anderiesen Le Riche, H.: Playful design for activation: co-designing serious games for people with moderate to severe dementia to reduce apathy (2017)
4. Stone, L.: Eating/feeding issues in dementia: improving the dining experience. End Life J. **4**(1), 1–7 (2014)
5. Chen, C.C.-H., Schilling, L.S., Lyder, C.H.: A concept analysis of malnutrition in the elderly. J. Adv. Nurs. **36**(1), 131–142 (2008)
6. Perivolaris, A., LeClerc, C., Wilkinson, K., Buchaman, S.: An enhanced dining program for persons with dementia. Alzheimer's Care Q. **7**(4), 258–267 (2006)
7. Timlin, G., Rysenbry, N.: Design for dementia: improving dining and bedroom environments in care homes. Helen Hamlyn Centre, Royal College of Art, London (2010)
8. Hicks-Moore, S.: Relaxing music at mealtime in nursing homes: effects on agitated patients with dementia. J. Gerontol. Nurs. **31**(12), 26–32 (2005)
9. Thomas, D., Smith, M.: The effect of music on caloric consumption among nursing home residents with dementia of the Alzheimer's type. Act. Adapt. Aging **33**(1), 10–16 (2009)
10. Houben, M., Brankaert, R., Bakker, S., Kenning, G., Bongers, I., Eggen, B.: Foregrounding everyday sounds in dementia. In: Proceedings of the DIS 2019 Conference on Designing Interactive Systems (2019)
11. Sjöstrand, J., Laatikainen, L., Hirvelä, H., Popovic, Z., Jonsson, R.: The decline in visual acuity in elderly people with healthy eyes or eyes with early age-related maculopathy in two Scandinavian population samples. Acta Ophthalmol. **89**(2), 116–123 (2011)
12. Gross, H., Blechinger, F., Achtner, B. (eds.): Handbook of Optical Systems, Survey of Optical Instruments. Wiley-VCH Verlag, Weinheim (2008)
13. Coughlan, T., et al.: Current issues and future directions in methods for studying technology in the home. PsychNology **11**(2), 159–184 (2013)
14. Longhurst, R.: Semi-structured interviews and focus groups. In: Key Methods in Geography, pp. 143–156. SAGE (2016)
15. Braun, V., Clarke, V.: Using thematic analysis in psychology. Qual. Res. Psychol. **3**(2), 77–101 (2006)

Surveillance Technology in Dementia Care: Implicit Assumptions and Unresolved Tensions

Yvette Vermeer[1,3](✉), Paul Higgs[1,3], and Georgina Charlesworth[2,3]

[1] Faculty of Brain Sciences, Division of Psychiatry, UCL,
Maple House, 6th Floor, 149. Tottenham Court Rd, London W1T 7NF, UK
y.vermeer@ucl.ac.uk
[2] Faculty of Brain Sciences, Department for Clinical, Education,
and Health Psychology, UCL, 1-19. Torrington Place, London WC1E 7HB, UK
[3] Interdisciplinary Network for Dementia Using Current Technology
(INDUCT), London, UK

Abstract. This paper examines the concept of "Surveillance Technology [ST]" as it is used in ageing and dementia research but which suffers from poor definition. We attempt to clarify this imprecision by contextualizing a brief history of the development of ST and provide a summary of the research in this area. We contrast this with the responses provided by a public and patient involvement group of people living with a dementia diagnosis, or experience of supporting people with dementia. ST operates in multiple interacting ways, all of which need to be taken into account in research, public and policy debate. As a technology it is often seen as a way of assisting individuals and therefore classified as an Assistive Technology [AT]. However, the meaning of ST used in dementia care has pragmatic implications beyond the meeting of the needs for "safety and independence"; ideas which is often used to justify its use. We argue that there is need to interrogate the terms "Surveillance" and "Technology" more carefully if ST is to be considered as empowering for people with dementia. This tension is brought out in the accounts present in a group discussion on ST and its use. This paper argues that there needs to be an acknowledgement that the purposes of such technologies need to be regularly reviewed in order for society to keep up with the rapidly changing pace of technology and the changing needs of users.

Keywords: Surveillance · Terminology · Safety · Technology · Dementia · Assistive · Patient Public involvement

1 Introduction

Public awareness of the challenges posed by an ageing population as well as the increasing demand for dementia care has become a mainstay of public debate [1, 2], as has the pressure placed on carers to manage risks of people living with dementia by taking appropriate safety measures [3]. This imperative is often interpreted as a need to find a technological solution to the problems of ageing [4]. Social policies and markets prioritize technological solutions [5]. In the field of dementia care technology is thought to delay institutionalization; encourage older adults to remain in their own home [6]; to save costs [7] and alleviate the impact of the decreasing number of kin

© Springer Nature Switzerland AG 2019
R. Brankaert and W. IJsselsteijn (Eds.): D-Lab 2019, CCIS 1117, pp. 101–113, 2019.
https://doi.org/10.1007/978-3-030-33540-3_10

prepared to be full-time carers by reducing caregiver burden [8]. In other words, technology may empower carers and people with dementia [9]. For example, the NHS Long Term Plan recently reported the aim to empower people and to change their experience of health and care [10]. This includes home-based and wearable monitoring equipment which will predict and prevent incidents that would otherwise result in hospital admissions. The NHS will ensure that these technologies can be used as well as meet the needs from a range of people. The plan points out "This could include... a location tracker to provide freedom with security for someone with dementia" [10: 17].

Surveillance Technology [ST], is often the term used for products used to locate and 'track' the whereabouts of people with dementia [11]. ST is also seen as a technological product that can keep people with dementia independent and safe [3]. Not surprisingly, carers have expressed positive responses to such products [12]. ST is used in dementia care for various reasons. For example, carers want to diminish own stress by locating the person with dementia who wanders [13, 14]. Wandering is considered problematic as people with dementia might get lost and hurt [15]. There are various STs available to locate people for safety reasons. To illustrate, Global Positioning System [GPS] which can be incorporated, into the coat of a person with dementia, identifies the location and signals that position of a person from the device to a carer [16]. There are many different types of electronic devices with GPS. 'Track your Ltd.', [17] is a simple tracking devices connected to a phone, whilst 'Dementia buddy', [18] is a tracker with an alarm button connected to a support platform for a monthly fee [19]. Another example is an electronic bracelet that sends a tracking signal for programs such as 'Project Lifesaver', [20] connected to the police [3]. However, some ST have not been proven to be cost effective [14], have failed to reduce uptake of health and social care services [21] and have no effect on improving the quality of life (QOL) of people with dementia in their own homes [22].

1.1 Terminology and Definition

ST has a terminology that keeps on expanding in society [23, 24]. Terms used for ST include: monitoring devices, personal and social alarms, telecare; electronic surveillance; information technology; tagging; tracking; wandering technologies; assisted living technologies; GPS device; ambient assisted living; Information and Communication Technology [ICT]; smart home technologies; and more [3, 12, 25–28]. It becomes problematic for both users and researchers when ST is inconsistently termed or defined as just technology [14]. For example, one study divided ICT into two functions of Assistive Technology (AT) and ST [29]. ATs were memory aids, calendars and devices for regulating kitchen equipment to compensate for cognitive defects. STs were safety alarms, electronic tagging devices and passive positioning systems such as mobile phones with GPS [29]. On the other hand, ST is often seen "as part of" [30]. For example, McCabe and Innes [12] described their GPS device for safer walking as AT. Another example is from Gibson and colleagues [31] and how carers and people with dementia made AT such as GPS devices work for them through personalisation, customisation and bricolage. The act of bricolage is combing household technologies with AT (e.g. placing duct tape over device buttons) [31].

The World Health Organisation (WHO) defines AT as: 'An umbrella term for any device or system that allows the individual to perform a task they would otherwise be unable to do or increases the ease and safety with which tasks can be performed' [2]. However, considering ST as part of AT may be a limited option [25]. For example the Cochrane review on AT products for memory support in dementia included tracking devices [32]. The authors had to use many search terms to find such devices and this resulted in the discovery of many false positives. They argue that there is a need for standardised terminology in order to better identify effectiveness studies for AT [32]. Similarly, Gibson and colleagues [31] acknowledged their limited wide definition of technology. Another study reported that a clear description of the meaning of video surveillance in practice would be useful. The authors themselves, however, used different terms throughout the article (e.g. surveillance, camera's, telecare, AT) [33]. Consequently, Tinker et al. [34] in their paper on terminology argue that ST should be more explicitly defined in order to implement changes in Gerontechnology.

It remains unclear, however, whether or not ST is part of AT. Studies show it operates in multiple interacting ways, which need to be taken into account in dementia studies as well as in public and policy debates. Terminological confusion may have a tendency to overlook tensions surrounding ST. To investigate such tensions, a suitable starting framework might be the description of ST as a monitoring system that allows carers to supervise a person with dementia for 24-h [3]. This paper examines the tensions that exist within the literature of ST in dementia studies by providing a brief history of 'Surveillance' and 'Technology', by outlining some of the tensions that exist in this area, tensions which lead ST to be differentiated from AT. Lastly, we discuss the comments received about ST from a Patient and public involvement group consisting of carers and people living with dementia.

1.2   Tensions with ST

Most discussion within this technological field focusses on how it is possible to surreptitiously use ST without fully engaging with the consent of the person with dementia; the justification being that increasing safety as overrides other ethical concerns [25]. For example, carers used bricolage to link tablets, webcams and home CCTV cameras to create a 'telecare' systems which over-rode any ethical concerns [31]. However, it has been pointed out that the use of technology often compromises autonomy and independence and promotes a false sense of safety [35]. It is also important to note that the belief that ST increases safety and reduces risks is asserted rather than being proven by research [25]. Niemeijer, [25: 124] has asked whether or not 'ST actually offer[s] more security'? ST can signal whether a fall happens; however, not it does not prevent the fall. A second tension that has received considerable critical attention is that technology such as ST should not be regarded as a substitute for human care [25, 36]. The perception of ST as the solution might undervalue carers and deplete the indispensable human contact that carers have with people with dementia [25]. A third tension featuring in much public and academic debate concerns the negative associations and moral implications of ST. The Oxford Dictionary describes surveillance as 'close observation, especially of a suspected person'. Gary Marx, [37], questioned if people with dementia are then seen as criminals. Family carers and people with dementia stressed the importance for consent to use ST by joint-decision making [12, 30]. For reasons that many concerns were reported about associating ST as a tool to manage people with dementia, children and criminals [12, 30, 38, 39]. Descriptions of ST as an malign tool [i.e. an Orwellian 'big brother watching you'] designed for social control is counterpoised to seeing it as a new technology that makes people secure [40]. Conversely, Judd [41] argues that the key to support people with dementia in order for them to have more control over their lives is to stress individual empowerment which valorises privacy and autonomy with less control from others.

1.3   A Brief History of ST

To understand the role of ST in dementia it is necessary to look at the idea of the emergence of what has been described as a 'surveillance society' [42]. Studies outside the field of gerontology tend to think of surveillance as a constant feature of modern society. For example, Marx, [37], describes a generalised focus on discovering personal information through surveillance as a feature of contemporary society. In this view the collection of data and the surveillance of people becomes deeply enmeshed in a myriad of social practices [37]. Similarly, Foucault's [43] well known discussion of the idea of the 'Panopticon' in his work on prisons and its role in the construction of what he termed the 'docile body' [44] is another example of the role that surveillance is supposed to have in wider society. In 1957, the first globally orbiting satellites were tracked by surveillance on the ground [45]. In the 1960s, electronic tagging and tracking was introduced as an alternative to custodial sentences [46].

Since that time the potential of surveillance has increased exponentially as technology has become more sophisticated and individuals have come to be more scrutinised in their everyday actions. Technology developed in one field rapidly extends to others. This has been as true in the field of social care as in other more obvious areas such as computer technology. Social care became an area ripe for technological intervention as the latter decades of the twentieth century saw an increase in the needs of an older population and a shift in the responsibility of providing care to the informal sector of family, friends, and neighbours [47]. This was accompanied by a discourse that the care provided by families was "good" whereas dependence on the state was "bad" [48].

From the 1980s onwards, two things occurred in the field of dementia research and technology. First, much academic research was conducted to see how these technological developments could be extended into the field of dementia care; however there was a dearth of take-up from designers and administrators [49]. Second, an impetus for developing the perfect ST also emerged leading to an ongoing perception that these products would meet a yet untapped market need which would both be profitable and cost effective [3, 50]. Later in the 1990s, [51] technology was seen as a way of providing a variety of solutions for the welfare state in the United Kingdom (UK) [51, 53]. The National Health Service and Community Care Act 1990 [54] promised a 'mixed economy of welfare', focusing on market forces for the delivery of technological services [55]. A justification for this was for older individuals to be cared for in their own homes for as long as possible [54]. However, reforms in UK care and social services also led to a narrow market-orientated approach based on consumerism and to a degree "user involvement" or "user empowerment" [48]. This meant users got the option to choose between competing providers and deflect products which did not meet their needs [57]. User empowerment, however, was often confused with consumerism [48]. In a supermarket analogy it is consumerism which ensures that users have a wide choice in products and some safeguards as to safety and quality. Hereby a user who can choose between products in a supermarket becomes a consumer. This is because consumerism does not really consult consumers what types of products they want to have in the supermarket, nor does it involve consumers in the management of that supermarket. Therefore, in such a [super]market analogy the consumers remain powerless [48]. Meanwhile, carers started to be included in research and studies reported how they favoured tracking people with dementia, which started an ethical debate on the morality of surveillance [58]. Welsh and colleagues [58], argue that a Panopticon of an ultimate efficient prison system to use surveillance on prisoners, without considering them as humans, should never be allowed.

In the late 1990s specially adapted technological designs became standard features of mainstream products [59]. This transformation of adaptation into mainstream technology designs became widespread and contributed to a larger trend that is based on universal design [59, 60]. This led designers to base their ideas on previously perceived needs generated by a market which results in designs that are reflections of what has been previously created [61, 62]. For example, while cassette tapes were initially created to support talking books for the blind they became mainstream when used by the general public, yet later these tapes were specially repurposed for the blind [59]. This can also be seen with the "Wristcare" design for dementia care [61]. The designers had years of experience with developing safety phones and later adapted these phones by adding monitoring features. The Wristcare was designed in the light of the growing ageing population and was anticipated to have big potential for an ageing market. The monitoring safety phone market was also anticipated to open up a new market among younger consumers [61].

Consequently in the last few years the market for ST has expanded as the number of carers increased [3] but without any real development of what users needed. Other commentators, however, have argued that the surveillance market was in reality underdeveloped and is now just starting to use technologies to improve services for older adults [4]. Nonetheless, one major development was that in the UK it became common to monitor people with dementia [16], so that by 2010 there were 1.7 million telecare users in a market valued at £106 million [62, 63]. Such devices are provided by local authorities, then private companies, followed by local and national technology resources [16]. This market is supported by the public sector with a small subsector selling directly to the public [16]. Policy makers continue to 'mainstream' ST within health-care given that there is a belief that it might alleviate the challenges of providing care without resort to institutional care and all of its costs [16]. Again, what is common to this process is that the development of ST has not addressed user involvement or indeed empowerment. However, as we show below, it is not that there is not a perspective from the users: it is just not heard or thought about.

2 Tensions About the Use of ST: Reactions from PPI

2.1 Patient and Public Involvement

There is an urgency to involve carers and people with dementia in patient and public involvement (PPI) [64]. PPI is research being carried out "with" or "by" members of the public. For example, members of the public can offer advice or comment on research materials as they have personal knowledge and experience of the research topic and might provide a more general perspective [65]. However, PPI is often criticised as an exclusive and tokenistic practice involving a narrow group of experienced members [66]. INVOLVE, [2012] created briefing notes for researchers involving the public and NIHR, [67] recommended to continuously improve the development of PPI by beginning with diversity and inclusion [66, 67]. Despite these criticisms, PPI can improve the quality and relevance of research and lead to the empowerment of those members involved. This is particularly important for groups which have traditionally lacked power and voice, such as people living with dementia [65, 66]. This study is aligned to the larger Horizon 2020 funded, INDUCT programme (Interdisciplinary Network for Dementia Using Current Technology). INDUCT aims to improve technology and care for people with dementia. In addition, the specific aim of this study is to gain an understanding of the perspectives and needs of people with dementia and family caregivers towards surveillance technology. A decision was made to create a PPI group in the UK. The group was based on the guidelines from INVOLVE, [66]. A role description was disseminated on the NIHR Join Dementia Research website. The role description asked for members of the public with personal experience of living with dementia, who wanted to influence policy and research and were interested in sharing their thoughts on ST and empowerment. In addition, the role description outlined what was expected from the PPI members as research advisors.

Table 1 describes the inclusion criteria for the research advisors. The PPI group included eight research advisors who are a family carer or themselves are living with dementia. The meeting took place in London in March 2018. During this meeting, the main author facilitated the discussion, one researcher had a supportive role and another researcher participated. Discussion included 'what is ST', 'can ST be empowering' and 'how would you categorise ST'. Hereby, the PPI group discussed ST and illustrates the existence of many tensions that are subsumed under the label of ST.

Table 1. Inclusion criteria.

Inclusion criteria for PPI members
The individual should have direct experience with dementia of being either:
− A person living with early set/moderate dementia
− A [former] family carer supporting a loved one with dementia
− Live at home
− Have some knowledge of ST, or use ST

2.2   What Is ST?

The PPI advisors spoke very passionately about surveillance. In particular, about the term surveillance and how it reminded them of police, prisoners, spies and the military. They emphasized that they feared this negative term might even put people off who want to use surveillance. The fear of how surveillance is used, as well as the tension surrounding its ethical implications was discussed. For example, people may not be aware of Facebook and CCTV monitoring them, with or without their consent. One advisor asked "am I actually in control or do third parties have access to my data? Another advisor commented with "surveillance is propensity for abuse". Therefore, the group agreed that regulations should be in introduced in relation to ST and the monitoring of people. One major reason given for this was disliking "big brother watching and collecting personal data". In spite of not liking the term, advisors felt they were all participating in surveillance in daily life without necessarily recognising it. Although there was a tendency to regard surveillance in a negative light, the group also discussed what benefits technology might bring about.

A person with dementia thought that her latest Apple watch which was connected to an iPhone was helpful giving her a feeling of safety. The group discussed how the iPhone is not designed to keep an eye on people but can be used to do so with apps. Illustrating personalisation, customisation and bricolage of everyday devices for everyday purposes. In her situation, she reported that, everything was co-jointly discussed and decided upon with her partner. The group agreed that consent and joint-decision making is something that would enable people to accept the use of technology more. Furthermore, technology was seen as a helpful tool to support the giving of care. However, some advisors described their concerns with the improvement of technologies. One major reason was that improved camera's in the home might be used as an excuse to reduce human interaction. For example, one advisor mentioned concerns about "helpers only walk into the home when they spot the problem on camera". This led to the discussion of seeing ST not as a substitute of care. They agreed that technology usage should improve the QOL of people with dementia and support carers and not only have the purpose to reduce costs for the government. This led to talking about the tension of [not] increasing safety. The group questioned if technology prevents wandering and if carers then only react when a person has already fallen, which is not useful. Rather technology should enable people to do things they would not be able to do without it. However, some stressed again that the help from formal and family carers is essential. Consequently, they wondered if a passive tracker would be helpful at all.

2.3   Can ST Be Empowering?

The advisors expressed different opinions on the issue of empowerment. One advisor expressed the view that empowerment through the use of technology is the capacity to be able to do the things they would not be able to do without it. Others described empowerment as anything that creates, promotes or enhances autonomy, QOL, skills and the power to do what one wants. For example, one advisor reported "my [tracking app on the] iPhone gives me power to walk outside and my husband has the power to know that I am okay". The advisor described how this power made her feel empowered.

However, some advisors felt that surveillance can quickly take away someone's power. The example of placing cameras in the home was described as taking away someone's power. One advisor asked "what happens when someone else has power over you". The discussion focused on the ethical implications of collecting personal data, which was considered disempowering. Descriptions were given of people in the later stages of dementia who had someone acting in their interest. Another example, giving another illustration of 'bricolage' one PPI member gave a description of using a home burglar alarm to provide an alert should his older relative with dementia open the front door. Carers discussed having the power to make decisions on behalf of the person with dementia. However, no consensus was reached on how society could ensure that this "power" is safely used. The group agreed that disempowerment is when someone else has power over you. Power should not be abused when making decisions on behalf of others and it was a priority that individual needs should be met.

2.4   How Would You Categorise ST?

Initially, the PPI group did not reach consensus when discussing what different categories there are of ST. Surveillance was sometimes termed as a "technology" or "concept". When the group questioned whether technology would fit their and other's individual needs, they decided upon the category of needs. For example, ST should be adaptable when dementia progresses to fit the needs of the persons using it. One carer described ST was initially easy to use. However, the person they supported started having troubles with the off button when the disease of dementia progressed. The advisors explained how they used existing technologies to support caregiving and other activities in daily life. Besides the earlier described iPhone, the advisors also mentioned products such as 'Amazon Echo' and 'Fitbit' which they used for surveillance. These products were discussed as "high-tech" and were perceived as a technology rather than just being forms of surveillance. Reasons given were that these high-tech products supported them to perform a task, or make certain tasks easier or safer. For example, the Amazon Echo played music whilst a timer was set for the stove.

Another topic was that of the effect of using ST. The group questioned what the purpose of ST should be and described that it should enable people to find their way home, or enable someone to find them. Again, the tension between increasing safety and independence emerged from this discussion. This category was discussed conjointly in terms of the reliability of the product; for example, batteries going low in times of need was an important issue. Given this point, the group agreed that ST is not just "Technology" as people are also involved in the practice of surveillance. For example, neighbours and carers checking in on a person living with dementia. In this case, advisors said it was important to leave the "technology" out of "surveillance technology". The importance of the role of carers was emphasized again and it was agreed that technology is just a support tool. Technology is considered to be an expensive tool for some and the focus should be on investing in healthcare instead.

3   Discussion

In this paper we examined theoretical attempts to define and describe ST which resulted in three tensions. ST might (not) (1) increase safety, (2) be a substitute for care, (3) have ethical implications. We followed this with an exploration of the concept of "Surveillance Technology" and what it means to people living with dementia and carers. The PPI group had an immersive understanding of ST which brought out some of the tensions implicit in the technology; ones that are rarely alluded to in the literature.

The PPI's intertwined discussion concurs with literature about the three tensions surrounding ST. The group discussed that ST can promote a false sense of safety by its passive use similar to Schulz et al. [35]. Furthermore, the PPI group questioned whether ST prevents wandering and falls corresponding with Niemeijer [25]. The group also discussed safety and how consent and joint-decision making is essential similar to previous studies [12, 30]. In addition, the group discussed the ethical implications of ST collecting data and how this can be disempowering. The PPI expressed how "Big Brother" (e.g. Facebook, CCTV) collects their data and hereby had power over them by dishonoring their privacy and autonomy. This contrasts with Judd's [41] argument to support people with dementia and to stress individual empowerment.

In line with the literature, the group describes that ST may not reduce costs, improve QOL and alleviate carers [7, 8, 22]. Rather, ST is just a supplement and instead they believed that more investment is needed in healthcare. Other similarities with the literature found that users associated ST with prisons [12, 30] and that all of society is involved of data collection and categorization of people [37]. This might explain why the group termed surveillance as technology yet, sometimes stressed the importance of 'surveillance' as a separate concept. When discussing this, we have to be aware that definitions are often bound by those making them. We see differences from those in the industry and those actually using it. This may mean that the unproblematic adoption of such technologies may well be disempowering as well as being unresponsive to the needs of the users.

3.1   Leave the "Technology" Out of "Surveillance Technology"

It therefore might be helpful to distinguish between "Technology" and "Surveillance". Technology is something that responds to a need as shown by the advisor's use of existing "High-tech" products for various purposes. These technologies might then be placed within AT as they allowed individuals to perform tasks with ease and safety. Surveillance, on the other hand has a more specific purpose. A previous study found that simple low-tech trackers were sold to track not only people with dementia, but also dogs and prisoners [68]. Companies are looking for a market and surveillance is what the market offers for dementia [61] If we use the supermarket analogy again it becomes noticeable that the ideology continues to be that dependence on the state is bad – and that families purchasing "surveillance products" is good [48]. However, literature and the PPI group described how low-tech products might not meet individual needs which creates tension. Within this user empowerment, which is confused with consumerism, consumers remain powerless, when surveillance is done to people anyway – or others can take away our power quickly. That is, the PPI group emphasized that surveillance is done to persons without asking and operates outside users. Hereby the question shifts from "is surveillance part of AT?" to "is it part of a market ideology"? As regards AT's terminology [2], the anxieties people have about what surveillance means, as well as how does it serve the purpose of supporting people, seems to suggest that it is the opposite from AT. When people see 'Surveillance' as not increasing safety or reducing costs it is viewed as unhelpful. This negative assessment has more to do with 'big brother' than with technology itself. For ST to be empowering in the field of dementia care: we need to address the intentions that can emerge from the term ST. The difference between ST and AT is that surveillance is done to people whilst high-technology as part of AT, aims to supports people in their daily activities. Therefore, surveillance should be differentiated from AT and its positioning should be re-oriented to keep up with the rapidly changing nature of what is possible with technology and how this meets the needs of its users.

We would argue that part of the tension that surrounds ST is that we need to move beyond the idea that consuming ST will empower people with dementia and their carers. Instead of consumerism the focus should be on empowerment. That it has been missing from the debate, other than in the form of framing aspirations, is an indictment of the shift away from the users and towards something that has a more unconcerned set of priorities. In conclusion we think that is important for gerontologists to become clearer about the implicit assumptions and unstated tensions that exist in the field of ST if only to ensure that such technologies do not lead to the persistence of exclusionary practices in the care of people with dementia.

References

1. Alzheimer's disease International and World Health Organization. Dementia: a public health priority (2012). WHO. http://www.who.int/mental_health/publications/dementia_report_2012. Accessed 19 Jan 2017
2. WHO Centre for Health Development: A glossary of terms for community health care and services for older persons (2004). http://www.who.int/iris/handle/10665/68896. Accessed 5 May 2018
3. Kenner, A.M.: Securing the elderly body: dementia, surveillance, and the politics of "Aging in place". Surveill. Soc. 5(3), 252–269 (2008)
4. Sixsmith, A.: New technologies to support independent living and quality of life for people with dementia. Alzheimer's Care Today 7(3), 194–202 (2006)
5. Kubitschke, L., et al.: ICT and Ageing: European study on users, markets and technologies–Final report (2010). Final Report. www.ict-ageing.eu. Accessed 7 Jan 2017
6. Brittain, K., Corner, L., Robinson, L., Bond, J.: Ageing in place and technologies of place: the lived experience of people with dementia in changing social, physical and technological environments. Sociol. Health Illn. 32(2), 272–287 (2010)
7. Duff, P., Dolphin, C.: Cost-benefit analysis of assistive technology to support independence for people with dementia–Part 2: results from employing the ENABLE cost-benefit model in practice. Technol. Disabil. 19(2, 3), 79–90 (2007)
8. McHugh, J., Wherton, J., Prendergast, D., Lawlor, B.: Identifying opportunities for supporting caregivers of persons with dementia through information and communication technology. Gerontechnology 10(4), 220–230 (2012)

9. Kenigsberg, P.A., et al.: Assistive technologies to address capabilities of people with dementia: from research to practice, Dementia **18**(4), 1568–1595 (2019)
10. Department of Health and Social Care. The NHS Long Term Plan (2019). https://www.gov. uk/government/news/nhs-long-term-plan-launched. Accessed 14 Feb 2019
11. Landau, R., Werner, S.: Ethical aspects of using GPS for tracking people with dementia: recommendations for practice. Int. Psychogeriatr. **24**(3), 358–366 (2012)
12. McCabe, L., Innes, A.: Supporting safe walking for people with dementia: user participation in the development of new technology. Gerontechnology **12**(1), 4–15 (2013)
13. Landau, R., Auslander, G.K., Werner, S., Shoval, N., Heinik, J.: Families' and professional caregivers' views of using advanced technology to track people with dementia. Qual. Health Res. **20**(3), 409–419 (2010)
14. Topo, P.: Technology studies to meet the needs of people with dementia and their caregivers a literature review. J. Appl. Gerontol. **28**(1), 5–37 (2009)
15. McGilton, K., Rivera, T., Dawson, P.: Can we help persons with dementia find their way in a new environment? Aging Ment. Health **7**(5), 363–371 (2003)
16. Gibson, G., Newton, L., Pritchard, G., Finch, T., Brittain, K., Robinson, L.: The provision of assistive technology products and services for people with dementia in the United Kingdom. Dementia **15**(4), 681–701 (2016)
17. Track your Ltd.: Track your (2013). http://www.trackyour.co.uk/. Accessed 8 Jan 2017
18. Dementia Buddy: Dementia Buddy, Dementia Buddy we care because you care (2016). http://dementiabuddy.co.uk/. Accessed 9 Jan 2017
19. Wan, L., Müller, C., Randall, D., Wulf, V.: Design of a GPS monitoring system for dementia care and its challenges in academia-industry project. ACM Trans. Comput. Hum. Interact. **23**(5), 1–36 (2016)
20. Project Lifesaver (2007). Project Lifesaver. http://www.projectlifesaver.org/site/. Accessed 21 Oct 2017
21. Steventon, A., et al.: Effect of telecare on use of health and social care services: findings from the Whole Systems Demonstrator cluster randomised trial. Age Ageing **42**(4), 501–508 (2013)
22. Cartwright, M., et al.: Effect of telehealth on quality of life and psychological outcomes over 12 months (Whole Systems Demonstrator telehealth questionnaire study): nested study of patient reported outcomes in a pragmatic, cluster randomised controlled trial. BMJ **346**, 653 (2013)
23. Berridge, C., Furseth, P.I., Cuthbertson, R., Demello, S.: Technology-based innovation for independent living: policy and innovation in the United Kingdom, Scandinavia, and the United States. J. Aging Soc. Policy **26**(July), 37–41 (2014)
24. Lyon, D.: Surveillance Society: Monitoring Everyday Life. Open University Press, Buckingham, Philadelphia (2001)
25. Niemeijer, A.R.: Exploring Good Care with Surveillance Technology in Residential Care for Vulnerable People. VU University Press, Amsterdam (2015)
26. Rialle, V., Ollivet, C., Guigui, C., Hervé, C.: What do family caregivers of Alzheimer's disease patients' desire in smart home technologies? Contrasted Results Wide Surv. Methods Inf. Med. **1**(1), 63–69 (2009)
27. Sixsmith, A.: Technology and the challenge of aging. In. Gutman, G. (ed.) Technologies for Active Aging, pp. 7–25. Springer, Boston (2013). https://doi.org/10.1007/978-1-4419-8348-0_2
28. Te Boekhorst, S., Depla, M.F.I.A., Francke, A.L., Twisk, J.W.R., Zwijsen, S.A., Hertogh, C. M.P.M.: Quality of life of nursing-home residents with dementia subject to surveillance technology versus physical restraints: an explorative study. Int. J. Geriatr. Psychiatry **28**(4), 356–363 (2013)

29. Olsson, A., Engström, M., Skovdahl, K., Lampic, C.: My, your and our needs for safety and security: relatives' reflections on using information and communication technology in dementia care. Scand. J. Caring Sci. **26**(1), 104–112 (2012)

30. Robinson, L., et al.: Balancing rights and risks: Conflicting perspectives in the management of wandering in dementia. Health Risk Soc. **9**(4), 389–406 (2007)

31. Gibson, G., Dickinson, C., Brittain, K., Robinson, L.: Personalisation, customisation and bricolage: how people with dementia and their families make assistive technology work for them. Ageing Society 1–18 (2018) https://doi.org/10.1017/S0144686X18000661

32. Van der Roest, H.G., Wenborn, J., Pastink, C., Dröes, R.M., Orrell, M.: Assistive technology for memory support in dementia. Cochrane Database Syst. Rev. **6** 1–26 (2017)

33. Mulvenna, M., et al.: Views of caregivers on the ethics of assistive technology used for home surveillance of people living with dementia. Neuroethics **10**(2), 255–266 (2017)

34. Tinker, A., et al.: Twelve years of ISG masterclasses: past, present, and future. Gerontechnol. J. **17**(4), 232–237 (2018)

35. Schulz, R., Wahl, H.W., De Matthews, J.T., Vito Dabbs, A., Beach, S.R., Czaja, S.J.: Advancing the aging and technology agenda in gerontology. Gerontologist **55**(5), 724–734 (2015)

36. Cahill, S., Macijauskiene, J., Nygård, A.M., Faulkner, J.P., Hagen, I.: Technology in dementia care. Technol. Disabil. **19**(2, 3), 55–60 (2007)

37. Marx, G.T.: What's new about the "New Surveillance"? Classifying for change and continuity. Surveill. Soc. **1**(1), 9–29 (2002)

38. Katz, C.: The state goes home: local hypervigilance of children and the global retreat from social reproduction. In: Monahan, T. (ed.) Surveillance and Security: Technological Politics and Power in Everyday (2006)

39. Monahan, T., Wall, T.: Somatic surveillance: corporeal control through information networks. Surveill. Soc. **4**(3), 154–173 (2006)

40. Percival, J., Hanson, J.: Big brother or brave new world? Telecare and its implications for older people's independence and social inclusion. Crit. Soc. Policy **26**(4), 888–909 (2006)

41. Judd, S.: Part four Interventions: technology. In: Marshall, M. (ed.) State of the Art in Dementia Care. Centre for Policy on Ageing, London (1997)

42. Lyon, D.: The Electronic Eye: The Rise of Surveillance Society. University of Minnesota Press, Minneapolis (1994)

43. Foucault, M.: Discipline and Punish: The Birth of the Prison (Sheridan, A. Ed. Translated.), second vintage books edition. May 1995. Random House, Inc., New York (1977)

44. Caluya, G.: The post-panoptic society? Reassessing foucault in surveillance studies. Soc. Identities **16**(5), 621–633 (2010)

45. Meyer, A.D.: GPS declassified: from smart bombs to smartphones by Richard D. Easton and Eric F. Frazier. Technol. Cult. **57**(1), 276–278 (2016)

46. Gable, R.: Left to their own devices: should manufacturers of offender monitoring equipment be liable for design defect. J. Law Technol. Policy **2009**, 333–362 (2009)

47. Gray, A., Normand, C., Whelan, A.: Care in the community : a study of services and costs in six districts (1988). https://ideas.repec.org/p/chy/respap/6cheop.html. Accessed 9 Jan 2019

48. Barnes, M., Walker, A.: Consumerism versus empowerment: a principled approach to the involvement of older service users. Policy Polit. **24**(4), 375–393 (1996)

49. Day, K., Carreon, D., Stump, C.: The therapeutic design of environments for people with dementia a review of the empirical research. Gerontologist **40**(3), 397–416 (2000)

50. Algase, D.L., et al.: Need-driven dementia-compromised behavior: an alternative view of disruptive behavior. Am. J. Alzheimer's Dis. Other Dement. **11**(6), 10–19 (1996)

51. National Health Service and Community Care Act 1990. Statutory Instruments. No. 1329 (C.37). National Health Service, UK, Wales, Scotland (1990)

52. Henman, P., Adler, M.: Information technology and the governance of social security. Crit. Soc. Policy **23**(2), 139–164 (2003)
53. Hudson, J.: E-galitarianism? The information society and New Labour's repositioning of welfare. Crit. Soc. Policy **23**(2), 268–290 (2003)
54. Phillipson, C.: Reconstructing Old Age: New Agendas in Social Theory and Practice. Sage, London (1998)
55. National Institute for Health Research. Help at Home - Use of assistive technology for older people. NIHR Dissemination Centre (2018). https://www.dc.nihr.ac.uk/themed-reviews/ Help-at-home-WEB.pdf. Accessed 20 Jan 2018
56. Means, R., Smith, R.: Community Care. Macmillan, Basingstoke (1994)
57. Welsh, S., Hassiotis, A., O'mahoney, G., Deahl, M.: Big brother is watching you–the ethical implications of electronic surveillance measures in the elderly with dementia and in adults with learning difficulties. Aging Ment. Health **7**(5), 372–375 (2003)
58. Cook, M., Hussey, A.: Assistive Technologies: Principles and Practice. Mosby, Baltimore (2002)
59. Newell, A.F.: Design and the digital divide: insights from 40 years in computer support for older and disabled people. Synth. Lect. Assist. Rehabil. Health Preserv. Technol. **1**(1), 1–195 (2011)
60. Hyysalo, S.: Representations of use and practice-bound imaginaries in automating the safety of the elderly. Soc. Stud. Sci. **36**(4), 599–626 (2006)
61. Strickfaden, M., Heylighen, A.: Who are they? Student voices about the 'Other'. In: Proceedings of the Include 2009. Helen Hamlyn Centre RCA, London (2009)
62. Deloitte: Primary care: working differently. Telecare and Telehealth - a game changer for health and social care (2012). https://www2.deloitte.com/uk/en/pages/life-sciences-and-healthcare/articles/telecare-and-telehealth.html. Accessed 9 Jan 2017
63. Goodwin, N.: The state of telehealth and telecare in the UK: prospects for integrated care. J. Integr. Care **18**(6), 3–10 (2010)
64. Brooks, J., Gridley, K., Savitchm N.: Removing the 'gag': involving people with dementia in research as advisers and participants. Soc. Res. Pract. (3-winter 2016/2017) 3–14 (2017)
65. INVOLVE. N.I.H.R.: Briefing notes for researchers: involving the public in NHS, public health and social care research. INVOLVE Eastleigh, UK (2012)
66. Ocloo, J., Matthews, R.: From tokenism to empowerment: progressing patient and public involvement in healthcare improvement. BMJ Qual. Saf. **25**(8), 626–632 (2016)
67. NIHR: Going the extra mile: improving the nation's health and wellbeing through public involvement in research. NIHR, London (2015)
68. Vermeer, Y., Higgs, P., Charlesworth, G.: Marketing of surveillance technology in three ageing countries. Qual. Ageing Older Adults **20**(1), 20–33 (2018)

Memento for Living, Working and Caring: An 'Archetypal Object' for Being with Dementia

Kathrina Dankl[1]([envelope])[iD], Stefan Moritsch[2][iD], Fritz Pernkopf[3],
Elisabeth Stögmann[4], Theresa König[4], and Sten Hanke[5][iD]

[1] Design School Kolding, Agade 10, 6000 Kolding, Denmark
kad@dskd.dk
[2] BKM Design Working Group, Diefenbachgasse 42/1/6, 1150 Vienna, Austria
[3] Fritz Pernkopf Industrial Design, Diefenbachgasse 42/1/6,
1150 Vienna, Austria
[4] Medical University Vienna, Währinger Gürtel 18-20, 1090 Vienna, Austria
[5] FH JOANNEUM Graz, Alte Poststraße 149, 8020 Graz, Austria

Abstract. Memento is a product family for people living with dementia, consisting of a notebook with an integrated pen, and a smartwatch. The design is the result of an extensive cross-disciplinary, multi-national development process focusing on learning from existing strategies of remembering of people with dementia and their families. Memento aims to support the mastering of an active social life by giving an overview of the day and reinforcing participation in leisure activities. It also assists in everyday scenarios such as the handling of appointments and medication intake. The project is a pitch, a speculative proposition, serving as an adaptable and expandable design concept for further contributions to the quality of life, care and wellbeing of people living with dementia.

Keywords: Ingenuity of ageing · Dementia in everyday life · Familiar and 'archetypical' objects · ICT for social inclusion

1 Introduction

Research shows that about 10% of the population develop dementia at some point in their lives, about 3% of people between the ages of 65–74 have dementia, 19% between 75 and 84 and nearly half of those over 85 years of age [6]. Dementia can thus be deemed one of the most common causes of disability among the old with severe consequences for living, working and caring. While information and communication technology (ICT) is already supporting the able-bodied majority society in a lot of daily life situations, it may also help to overcome some of the growing limitations which appear with dementia. For persons with mild cognitive impairment and early stages of dementia, a potential solution has to function in a boundary context, requiring a high

© Springer Nature Switzerland AG 2019
R. Brankaert and W. IJsselsteijn (Eds.): D-Lab 2019, CCIS 1117, pp. 114–127, 2019.
https://doi.org/10.1007/978-3-030-33540-3_11

demand regarding the design of the hardware and software solution to fit into everyday life. Consequently, actual products/services shall be "invisibly blending" into persons' lives while offering functionalities enabling social inclusion through everyday support.

The research covered by this paper is carried out by a multi-national group of design, software and hardware developer as well as neurology and psychology experts from Austria, Cyprus, Italy, and Spain for a project time-span of 36 months. The multi-disciplinary project investigated to which extent digital platforms such as connected hardware devices and software services can help persons with dementia in the early stages to keep an active social life and to cope with challenges they experience. By evidence of the design research process, Memento presents a possible design solution based on norm-core products, archetypal objects such as a leather notebook and wristwatch to integrate seamlessly into everyday life. By archetypal objects, we relate to models and pattern of objects that are collectively known for specific values and functions. Notebook and watch are considered as such. The scope of this paper is to give an overview of the design research activities that were formative for the product family Memento.

2 Related Work

ICT solutions designed and developed for persons with dementia so far focus on three different categories. The first category includes solutions, which foster recreational activities, which are meaningful and enjoyable for people with dementia. The aim is to facilitate well-being and to delay the cognitive impairment progression or to reduce the need for antipsychotic medication [14]. Developments here include arcade games and creative games [2, 30], ICT technology to play music [16] or solutions in the area of social involvement (e.g. Video Calling [18], Facebook) and entertainment (e.g. games, puzzles, and movies) [13].

The second category is focusing on telecare solutions and mobile communication technologies like patient location tracking for indoor and outdoor usage [29], ICT for detection of falls for older dementia patients [26] and health status detection [9]. These solutions are often developed to support informal and formal caregivers but need to be used and accepted by people with dementia themselves.

The third category of ICT solution is focusing on functional assistance. The solutions designed are aiming to compensate for disabilities which patients in the early stage of dementia experience (e.g. external memory aids in the form of reminders (to take medication or keep appointments [8, 11, 19, 20]) or cognitive interventions with internet-based multimedia systems, including familiar equipment such as TV or PC [12]). Studies have shown that people with dementia are capable of handling simple electronic equipment and can benefit from it in terms of more confidence and the positive effect by indirectly reducing the caregiver's burden [1].

The following challenges have been indicated when designing ICT solutions for persons with dementia. Design recommendations suggest considering the gradual decline of patients' memory, reasoning or judgment in a user-centred design approach. Furthermore, it should be considered that persons with dementia do vary in behaviours that are also changing continuously. So common dementia symptoms are sudden mood changes, paranoia, lack of motivation and confusion [24]. Caregivers and care professionals should, therefore, be included and consulted throughout the whole design process and participatory design methods require adaption [17, 23].

However, studies have reported that designers may not always have the resources to involve people with dementia extensively in the initial stages of design. In addition, the effort needed when developing solutions for persons with dementia is underestimated [10]. Very often studies lack the training with persons with dementia which results in a rejection of the technology. Especially together with an inappropriate design, it often makes the products difficult to use for this specific user group. A comprehensive design includes the hardware design as well as the user interface design. ICT solutions' usefulness has also been met with scepticism by caregivers. Often the provided solution is not perceived as a solution for the real challenges faced by persons with dementia. These obstacles, discussed in the literature could be avoided by using design methods, more suited to the user group and an integrative design approach which makes use of known technologies and applies familiar concepts. It has been shown that persons with dementia are more at ease with familiar objects and unfamiliar design can be deterrent for using technology [5]. Also, ICT developments need to support learning and have to fit within the user's habitual practice [3]. A missing design process or one not meeting these criteria is likely to lead to product developments, not accessible and useable. Even more, products can then evoke negative emotional reactions, including anxiety, frustration, and the feeling of incompetence as well as the feeling of being stigmatized [3, 4, 25].

By evidence of the literature review on ICT for persons with dementia, we conclude that current products offer solutions for specific categories such as location tracking or games. There is still room for a product that unites these aspects while keeping the simplicity and contemporary aesthetics as a leading design principle. We also conclude that there is a gap in the marketplace for solutions that scaffold people's existing coping strategies and that build upon familiar objects to enhance implementation and integration rates.

3 Method

Our design research approach follows the concept of the 'ingenuity of ageing' which takes the experiential everyday knowledge of persons with dementia and their families as the point of departure for design research and concept. The concept of the 'ingenuity of ageing' has been developed as a response and counter concept to viewing ageing as a downward process of decline only. On the contrary, it stresses the strategies, originality, and inventiveness of older adults as a valuable resource for future design solutions. The DESIS Network's publication "Ageing, Ingenuity & Design" for instance, gives an insight into a number of international cases working with this principle [7, 15].

Research sites were Austria and Italy over a time span of 36 months with more than 40 participants. People with dementia and their families were invited to participate in the study according to the following criteria: According to the anticipated end-users of Memento and following the NIA AA criteria [21], subjects with a diagnosis of mild cognitive impairment (MCI) due to AD or mild AD with an Mini-Mental State Examination (MMSE) 28–24, together with their informal caregivers, were invited to participate in design ethnography and collaborative workshops. Further parameters, such as cognitive reserve (Cognitive Reserve Index [22]) and the technical proficiency of participants were taken into consideration. Written informed consent was provided according to the local ethical committee of each institution.

The research design used design ethnography combined with a set of participatory workshops throughout the whole product development process. First ethnographic data was collected at visits in the homes of twelve persons with dementia and their informal caregivers in Italy and Austria; the design ethnography was carried out over a time span of two months. Second, a cross-disciplinary workshop with stakeholders from design, medicine, hardware and software design was carried out to discuss and analyse design ethnographic insights. Third, a co-creation workshop was held together with persons with dementia and their informal caregivers aiming at the development of use cases and scenarios. Fourth a design concept workshop and fifth an interface design workshop explored features and everyday fit from the perspective of primary, secondary and tertiary users. The design methods used were selected according to collaborative design principles, utilizing cultural probes, generative toolkits, and design prototypes as ways for participatory making [27, 28]. Making is thereby characterized as a creative activity where participants are designing together with the design team, via given tasks and mini-projects with the goal to design for social inclusion, integration, and everyday implementation (Table 1).

Table 1. Overview of design research process

Research mode	Participants	Methods
Design ethnography	12 persons with dementia, 6 caregivers	Contextual interviews, visual ethnography, cultural probes
Cross-disciplinary workshop	10 persons from different stakeholder groups (hardware design, medical research, design research, user interface design)	Personas, problem scenarios, activity scenarios, draft use case development
Co-creation workshop	8 persons with dementia, 3 caregivers	Generative tools, prototyping use cases
Design concept workshop	10 persons with dementia, 8 caregivers	Validation of first prototypes, generative tools for co-creating the concept design
User Interface workshop	5 persons with dementia, 4 informal care givers, 5 formal care givers such as leaders/employees of nursing homes and day centers, 2 neurologists, 3 neuropsychologists	Validation of first UI prototypes, generative tools for co-creating the user interface design

The grander scope of the project and the aim of its research design, was to explore people's own strategies for managing dementia in their everyday life and to transfer this expertise to a convincing design proposal, using iterative stakeholder involvement.

3.1   Design Ethnography, Cross-disciplinary and Co-creation Workshop

The design ethnography explored people's own strategies for managing dementia in their everyday life, investigating what means or objects are used to organize family life, friends, work or leisure activities. We would like to show the transfer of ethnographic findings into the final design proposal via three selected examples. (1) Research showed that informants use analogue tools such as calendars, cribs, notes or post-its to a large extent, the classic desk or wall calendar was present in every household we visited. (2) Informants' strategies for order and sense-making in calendars was another observation that caught the design researcher's attention. Different colors and edgings were used to distinguish between more or less important events, private or professional ones. (3) Newspapers were used by informants' to check date and day.

These first design observations lay the foundation for later design decisions on the format, prioritising events and essential information for the home screen (Fig. 1).

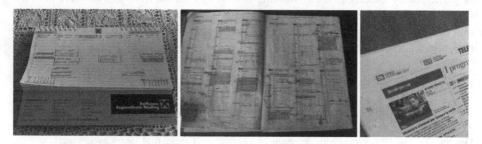

Fig. 1. Observations on how informants keep track of events with simple desk calendars, prioritize events in calendars and use newspapers as a basic information source for date and day

As a second step in the design process, ethnographic findings have been analyzed and transferred into scenarios and draft use cases via an internal cross-disciplinary workshop. It showed that the main challenges faced by the user group were in the three sections orientation, organization, and information. Draft scenarios thus included potential applications of Memento for shopping, feeling lost outside and being in need for immediate support, getting ready for leisure activities, a situation where pin codes are required, for the organization of appointments, for medication intake, to support in situations of feeling lost at home as well as outside.

These draft use case scenarios were used in a co-creation workshop with persons with dementia and informal caregivers together with generative tools (suggestions included tablet, smartphone, watch, earphone, as well as 'open' props) to discuss potential smart objects that could be supportive in these situations. Interactions with a smartwatch (cannot get lost easily), a smartphone as well as a device usable on the go as well as in a home setting, were most often mentioned and therefore carried forward to the design concept phase.

3.2 Design Concept Workshop

Based on research evidence, in this workshop first prototypes were presented to people with dementia and informal caregivers, which consisted of an all-day device and a watch (Fig. 2).

Fig. 2. First design prototypes consisting of the main device and smartwatch

In general, the feedback for both the main device and the watch were positive. The possibility to personalize the system seemed important in order to take into account the users' personality, habits, and level of cognitive impairment. The synchronization of different devices has been appreciated and caregivers proposed a synchronisation with their smartphones. Some additional functionalities were suggested (e.g. webcam on the main device to see the user when needed or stimulation programs such as games or suggestions). Some users were worried that Memento's use can reduce their attention and memory functions and they are afraid of becoming dependent on the system. At the same time, the caregivers appreciate the advantage for the user to become more independent from their support. All participants appreciated the size of the main device and imagined to transport it in a bag or a pouch. A female user commented that the main device is very similar to an agenda. The main device is thought especially for at-home use as a calendar or agenda. Writing was considered to be very comfortable by all of the participants and was experienced as writing on paper. Typing worked well on the main device as well. One of the users mentioned, that both handwriting and typing gets troublesome with time. Some caregivers suggested the possibility to use speech commands for the watch as well as the main device. While some users would be happy to receive messages containing their name (e.g. "John! It's time to take your medications!"), others stated they would not. In general, the judgement on comprehension of the system was very positive. By ethnographic evidence we know that informants have calendars located at specific places (e.g. the dining table or the kitchen counter), in the workshops informants remarked that the Memento main device would fit in these places which suggests an understanding of Memento system as a familiar object typology. Importantly, the current date should be highlighted. A caregiver reported that her husband repeatedly spends a lot of time in front of their family calendar throughout the day, trying to figure out what day it was. This is an example for an observation that has been made early in the design ethnography phase (the use of newspaper as a medium to check date and day) and has been validated in the consecutive workshops.

In general users and caregivers appreciated the cover of the main device. One user also stated that it would be nice to design their own cover (e.g. "AC Milan") and to store some cards in it. Two female users and one male commented on the watch design as being potentially stigmatizing. A female informant asserted: "I could hold the watch in my pocket so my friends don't ask me what it is!" Reasons were mainly due to size (especially for females) and unfamiliar design that reminded informants of assistive technology; however good readability of text was mentioned too. Caregivers, who are obviously not the future wearers, were less afraid that users might not wear the watch for shame. In terms of watch functions, short written messages or images were appreciated as reminders; vibration is considered better than acoustic signals. A GPS system was appreciated by both users and caregivers. However, not all users found the possibility to receive support for finding destinations interesting. To sum up, the findings of the workshop pointed to adaptions of the watch size and style to fit users' preferences and physiognomy as well as to avoid stigmatization. The prototype's watch design seemed to be too advanced. Potential directions include male/female version, classic/sportive version, or an orientation more towards classic watches.

3.3   User Interface Workshop

The user interface workshop united persons with dementia, formal and informal caregivers, physicians and neuropsychologists and aimed at a critical assessment of the overall UI approach by all stakeholders An overlapping feedback received from professionals and approved by primary users was the request for an affirmative and animating approach including games, pictures and a personal welcome. Participants envision Memento as a customizable system adapting to their needs and preferences. However, there are also essentials for the home screen such as the daily overview of events, the actual date, time, today's weather. Memento should be a learning system adapting according to disease progression. Caregivers mentioned the weather information as an example: "The home screen shall show weather and temperature but could be adaptable in later stages towards "You need a jacket!" (formal caregiver).

During the workshop, the UI for the three sample use cases *appointments*, *medication* and *getting ready* have been discussed as well. The most important findings for the use case appointments concern the categorization of importance: "One appointment a day is usually really important compared to others." (informal caregiver) also, confirmation of appointments "Done" and reminders are considered essential. Appointments should also be part of a 'family cloud' for easier coordination of the whole family. The most important findings for the use case medication have been who can entry new medication and the overall usability, to ensure the safety of the system. The general accord was that technically-savvy users would also register drugs themselves, in other cases, they would be registered by physicians and carers, while persons with dementia receive a reminder for its intake.

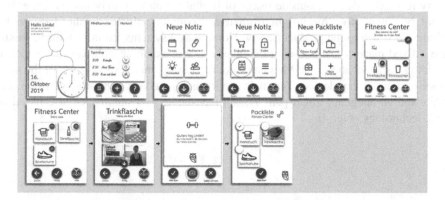

Fig. 3. First UI prototype for the use case *Getting Ready* for participating in leisure activities

The use case *getting ready*, aiming at supporting persons with dementia to participate in leisure and travel activities, by offering packing lists for necessary items, received widespread acceptance from all participants (Fig. 3). This use case was also seen as a very inclusive one, with relevance for the mainstream society, for instance for re-occurring events such as "City trip", "Trip to second home", "Trip with baby" could be a helpful feature for many. The comments received, concern the inclusion of pictures: "Image of the packing list with the actual personal items, would be good" (neuropsychologist). And the function "back pack", when the user returns from the event should be included.

4   The Transfer of Research Findings into a Design Concept

The study provided a series of guidelines for the design of digital technology for persons with dementia and their caregivers. These include the adaption of familiar analogue tools and personal habits for the digital sphere, opportunities for inside and outside usage and opportunities for adaptation and customization. Initial observations from the design ethnography such as informants' use of desk calendars for keeping track of events, strategies for prioritizing events in these calendars and the use of newspapers as a basic information source for date and day have been validated by iterative user involvement and co-creation activities. They have been transferred into the design concept in the shape of its desk calendar-like format and interface choices for home screen and prioritizing options. It is a key challenge to use the possibilities of ICT on one hand and, on the other hand, to ensure the most self-evident and appropriate integration of existing routines regarding memory and orientation strategies of users and caregivers. The 'archetypal objects' and the technology used, try to come as close as possible to the analogue commodities entrusted to the user group, thereby lowering the threshold of inhibition against new technologies and still being able to use all the advantages of these technologies to support persons with dementia and their needs.

By research evidence, outside usage of digital technology only makes sense, if it cannot be lost easily; this insight from users, consequently led to the decision for including a watch to the product family. Home-based systems, on the contrary, should have a fixed place in the household similarly to a standing or wall calendar which is providing a safe location. The Memento product family, therefore, consists of the main device and an all-day device. The main device is a notebook consisting of two E-Ink tablets and an integrated smart-pen. The all-day device is a smartwatch also based on E-Ink technology (Fig. 4).

Fig. 4. Memento product family

The main advantages are that the device can thus come very close in its appearance and materiality to an analogue notebook and still exploit all technological possibilities. The deliberate reduction to a black-and-white or grayscale user interface supports the central design strategy to develop a preferably reduced system. The advantages of e-ink tablets such as good readability even in daylight and low power consumption increase the plausibility and functionality of the system.

The notebook and wristwatch integrate inconspicuously into everyday life and thus prevents stigmatization of the user as a "patient". This design strategy also makes it possible to adapt or customize the design to style preferences of different user groups (Fig. 5).

Fig. 5. Styles are adaptable to user preferences

If the notebook is not in use or needs to be loaded, it can be set up as a desk calendar or wall calendar (Fig. 6) in one place defined for this purpose. If required, it can announce the time, date or the next appointment visually as well as acoustically.

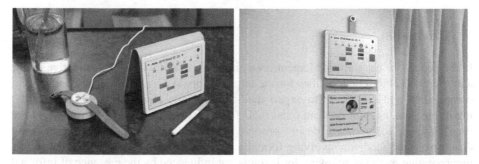

Fig. 6. The main device hung on the wall or positioned at a table or sideboard, functioning as a simple family calendar

The smartwatch is made of the same materials as the main unit and serves as a daily companion and reminder. Its design has been adapted according to user feedback. As a daily routine, the clock is taken down at night and placed on the base station. Overnight it is charged on the nightstand and can take over the function of an alarm clock (Fig. 7).

The focus for the user interface (UI) has been on two levels: primary, to use the home screen for emotional binding by offering all essential information such as time and today's events. As a next expansion step, the UI allows for personalization (for instance the elements shown on the home screen can be chosen by users according to their preferences). Additional, the UI focuses on breaking-down each use case into a handful of simple steps. This combines the reduction of levels as well as the reduction of content in each step. The reduction of levels has been a trade-off between avoiding frustration and at the same time providing cognitive training for primary users. As in the product design, concept simplicity was the guiding principle for the layout of the UI.

Fig. 7. The watch design is orientated towards a modern classic, loaded at the docking station.

5 Discussion

In the process of developing Memento, we aimed for a solution that is instinctive to use and offers specific functionalities for the target group. We made use of the consortium composition and the access to expert medical dementia clinics in Austria and Italy, involving persons with dementia and their families from the start and throughout the user-centered, collaborative design process. Special attention has been put on using design research methods involving formal and informal caregivers together as well as incorporating methods, allowing for insights not influenced by the presence of informal or formal caregivers.

Although ICT developments primary addressing age-related challenges like memory decline do exist, Memento tries to address people with dementia in early stages specifically and puts a focus on inclusiveness by uniting functions while keeping the product simple. Memento allows for a variety of use cases that address social inclusion, work, and leisure as well as more specific use cases supporting, for instance, medication intake. By providing stimulations via different devices (main device and smartwatch; as well as existing devices shall be part of the ICT ecosystem) we tried to approximate a new solution which connects with known habits and blends naturally into every day of the target group.

When designing for dementia, limits need to be considered as well. ICT solutions cannot stop or reverse dementia progress but might provide a tool which allows for an unobtrusive compensation of certain degradations in early stages and therefore support people to participate more actively in daily life routines and social interactions. To make this happen, developers might need to step back, since ICT developments are often driven by engineering motivations, rather than a collaborative endeavour driven by stakeholders with special needs.

Further ICT development for dementia might to an even greater extent gather knowledge on intuitive usage scaffolding the *ingenuity of ageing*. Especially in the UI design, there might be room for self-explaining interactions based on well-known and integrated objects such as an empty notebook, which explains function and usage by itself. Memento is an example of ICT that moves away from 'assistive technology' and instead presents a product family that responds to inclusivity and contemporary aesthetics. We see the need for critical engagement in this direction to remove the stigma and to enable autonomous life and work with dementia as long as possible.

Furthermore, we question the time span of funded projects, which is often limited to three years. We suggest that research should be long term, to allow for evaluation and further development of solutions. It would be rewarding to study if design proposals such as Memento help to retrain and trigger behaviour change and to what extent people combine smart and analogue solutions. This is especially relevant in the case of proposals where behaviour change techniques are applied (e.g. stimulating a personal plan for certain activities) or where solutions act beyond simple messaging device such as reminders.

6 Conclusion

The steady rise of persons with dementia and more routine use of digital technology provide timely opportunities for ICT-solutions supporting living, working and caring for/with people with dementia. This extensive, multi-national research study used existing strategies of remembering and points to a number of factors that must be reflected for design: the community uses analogue tools for remembering such as calendars, notes, post-it's the most; the most essential challenges faced by our informants can be clustered into the three sections information, orientation, and organization.

The design concept of Memento reflects these findings with a product family of the main device and an all-day device. Both objects aim at invisibly integrating into every day while strengthening autonomy via the exploitation of technology. Memento gives an overview of the day, enables the easy set-up of appointments as well as getting ready for social and leisure activities. This potential for independence and inclusion is provided via an inclusive product aesthetics and functions that enhance a sense of security. Design proposals offer alternative, tangible realities and make possible futures debatable. As such, Memento wishes to contribute actively to a discourse on ICT supporting living, working and caring of people with dementia.

References

1. Allen, R., Cook, S., Hignett, S.: How do people living with dementia use technology? (2016)
2. Alm, N., et al.: Engaging multimedia leisure for people with dementia. Gerontechnology 8(4), 236–246 (2009). https://doi.org/10.4017/gt.2009.08.04.006.00
3. Arntzen, C., Holthe, T., Jentoft, R.: Tracing the successful incorporation of assistive technology into everyday life for younger people with dementia and family carers. Dementia 15(4), 646–662 (2016)

4. Brittain, K., Corner, L., Robinson, L., Bond, J.: Ageing in place and technologies of place: the lived experience of people with dementia in changing social, physical and technological environments. Sociol. Health Illn. **32**(2), 272–287 (2010)
5. Cahill, S., Begley, E., Faulkner, J., Hagen, I.: " It gives me a sense of independence"–findings from ireland on the use and usefulness of assistive technology for people with dementia. Technol. Disabil. **19**(2, 3), 133–142 (2007)
6. Carlton-Foss, J.: Method and system for fall detection, July 2012
7. Coleman, R.: But will the neighbours be jealous? "Ageing, ingenuity & design. In: Lee, Y., Moore, P. (eds.) International Cases Collection, pp. 36–49 (2015)
8. Du, K., Zhang, D., Zhou, X., Mokhtari, M., Hariz, M., Qin, W.: HYCARE: a hybrid context-aware reminding framework for elders with mild dementia. In: Helal, S., Mitra, S., Wong, J., Chang, Carl K., Mokhtari, M. (eds.) ICOST 2008. LNCS, vol. 5120, pp. 9–17. Springer, Heidelberg (2008). https://doi.org/10.1007/978-3-540-69916-3_2
9. Guigoz, Y., Lauque, S., Vellas, B.J.: Identifying the elderly at risk for malnutrition. The mini nutritional assessment. Clin. Geriatr. Med. **18**(4), 737–757 (2002)
10. Hendriks, N., Truyen, F., Duval, E.: Designing with dementia: guidelines for participatory design together with persons with dementia. In: Kotzé, P., Marsden, G., Lindgaard, G., Wesson, J., Winckler, M. (eds.) INTERACT 2013. LNCS, vol. 8117, pp. 649–666. Springer, Heidelberg (2013). https://doi.org/10.1007/978-3-642-40483-2_46
11. Kamimura, T., Ishiwata, R., Inoue, T.: Medication reminder device for the elderly patients with mild cognitive impairment. Am. J. Alzheimer's Dis. Dementias® **27**(4), 238–242 (2012)
12. Lauriks, S., et al.: Review of ICT-based services for identified unmet needs in people with dementia. Ageing Res. Rev. **6**(3), 223–246 (2007)
13. Lazar, A., Thompson, Hilaire J., Demiris, G.: Considerations in evaluating technologies in memory care units. In: Zhou, J., Salvendy, G. (eds.) DUXU 2015. LNCS, vol. 9194, pp. 114–122. Springer, Cham (2015). https://doi.org/10.1007/978-3-319-20913-5_11
14. Lazar, A., Thompson, H.J., Demiris, G.: Design recommendations for recreational systems involving older adults living with dementia. J. Appl. Gerontol. **37**(5), 595–619 (2018)
15. Lee, Y., Moore, P. (eds.): DESIS Network Presents "Ageing, Ingenuity & Design" International Cases Collection 2015, HKDI (2015)
16. Lim, F.S., Wallace, T., Luszcz, M.A., Reynolds, K.J.: Usability of tablet computers by people with early-stage dementia. Gerontology **59**(2), 174–182 (2013)
17. Lindsay, S., Brittain, K., Jackson, D., Ladha, C., Ladha, K., Olivier, P.: Empathy, participatory design and people with dementia, pp. 521–530(2012)
18. Lund, D.A., Hill, R.D., Caserta, M.S., Wright, S.D.: Video Respite™: an innovative resource for family, professional caregivers, and persons with dementia. Gerontologist **35**(5), 683–687 (1995)
19. Maier, A.M., Özkil, A.G., Bang, M.M., Forchhammer, B.H.: Remember to remember: a feasibility study adapting wearable technology to the needs of people aged 65 and older with mild cognitive impairment (MCI) and Alzheimer's Dementia (2015)
20. McGoldrick, C.: MindMate: a single case experimental design study of a reminder system for people with dementia (2017)
21. McKhann, G.M., et al.: The diagnosis of dementia due to Alzheimer's disease: recommendations from the National Institute on Aging-Alzheimer's association workgroups on diagnostic guidelines for Alzheimer's disease. Alzheimer's Dement. **7**(3), 263–269 (2011)
22. Nucci, M., Mapelli, D., Mondini, S.: Cognitive Reserve Index questionnaire (CRIq): a new instrument for measuring cognitive reserve. Aging Clin. Exp. Res. **24**(3), 218–226 (2012)

23. Orpwood, R., Bjørneby, S., Hagen, I., Mäki, O., Faulkner, R., Topo, P.: User involvement in dementia product development. Dementia **3**(3), 263–279 (2004)
24. Prince, M., Jackson, J.: Alzheimer's Disease International. World Alzheimer Report (2009)
25. Riikonen, M., Mäkelä, K., Perälä, S.: Safety and monitoring technologies for the homes of people with dementia. Gerontechnology **9**(1), 32–45 (2010)
26. Rimminen, H., Lindström, J., Linnavuo, M., Sepponen, R.: Detection of falls among the elderly by a floor sensor using the electric near field. IEEE Trans. Inf. Technol. Biomed. **14** (6), 1475–1476 (2010)
27. Sanders, E., Stappers, P.: Convivial toolbox: generative design research for the fuzzy front end (2013)
28. Sanders, E.B.-N., Stappers, P.J.: Probes, toolkits and prototypes: three approaches to making in codesigning. CoDesign **10**(1), 5–14 (2014)
29. Sposaro, F., Danielson, J., Tyson, G.: iWander: an Android application for dementia patients, pp. 3875–3878 (2010)
30. Yamaguchi, H., Maki, Y., Takahashi, K.: Rehabilitation for dementia using enjoyable video-sports games. Int. Psychogeriatr. **23**(4), 674–676 (2011)

Social Robot and Sensor Network in Support of Activity of Daily Living for People with Dementia

Sara Casaccia[1(✉)], Gian Marco Revel[1], Lorenzo Scalise[1],
Roberta Bevilacqua[2], Lorena Rossi[2], Robert A. Paauwe[3],
Irek Karkowsky[4], Ilaria Ercoli[5], J. Artur Serrano[6],
Sandra Suijkerbuijk[7], Dirk Lukkien[7], and Henk Herman Nap[7]

[1] Department of Industrial Engineering and Mathematical Sciences,
Università Politecnica delle Marche, Ancona, Italy
s.casaccia@staff.univpm.it
[2] IRCCS INRCA, Ancona, Italy
[3] RDM Dokkantoor, Rotterdam, The Netherlands
[4] Sensara B.V, Rotterdam, The Netherlands
[5] JEF srl, Civitanova Marche, Italy
[6] Department of Neuromedicine and Movement Science, Faculty of Medicine
and Health Sciences, NTNU/Norwegian University of Science and Technology,
Trondheim, Norway
[7] Vilans, Utrecht, The Netherlands

Abstract. In this paper, an eHealth system is described to improve the lifestyle of people with dementia and their caregivers. In the eWare project, a social robot is integrated with a sensor network to measure ADLs with the goal to provide context relevant suggestions to the person with dementia and reduce the caregiver burden. Furthermore, the context relevant messages can remind people with dementia to perform the activities that they want and need to perform, but forgot due to a decline of brain. The developments are based on iterative co-design and in-situ evaluations with people with dementia and their (in)formal carers. The architecture configuration of eWare was tested in laboratory experimental tests to provide a final ecosystem that will be further evaluated during the pilot cases of the project.

Keywords: Dementia · Social robot · Measurements

1 Introduction

The estimated number of people living with dementia in the world is about 46.8 million with a person diagnosed every 3.2 s [1]. In prospective, this number is going to double every 20 years reaching about 75 million in 2030. Typically, people with dementia have a lifestyle which is not different from other people, and have similar daily needs in respect to well-being and health. Daily needs that are increasingly more difficult to fulfill with the support of care professionals due to shortages and budget cuts. Furthermore, informal carers are already overburdened. ICT solutions can support people

© Springer Nature Switzerland AG 2019
R. Brankaert and W. IJsselsteijn (Eds.): D-Lab 2019, CCIS 1117, pp. 128–135, 2019.
https://doi.org/10.1007/978-3-030-33540-3_12

with dementia in improving their quality of life, and staying independent and active [2, 3]. This work is focused on an eHealth system, based on a social robot to support people with dementia in the mild to middle stage of dementia - who live alone at home - in their daily activities, and to be independent. The social robot has the potential to improve their wellbeing and reduce care-related stress among their caregivers. The system is characterized by the integration of a lifestyle monitoring technology (Passive Infra-Red and door contact sensors) and social support robotics, providing people with dementia context-relevant reminders based on predefined goals such as taking breakfast or going to bed within a certain time interval. In Fig. 1 is shown the specification of utilities for the project. Carers are informed via an app whenever goals have been met or not. The work has been performed within the framework of the eWare project [4] AAL-2016-071, financed by European Commission, National Ministries (The Netherlands, Italy and Switzerland) and National Funding Agencies (Norway).

Fig. 1. Specification of utilities

2 System Architecture and Methodology

The innovative aspect of eWare is the integration of sensors - to monitor the Activities of Daily Living (ADLs) of the older adult at home [5, 6] - and a small social robot to provide context-relevant suggestions to the user. Feedback is sent through a web-app to the caregiver to provide information about the older adults at home. In particular, the robot interacts to the person with dementia in achieving their Activity of Daily Living (ADL) goals. Goals such as having breakfast within a pre-defined time frame, eating dinner, leaving the house for activities, or going to bed. People with dementia often have difficulties in initiating activities and the day-night rhythm can shift.

To design an eHealth solution that supports people with dementia and their carers, active iterative involvement of these users is preferred in design to ensure compatibility with preferences, needs, and abilities. Currently, there is an increasing effort in actively involving people with dementia in the design of supportive technologies [7]. In particular for the design of navigation aids and social robotics.

The eWare system for people with dementia is realized combining two eHealth solutions already existing on the market. Life-style monitoring represents the newest category of monitoring system for application in elderly care. Passive Infrared sensors (PIR) combined with door contact sensors are used to monitor the activities of daily living of older people living alone at home [8, 9]. The innovative idea of this system is to combine the elaborated information coming from the life-style sensors network to give feedback to the user through a social robot. Introducing to people with dementia a social robot to provide suggestions and feedback regarding their daily goals is becoming an new way people with dementia in improving their quality of life and caregivers in reducing stress burden.

In the upcoming sections, we describe the technical development of the eWare system and a first experimental test with actual end-users.

2.1 Lifestyle Monitoring

A commercial sensor network of PIR sensors has been selected (Sensara Lifestyle monitoring system; https://sensara.eu/) for the purpose of the eWare project. The lifestyle system configuration is characterized by five wireless sensors (3 Passive Infrared (PIR) sensors and 2 doors contact sensors), which are installed in the home of the customer. The sensors are battery operated and need to be attached to the wall at about 1.40 m height. PIR sensors are installed in toilets/bathroom, kitchen, exit door(s), hall and the living room. Door contact sensors (On/Off sensors) are installed in the kitchen, for example in frequently used drawer or on the door of the fridge, etc. Sensors communicate with software in the cloud using a wireless receiver with a connection range sufficient to cover the monitored apartment. This receiver requires a wired power source and an internet connection.

Due to a self-learning algorithm, the lifestyle monitoring system supports different customer lifestyles. The algorithm collects data and can learn a baseline lifestyle pattern during the first two weeks of use (learned behavior period). Special filtering functions are implemented in order to make the system robust to interfering inputs such as visitors, holidays, pets, false sensor messages, etc. Based on the self-learning algorithm, this system configuration can provide useful information about the lifestyle of the users, e.g. level of activity, going inside/outside, in or out of bed, kitchen and toilet activity, walking speed. The end-user is the owner of the data and can invite (in)formal carers to follow its lifestyle. If the end-user is not able to perform this task, then a responsible family member can invite others. An associated privacy wizard allows for controlling access to the provided information.

2.2 Tessa Social Robot

For the purpose of the eWare project, Tinybot's Tessa is used, which is a small talking conversation robot [1] (https://www.tinybots.nl/). The definition of Social Robot is continuously debated, as reported also in [10]. The authors, in particular, have defined a social robot as an autonomous or semi-autonomous robot that interacts and communicates with humans by following the behavioral norms expected by the people with whom the robot is intended to interact. The high degree of personalization of the interaction represents the kernel of the Tessa robot social capability. Despite this, of course, there are several improvements that can be made, regarding for instance the social interaction capability and the social presence of Tessa, but, taking into account the peculiarity of the target group involved in the project, it was decided to provide a low-complex and easy to use robot, that has been specifically designed for- and with people with dementia. Tessa has been developed to provide social support and agenda functionalities for individuals with dementia and their informal caregiver. Tessa consists of a stationary social robot that provides a stimulus for individuals with dementia by delivering spoken verbal reminders, friendly suggestions, and playing personal music. Both formal and informal caregivers can personalize Tessa through an easy-to-use app, as well as add their own reminders, suggestions, and music.

3 Method and Results

3.1 Preliminary Pilot

Active involvement of people with dementia, their informal and formal carers was to ensure a match with the individual end-user goals and needs of the eWare eco-system in iterative test-retest procedures. Insights from different sessions and focus groups, a persona profile and the structure of the services were developed. In this paper is reported, the preliminary studies with the end-users, with aim of understanding the interaction features of the robot and of the UI, taking into account the peculiarities of the communication modalities of people with dementia (see Fig. 2).

Fig. 2. Active involvement of end users.

Following the national guidelines of the country involved, the Ethical approvals were collected for the evaluations and informed consents were collected. During the sessions people with dementia (primary end-users), (in)formal carers (secondary end-users) and (location) managers (tertiary end-users) were involved. The initial participatory sessions took place in three countries, Italy, Switzerland and The Netherlands, involving the future primary-, secondary- and tertiary end-users of eWare. The results from active involvement of the end users iteratively lead to improvements of the eWare eco-system. From the active involvement sessions, needs were gathered for the person with dementia in respect to support in ADLs and these were translated into system requirements (Table 1) for creating ADL goals with the eWare system.

Table 1. System requirements.

	Tessa	Movement sensor	Door sensor	Bed sensor	Other sensors
Activity Guidance	v	v	v		
Activity Level Monitoring	v	v	v	–	–
Reminders & Simulation	v				
Provide Daily Information	v				
Inactivity Detection	v	v	v	Optional	
Monitoring Mood	Optional				
Wandering		v	v	Optional	
Activating Cognition	v				
Sleep Quality Monitoring	Optional	v		v	
Safety Monitoring	Optional				v
Real-time Tele-monitoring	Optional				v

After the active involvement sessions, rich qualitative and quantitative insight was gathered in multiple in-situ evaluations with nine older people with early to middle stage dementia, four informal caregivers, and one formal caregiver. Life-style monitoring sensors and Tessa were placed inside the home of older people with mild to moderate dementia for three weeks. All participants were interviewed, except for one due to personal circumstances. The in-situ evaluation used a Wizard-of-Oz test set-up, in which the participants interacting with the robot believe it is fully autonomous, but which is actually operated by an unseen human being [11] and had a twofold purpose to the eWare project. First, the intention was to gain rich insights in the actual services that people with dementia would like to use in the eWare system and to see how they would respond to the interaction with the Tessa. Second, a Wizard-of-Oz experiment was also intended to see whether the sensor system would give enough information about the lifestyle for the AI to evoke meaningful insights for the robot to respond to. The experiment lasted for three weeks at four different households. People with dementia and their informal carers provided relevant input for functionalities and improvements of eWare as a response after trying out this Wizard-of-Oz version. The main results of the sessions in-situ evaluations were:

- Personalisation was considered important by all participants, but more so on the level of 'when' and 'how', rather than 'what.' For example, such as using the name of the person ("Good morning, Jane. Would you like some breakfast?")

ADL tasks chosen were very similar, but timing and messages differed.

- The Tinybot's voice was universally liked, and its appearance was considered adequate. Participants focused on its appearance more in the participatory sessions than the field study participants. "Sure. It is fine. I think it is a nice little egg." – one of the participants with dementia in our in-situ evaluation study.
- The Tinybot was considered less suited for care receivers leading an unstructured life, and for houses with multiple inhabitants and multiple floors. This was confirmed in the field study.
- Field study participants wanted and expected more interaction between care receiver and Tinybot. This element did not come forward as prominently in the participatory sessions.

3.2 Further Developments

Results of the pilot are necessary to define the final architecture of the system. From the initial configuration, the final architecture is characterized by:

- Lifestyle monitoring Adapter –It is based on the public API called "Customer-API", which allows retrieval of the lifestyle information of the users of the system, which use LAN (gateway and PIR and door sensors). This information includes information about the attached users, their ADLs.
- Robot Adapter –It is based on an API which allows firing various actions (i.e. playing messages, asking questions, playing music) and receiving feedback from the end-users (residents/ elderly).
- System Database – it is the central data storage for the whole system and combines data received from the Lifestyle monitoring system, the robot and some system operating data.
- System Web UI – This component allows users (caregivers) to access all relevant configuration and user data, including the list of users of the system, the lifestyle information for the active user of the system, the list of active Tessa's and the associated social robot general configuration, the list of campaigns for all active social robots and the configurations of these campaigns, log files for the executed campaigns, including the received response from the end-users (residents).
- System Main Application – This software module is responsible for the overall orchestration and administration tasks within the system, like for example system startup and scheduling the system activities.
- System Artificial Intelligent (AI) Module – This software component implements the added "intelligence" of the system.

3.3 Goals Setting for People with Dementia

Based on the final architecture, the main aspect of the developed system is the setting of the goals for the resident. Goals are the combination of ADL events (sensor events of the life-style monitoring system) and reminder messages from the social robot. Together with the person with dementia, the informal and formal caregiver, the goals are set. Cards to guide this discussion are developed in the project. Next, the caregiver can set goals for the resident through the web-app. For example, having regular breakfast, or going outside more often for a walk. The system uses the sensor data to send relevant suggestions and motivating compliments via social robot. Goals are set within a time window (a minimum and maximum time). For example, a goal can be set for having regular breakfast between 7am and 11am. The caregiver can write these messages directly in the system app when planning a goal.

To give relevant suggestions through the social robot, the caregiver can write three different messages for each goal. Tessa will say these messages under certain conditions whether a goal has or has not been achieved yet within the set time. A message in a green font represents the success message. The robot will say this message when the goal has been achieved. A message in a yellow font represents a reminder: the robot will say this reminder halfway if a goal has not been achieved yet. A reminder in a red font represents a more urgent reminder if a goal still has not been achieved yet after the yellow reminder.

4 Discussion and Conclusion

The final functional system of eWare is designed to support people with dementia in achieving their Activity of Daily Living (ADL) goals. Goals such as having breakfast on time every day, eating dinner at appropriate times, leaving the house for activities, or going to bed at the right time. Individuals with cognitive disabilities such as dementia often have difficulties in initiating activities. Caregivers can promote healthy behaviour patterns for the person at home, fixing goals for the week and knowing the ADLs of the days. Using this protocol, the caregiver can monitor which ADLs have been triggered and which reminders Tessa has spoken. So based on this information, the caregiver can decide whether to change the goals or change something in the environment of the person with dementia. This always happens in close communication with the person with dementia themselves. The goals cannot be enforced, but with better information the caregiver can provide better support to make sure the older user achieves goals.

From the literature, it is evident the advantage in using social robots to take care of people with dementia [12] but, integrating the social robot with a sensor network may provide a more powerful system in helping people with dementia and their caregivers. People with dementia can benefit from this integrated system thanks to the advices received from the social robot, but funded on the measurement of ADLs, they are encouraged in maintaining their independence and intrinsic capacity receiving support and reminding for their daily activities, as reported in (Organization 2015). This way they won't get blunt reminders that do not comply with what actually happens in their homes.

The integrated system was realized based on in-situ evaluations and interactive sessions with people with dementia and their (in)formal carers. The eWare system has been tested through regression-tests: after every change functional and non-functional tests were re-run to ensure that previously developed and tested software still performed. Regression tests provided the complete functionality of the system ensuring that the architecture is functioning; this allows us to hypothesize the feasible application of the eWare system on people with dementia.

Acknowledgements. The authors thank the care professionals and solder people who participated in the studies, and the eWare project partners for their support. We gratefully acknowledge support from the European Commission's Active and Assisted Living programme, co-financed by the consortium national funding agencies. The authors also thank Eva de Jong, Peter Ruijten and Raymond Cuijpers to collaborate in some activities described in the paper.

References

1. Bouwhuis, D.G., Human Technology Interaction: Current use and possibilities of robots in care (2016)
2. Chen, K., Chan, A.H.S.: A review of technology acceptance by older adults. Gerontechnology **10**, 1–12 (2011). https://doi.org/10.4017/gt.2011.10.01.006.00
3. Kamphof, I.: Seeing again. Dementia, personhood and technology. In: Ageing and Technology (2016)
4. eWare – Early Warning Accompanies Robotics Excellence. https://aal-eware.eu/wp/. Accessed 12 Dec 2018
5. Monteriù, A., Prist, M.R., Frontoni, E., et al.: A smart sensing architecture for domestic monitoring: methodological approach and experimental validation. Sensors **18**, 2310 (2018). https://doi.org/10.3390/s18072310
6. Pietroni, F., Casaccia, S., Revel, G.M., et al.: Smart monitoring of user and home environment: the Health@Home acquisition framework. In: Casiddu, N., Porfirione, C., Monteriù, A., Cavallo, F. (eds.) Ambient Assisted Living, pp. 23–37. Springer, Cham (2019). https://doi.org/10.1007/978-3-030-04672-9_2
7. Suijkerbuijk, S., Nap, H.H., Cornelisse, L., et al.: Active involvement of people with dementia: a systematic review of studies developing supportive technologies. J. Alzheimer's Dis. **69**, 1041–1065 (2019). https://doi.org/10.3233/JAD-190050
8. Casaccia, S., Pietroni, F., Scalise, L., et al.: Health@Home: pilot cases and preliminary results : Integrated residential sensor network to promote the active aging of real users. In: 2018 IEEE International Symposium on Medical Measurements and Applications (MeMeA), pp. 1– (2018)6
9. Gochoo, M., Tan, T., Liu, S., et al.: Unobtrusive activity recognition of elderly people living alone using anonymous binary sensors and DCNN. IEEE J. Biomed. Health Inform. 1 (2018). https://doi.org/10.1109/JBHI.2018.2833618
10. Bartneck, C., Forlizzi, J.: A design-centred framework for social human-robot interaction. In: RO-MAN 2004. In: 13th IEEE International Workshop on Robot and Human Interactive Communication (IEEE Catalog No. 04TH8759). pp. 591–594 (2004)
11. Martin, B., Hanington, B.M.: Universal Methods of Design: 100 Ways to Research Complex Problems, Develop Innovative Ideas, and Design Effective Solutions. Rockport Publishers, Beverly (2012)
12. Mordoch, F., Osterreichei, A., Guse, L., et al.: Use of social commitment robots in the care of elderly people with dementia: a literature review. Maturitas **74**, 14–20 (2013). https://doi.org/10.1016/j.maturitas.2012.10.015

Dementia Lab Ideas

SoundscapePillow; a Design for Creating Personalised Auditory Experiences for People with Dementia

Daniel van Pel, Maarten Houben$^{(\boxtimes)}$, and Berry Eggen

Industrial Design, Eindhoven University of Technology,
Eindhoven, The Netherlands
m.houben1@tue.nl

Abstract. This paper explores how we can design personalised auditory experiences for people with dementia (PwD). We introduce a new product design called the SoundscapePillow. The SoundscapePillow is a long tubular shape changing pillow that enables personalised auditory experiences for PwD by listening to (nature) soundscapes. The built-in sound system produces these soundscapes to empower the PwD to relax, to reduce agitation, and to remember experiences from the past. In combination with an accompanying App the experience can be personalised for the PwD. The concept was put in practice by conducting two small scale explorative user tests with a prototype of the concept. This paper discusses the insights gained from the design process of the SoundscapePillow, the concept itself, and what future work is needed.

Keywords: Dementia · Design · Technology · Soundscapes · Research through design

1 Introduction

Dementia is a term for a wide range of conditions. The most prevalent ones are Alzheimer's disease and cardiovascular dementia [1, 2]. Dementia comes with many problems and complications, and results in cognition and mental functioning being impaired. The most common known one is loss of memory, but dementia can lead to anxiety and depression as well [3].

Due to lack of a cure for dementia, other, non-pharmaceutical interventions are needed. These can reduce stress, boredom, frustration and improve quality of life without the use of medicine or drugs [4]. An example of such a non-pharmaceutical intervention is by the use of sound. Sound around us is typical for our environment and using this has shown potential to be used for triggering memories and conversations for people with dementia (PwD) [5–7]. Most interventions, or designs, are technology driven and have potential to be a success in theory, but this one size fits all approach is not effective since all PwD experience dementia differently [8]. Therefore technology needs to be adaptable to the specific needs, likes, preferences and social context of PwD [9].

© Springer Nature Switzerland AG 2019
R. Brankaert and W. IJsselsteijn (Eds.): D-Lab 2019, CCIS 1117, pp. 139–145, 2019.
https://doi.org/10.1007/978-3-030-33540-3_13

In this paper we present the design of the SoundscapePillow to facilitate adaptable and customisable listening experiences for PwD. This is done by firstly, discussing the design process. Secondly, by presenting the design. And lastly, by drawing conclusion from the design and considering what future work is needed.

2 SoundscapePillow

A research through design [10] approach was used to structure the design process. Firstly, Interviews were conducted with experts on the subject of design for dementia, and with caregivers in order to gain insight in day-today practice of dementia care. Afterwards, a prototype was created and two user tests were conducted with PwD in different stages of dementia. Additionally, the PwD their preferences regarding soundscapes was explored using interviewing techniques based on the decision tree by Hendriks et al. [11]. With these insights the first version of the prototype was extended based on exploratory tests with PwD.

2.1 Concept

The SoundscapePillow is a long tubular shape changing pillow that can be used for listening to (nature) soundscapes. (See Fig. 1). The built-in sound system can produce these soundscapes with the aim of helping the PwD to relax, to reduce agitation, and to remember experiences from the past. The pillow is highly adjustable, customisable, and personalisable, in order to suit the needs of the PwD.

Fig. 1. The SoundscapePillow, creating personalised auditory experiences by the use of a shape changing pillow that can play soundscapes in combined with an app.

2.2 Pillow

The pillow can be bent into different shapes, and will keep its shape after bending. This, in combination with its length, allows the pillow to be used in multiple ways. see

Fig. 2. The way the pillow is used has influence on the interaction the PwD has with it, and can create different experiences.

Fig. 2. The shape changing pillow that can be bent and folded allows for multiple interaction possibilities.

2.3   SoundscapePillow App

Aside from the shape changing pillow an accompanying app is also part of the adaptable and personalised experience. This app allows you to select and play the soundscapes through the SoundscapePillow. Simply connect the pillow with a device which has the app. Any tablet or smartphone with bluetooth capabilities will do.

The app allows you to create profiles for individuals to save user preferences and use history to improve the personalised experiences. Due to the intelligence of the SoundPillow being inside the pillow, and not within the app, every device connected to the pillow will be able to see all profiles that are created and the corresponding data. See Fig. 3.

When signed in to a profile, the interface allows for easy access to all soundscapes organised in groups based on location (Beach, Forest, Farm etc...). The groups have icons and colours corresponding to the group name for easier navigation. Within these groups the soundscapes can be found. See Fig. 4. The soundscapes have titles and images which try to give an impression of what the soundscape will sound like. Additionally, auditory elements of the soundscape are shown underneath the title.

Selecting a soundscape will show a screen which has the basic functionalities of playing, pausing, volume control, and favouriting. When a soundscape is liked by the PwD the user can choose to set the soundscape as a favourite for the current profile by clicking the star icon. The favourited soundscapes are shown on the first tab of the user interface for quick accessibility. See Fig. 5.

Fig. 3. The list of profiles within the SoundscapePillow (left). When a profile is selected the user sees more information and can sign in (right).

Fig. 4. All Soundscapes grouped on location (left). Within the groups there are multiple soundscapes (right).

When the device is not connected to the pillow the app has the functionality to record sound using the microphone of the device. Family members and caregivers can record specific sounds which can personalise the experience for the PwD. As soon as the device with the recordings is connected to a SoundscapePillow the recordings will be transferred to it, and are now able to be played from within the app. When the SoundscapePillow is connected to another device the recordings can be played from there as well.

Fig. 5. A selected soundscape with its controls (left). The favourited soundscapes are shown in their own tab for easy access (right).

2.4 Soundscapes

The soundscapes in the pillow are a large collection of everyday sounds and categorised in the following groups: Beach, Forest, Farm, Urban, Home, Garden, Ambient, Mountain and Recordings.

The pre-existing soundscapes are created specifically for the SoundscapePillow and put together by combining different recordings and samples. By using sound-design the elements are positioned in a 3d space and move through it. The illusion of being in the environment is created using automation of volume, panning and reverb.

When a soundscape is played, the volume is gradually brought up to the volume level that is set. When a different soundscape is played, or the playing soundscape is paused, the volume level is gradually brought down. This is to make sure the PwD doesn't get surprised by the sudden change in volume and sounds in the environment.

2.5 Basic Controls

To make controlling the basic functions of SoundscapePillow easier, a label with four buttons is attached to the inner case. "Power", which turns the pillow On/Off, "Volume up", "Volume down" and "Next Soundscape". These buttons are represented by corresponding icons. See Fig. 6.

With these 4 buttons the SoundscapePillow can be quickly adjusted without the need of using the app. This reduces the amount of effort needed by the care giver and family members, as well as makes it possible to adjust the pillow while someone else is already connected to it. Another benefit of having the control without the app is that people who are not able to use a smartphone or tablet can still use the SoundscapePillow to play soundscapes. Although, without the option to use the benefits that come with the profiles and organisation of the soundscapes in the app.

Fig. 6. Four buttons on the pillow allow for basic control without the need of the SoundscapePillow App.

3   Conclusion and Future Work

This paper explores how design can be used for personalising care for PwD. The SoundscapePillow is an example of such a design and uses auditory experiences that can be personalised to the PwD. We believe that personalising care by the use of design, with the SoundscapePillow as an example, can contribute to the wellbeing of PwD. This paper aims to raise a discussion on how the challenges of dementia can be tackled using a combination of technology and design. The next steps are to verify the observations from user tests regarding the effectiveness of the SoundscapePillow in a larger study. The study should aim to find insights of whether the SoundscapePillow is able to reduce stress, reduce agitation, and help with remembering experiences of the past. We believe that there is a great potential for the design, but only after these answers are found can be concluded whether it would be successful in helping the people with dementia in practice.

Acknowledgements. Special thanks to Ben Janssen, Jasperina Vennema, Jan van Gils, Anne-loth Spaan, Eveline Wouters, and all participants.

References

1. Prince, M., Albanese, E., Guerchet, M., Prina, M.: World Alzheimer Report 2014 Dementia and Risk Reduction (2014)
2. Prince, M., Prina, M., Guerchet, M.: World Alzheimer Report 2013 Journey of Caring (2013)
3. Chenoweth, L., et al.: Caring for aged dementia care resident study (CADRES) of person-centred care, dementia-care mapping and usual care. Lancet Neural **8**, 317–325 (2009)
4. Olazaran, J., et al.: Nonpharmacological therapies in Alzheimer's disease: a systematic review of efficacy. Dement. Geriatr. Cogn. Disord. **30**(2), 161–178 (2010). https://doi.org/10.1159/000316119
5. Schine, J.: Movement, memory & the senses in soundscape studies. J. Can. Acoust. Assoc. **38**(3), 100–101 (2010)

6. Nagahata, K., Fukushima, T., Ishibashi, N., Takahashi, Y., Moriyama, M.: A soundscape study: what kinds of sounds can elderly people affected by dementia recollect? Noise Health **6**(24), 63–73 (2004)
7. Houben, M., Brankaert, R., Bakker, S., Kenning, G., Bongers, I., Eggen, B.: Foregrounding everyday sounds in Dementia. In: Proceedings of the DIS 2019 Conference on Designing Interactive Systems (2019). https://doi.org/10.1145/3322276.3322287
8. Kitwood, T.: The experience of dementia. Aging Ment. Health **1**, 13–22 (2010). https://doi.org/10.1080/13607869757344
9. Brankaert, R.: Design for Dementia: A design-driven living lab approach to involve people with dementia and their context. Ph.D., Eindhoven University of Technology (2016)
10. Koskinen, J.Z., Binder, T., Redström, J., Wensveen, S.: Constructive design research. Design Research Through Practice, pp. 1–13 (2012)
11. Hendriks, H., Vliet, D.V., Gerritsen, D.L., Dröes, R.-M.: Nature and dementia: development of a person- centered approach. Int. Psychoger. **28**(9), 1455–1470 (2016)

Feasibility of Virtual Reality in Elderly with Dementia

G. Andringa[1]([✉]), P. L. Nuijten[1], M. M. Macville[1], E. G. A. Mertens[1],
J. J. Kaptein[1], A. C. M. Bauer[1], L. R. van den Doel[1], and A. G. Roos[2]

[1] Department of Science, University College Roosevelt,
Middelburg, The Netherlands
g.andringa@ucr.nl
[2] Arend Roos, Middelburg, The Netherlands

Abstract. Virtual reality (VR) is a promising tool in health care, yet its application and feasibility in people with dementia is largely unexplored. The aim of our study was to explore the feasibility of VR in people with dementia in a daycare setting by means of a) a literature study and b) a pilot study using the VR game "Balloons". Our literature study of eight primary research articles using VR in demented elderly showed that practical and personal feasibility issues were limited. Only few subjects experience cybersickness or anxiety and practical issues are rarely encountered. Our pilot study testing the game "Balloons" in ten elderly subjects visiting a daycare center underscored our literature study. The limited number of studies available, especially with respect to fully immersive set-ups, warrants further studies for successful implementation of VR in day-care.

Keywords: Dementia · Virtual reality · Feasibility

1 Introduction

With the number of elderly on the rise and shortages in the health care system, new ways of supporting people with dementia and their caretakers are called for. Virtual reality (VR) is rapidly gaining interest as one of the tools in the observed technological revolution in health care and may provide an innovative and effective means to provide support in training activities for daily living or cognitive skills in general. VR allows for great control as well as flexibility and may provide a tool to cater the individual needs of the people with dementia and their immediate environment. However, while VR has been widely applied already in both mental health care and physical rehabilitation, its application and feasibility in people with dementia is largely unexplored.

The aim of our study was to explore the feasibility of VR in people with dementia in a daycare setting by means of (a) a literature study and (b) a pilot study using the VR game "Balloons" in 10 elderly visiting a day-care facility.

R. Brankaert and W. IJsselsteijn (Eds.): D-Lab 2019, CCIS 1117, pp. 146–149, 2019.
https://doi.org/10.1007/978-3-030-33540-3_14

2 Methods and Results

2.1 Literature Study

For the literature study, articles were selected using the following key terms: "virtual reality", "VR", "demented elderly", "older adults with dementia", "dementia", "Alzheimer's disease", "cognitive decline", "feasibility", "pilot", and "acceptability". Studies were only included if they were primary sources and focused on feasibility for VR in elderly with (any form of) dementia. Eight studies complied with our criteria [1–8]. The studies, using non-immersive and semi-immersive VR, showed that participants experienced medium to high level presence in the virtual environments, suggesting reasonable immersion. The majority of studies reported no or low levels of simulator sickness. Furthermore, seven studies reported demented elderly feeling safe, where one study reported minor anxiety. In addition, VR was found to be a positive and enjoyable experience. Interestingly, in a study comparing a VR version to a paper version of a attention task, it was found that almost 70% of the participants preferred the VR condition as a result of its immersive, motivating, and engaging nature, even when the VR task was more difficult [7]. Generally, few problems arose when using the equipment, however, the interface devices chosen should be dependent on the tasks used in the virtual environment, and a seated position during the experience is preferred. The duration spent in the VR was highly variable, and only one study used repeated sessions. Overall the results with respect to practical and personal feasibility are premature but promising, while topics such as session length and frequency and immersion level as largely unexplored fields.

2.2 Pilot Study

In our pilot study, we used a semi-experimental set-up to explore the feasibility of the game "Balloons" in elderly at a day-care center in Yerscke, the Netherlands. Ten elderly (3 males, 7 females) were included of which four suffered from dementia. All participants provided informed consent. Informal caretakers were informed when applicable. Most of the participants indicated having no or little experience with digital tools and none had used VR before. Participants remained seated during the experiment and could interact with the environment through a controller that was shown as a blue stick in the virtual environment. After a brief period of habituation, participants played four rounds of the game. Time and score were collected, and several of the experiences were videotaped. Subsequently, the participants were asked to participate in a semi-structured interview to gain insight into personal factors of feasibility, namely cyber sickness (rated by the cybersickness questionnaire [9]), anxiety, and perceived enjoyment and motivation, and practical factors of feasibility, namely their ability to handle the equipment and their understanding of the game.

The aim of the game was to prick blue and green balloons while neglecting red balloons coming from three pipes in random order and color. The game was designed in Unity version 3.5.0.3. and run on a Microsoft Windows 10 Pro computer in Steam VR version 1.3.23. It was connected to an HTC Vive headset with a 2160 × 1200 resolution, and two wireless motion-tracked controllers. Sounds were played on computer speakers, and motions were tracked through two motion sensor stations placed 2,5 meters opposite to each other. Nine out of ten participants completed the experiment. One subject suffered from claustrophobia and did not finish the game. In the nine subjects, no practical problems were observed; participants were able to use the controller and headset. Participants played between 2.17 and 4.35 min, and no negative effects such as cybersickness symptoms, wrist pain or anxiety were reported in the interviews. Furthermore, the majority of participants were highly motivated during the game and expressed enjoyment and satisfaction afterwards. Moreover, the experiences did not seem to differ between the healthy elderly, the demented elderly, and the elderly with advanced dementia. The competence levels of the participant varied widely. The instructions were well understood by the participants.

3 Discussion

Both our literature study as well as our pilot suggest that VR can be used as a feasible tool in elderly people with dementia. While most elderly (aged 80 and over) have little experience with digital means, practical factors, such as limitation in use and understanding of the digital tool are limited. In addition, personal factors do not seem to form a serious problem either; as most subjects find the experience enjoyable and report little or no cybersickness.

The high level of control over the VR experience, the flexibility of VR to cater individual needs, the possibility to create an environment that allows for full immersion and effective learning and the ability to extract information are all clear advantages of VR over classic tests and games. The limited number of the studies available, especially with respect to fully immersive set-ups and use of repeated sessions, warrant further studies into the relation between comfort and motivation on the one hand and the duration and level of immersion on the other. These topics are the current focus of our research.

References

1. Flynn, D., Schaik, P.V., Blackman, T., Femcott, C., Hobbs, B., Calderon, C.: Developing a virtual reality-based methodology for people with dementia: a feasibility study. CyberPsychol. Behav. **6**(6), 591–611 (2003)
2. Mcewen, D., Taillon-Hobson, A., Bilodeau, M., Sveistrup, H., Finestone, H.: Two-week virtual reality training for dementia: Single case feasibility study. J. Rehabil. Res. Dev. **51**(7), 1069–1076 (2014)
3. Manera, V., et al.: A feasibility study with image-based rendered virtual reality in patients with mild cognitive impairment and dementia. PLoS One **11**(3) (2016)
4. Vallejo, V., et al.: Usability assessment of natural user interfaces during serious games: adjustments for dementia intervention. J. Pain Manage. **9**(3), 333–339 (2016)
5. Siriaraya, P., Ang, C.S.: Recreating living experiences from past memories through virtual worlds for people with dementia. In: Proceedings of the 32nd annual ACM conference on Human factors in computing systems - CHI 2014 (2014)

6. Burdea, G., Rabin, B., Rethage, D., Damiani, F., Hundal, J.S., Fitzpatrick, C.: BrightArm therapy for patients with advanced dementia: a feasibility study. In: 2013 International Conference on Virtual Rehabilitation (ICVR), pp. 208–9 (2013)
7. Burdea, G., et al.: Feasibility study of theBrightBrainerTM integrative cognitive rehabilitation system for elderly with dementia. Disabil. Rehabil. Assistive Technol. **10**(5), 421–432 (2014)
8. Moyle, W., Jones, C., Dwan, T., Petrovich, T.: Effectiveness of a virtual reality forest on people with dementia: a mixed methods pilot study. Gerontologist **58**(3), 478–487 (2017)
9. Robert, P., et al.: Is it possible to use highly realistic virtual reality in the elderly? A feasibility study with image-based rendering. Neuropsychiatric Disease and Treatment, p. 557 (2015)

Wijstijd, Supporting Time Orientation Designed for and with People with Dementia

Thilly Maria Johanna Coppelmans$^{(\boxtimes)}$ (iD)

University of Technology Eindhoven, Eindhoven, AZ 5612, The Netherlands
thilly.coppelmans@gmail.com

Abstract. The number of elderly living with dementia globally is expected to increase over the coming years. This project focusses on designing for people with dementia. Some common difficulties in the early stage of dementia are related to orientation in time. Difficulties such as trouble with planning or organizing, forgetting things someone has just read and a decrease in the awareness of time. Within the development process of this project, the users played an important role. This article highlights this involvement of the end users within the design process and the design decisions made from this involvement. The result of this project is the Wijstijd. It focuses on the problems surrounding time orientation for people with dementia in the early stages. The project is a graduation project at the University of Technology, Eindhoven.

Keywords: Dementia · Time-orientation · Co-design · User involvement · User-centered design

1 Introduction

The number of elderly living with dementia is expected to grow over the coming years (Wimo et al. 2003). This project is about designing for people with dementia. Dementia is a general term for a group of diseases that result in a decline in mental ability. It is a progressive disease, which creates a design space to assist the target group, instead of focusing on creating a medicine.

In 2016, 70% of the people with dementia in the Netherlands lived at home and was being taken care of by an informal caregiver (Alzheimer Nederland 2016). An informal caregiver improves the quality of life for a person with dementia, which allows them to stay at home (Hattink et al. 2016). Unfortunately, they carry a heavy burden, which is one of the biggest reasons for a person with dementia to go to a nursing home (Alzheimer Nederland 2016).

Assistive technology can help to reduce this burden for an informal caregiver (Hattink et al. 2016). Therefore, this project focusses on creating an assistive technology that will support the independence of the person with dementia and lowers this care burden for an informal caregiver. A reason to focus on supporting people with dementia at home with technology is that it saves costs compared to going to a nursing home (Nijhof 2013). Additionally, this could save a lot of costs, seeing that the median survival time is 3,4 years if diagnosed at the age of 90, up till 8,3 years when diagnosed at age 65 (Brookmeyer et al. 2002).

© Springer Nature Switzerland AG 2019
R. Brankaert and W. IJsselsteijn (Eds.): D-Lab 2019, CCIS 1117, pp. 150–155, 2019.
https://doi.org/10.1007/978-3-030-33540-3_15

Some common difficulties in the early stage of dementia are related to orientation in time. Difficulties such as trouble with planning or organizing, forgetting things someone has just read and a decrease in the awareness of time (Alzheimer Association 2019) (Alzheimer Nederland 2016). These difficulties with time orientation can also be associated with understanding the length of time periods and understanding the time of day, which interferes with a person's ability to structure their day and make plans (Topo et al. 2007). Time disorientation is also directly linked to an increased risk of dementia (Dumurgier et al. 2016). However, it is also shown that there is a need for support surrounding these problems of orientation and dealing with memory loss (Brankaert 2016).

This project focusses on people in the early stage of dementia. By supporting them with understanding their daily schedule in relation to the current time, the project supports their independence.

2 Approach

Within this project, the design will be focused on increasing the independence of a person with dementia. The approach of this project is to involve the users within the design process. Doing this allows for a better understanding of the context and the problems the user is facing. A growing approach within the care sector linking to this is Person-Centered Care (PCC); "Providing care that is respectful of and responsive to individual patients preferences, needs, and values, and ensuring that patient values guide all clinical decisions" (Brummel-Smith et al. 2016).

Within this project, the user focus is incorporated throughout the process to focus on the users' needs and preferences. In addition, the final product is tested within the context of the user.

This approach links closely to the living lab approach. This approach shows that in order to design for impaired users – people with dementia – it is important to involve the users actively in different stages of the process (Brankaert 2016).

An important principle in the user-centered design approach for people with dementia is reminiscence. Reminiscence refers to a process in which a person recalls experiences or events from the past (Dempsey et al. 2012).

3 Result

3.1 The Wijstijd

The result of the graduation project is the Wijstijd. The Wijstijd is a clock which visually links your appointments for today to the current time. It consists of an analogue clock with a screen underneath. The different functions support the user by showing the current time and time of day, visualizing when the next appointment will take place and reminding them when they need to leave for this appointment. These different functionalities can be adjusted to what a person with dementia needs in their current situation. This allows the Wijstijd to adjust throughout the progression of dementia (see Fig. 1).

Fig. 1. The WijsTijd prototype in context

3.2 Supporting Insights

Bellow the different aspects of the Wijstijd will be highlighted and explained in relation to the different insights gathered from the user involvement throughout the project.

Overview
The Wijstijd will give an overview of your upcoming appointments. These will be shown by means of different colors on the face of the clock, which correspond with the time of the appointment. The lights also correspond with the screen, which always shows the next appointment in a corresponding color. When the user comes closer to the Wijstijd, the screen will show an overview of the coming three appointments for the current day.

The insights gathered that support these functions where gathered during a focus group session with people with dementia and their caregivers. Here the participants mentioned that they would like to have a clear overview of one day, to eliminate confusion on which day it currently is.

Adaptability
Because dementia is a progressive disease, the Wijstijd is developed in such a way that it is adjustable to the different needs of a person with dementia. Ideally a person with early stage dementia, or even before diagnosis, would start using the Wijstijd. In this way the Wijstijd starts out as an extra support for their daily schedule by means of showing their appointments and reminding them. This however can change into supporting in a person's daily schedule, such as when to eat dinner, or even just by supporting their day and night rhythm by means of a sun and moon rising and going down on the screen.

The insight to show the sun and moon rhythm to support day and night came forward during an interview with users on an early prototype of the Wijstijd (Fig. 2).

Fig. 2. The interface design of WijsTijd

Reminder

30 min before an appointment starts, a sound will remind the user that it is time to leave for their appointment.

During a focus group session with people with dementia and their caregivers, the concept of a reminder was highly appreciated. In later prototypes this was also supported during interviews and feedback sessions with users.

Online Calendar

The input for the appointments can be done via an online calendar. This allows family members and caregivers to input appointments, even from a distance.

This functionality is supported within multiple interviews where this subject of adding appointments was discussed. Here it was shown that especially the partner will be inputting the appointments which should be easy and fast.

Appearance
The clock is made from wood in a style based on old standing table clocks. The Wijstijd is also rather big in size so it could be easily seen from across the room.

The appearance is mostly linked to the concept of reminiscence. This was also apparent when presenting the Wijstijd or earlier prototypes with similar features. The wood and analogue clock helped the person with dementia with recognizing that it was a clock.

Clock face
The hands of the clock are adjusted to clarify the difference between the big and small hand. The hour hand has a circle attached to it. This circle will put a focus on the current hour.

When presenting different clock faces to people with dementia, the circle was shown to help with understanding the difference between the big and small hand. The problem of confusing the two hands came forward during interviews when a person was asked to tell what time it was. Here the hour and minute hand where often mixed.

4   Conclusion

Having a user centered approach during the project helped with the development of the Wijstijd. There where aspects, such as the difference between the big and small hand, that would not have come up as a problem when the users where not repeatedly involved within the process.

This shows that it is important to involve the end users and the people surrounding them, such as the caregivers, within the design process. This allows the designer to fully understand the problems the users are facing and to keep testing assumptions on which design will and which won't work.

References

Alzheimer Association: What is Alzheimer's Disease? (2019). https://www.alz.org/alzheimers-dementia/what-is-alzheimers. Last accessed 23 Aug 2019

Alzheimer Association: What is dementia? (2019). https://www.alz.org/alzheimers-dementia/what-is-dementia. Last accessed 23 Aug 2019

Alzheimer Nederland: Factsheet; Cijfers en feiten over dementie (2016)

Alzheimer Nederland: Symptomen van dementie (2016). https://www.alzheimernederland.nl/dementie/herkennen-symptomen/symptomen. Last accessed 1 Oct 2016

Brankaert, R.: Design for Dementia, A design-driven Living Lab approach to involve people with dementia in their context, 84, pp. p. 53–69 (2016)

Brookmeyer, R., Corrada, M.M., Curriero, F.C., Kawas, C.: Survival following a diagnosis of Alzheimer disease. Archives Neurol. 59(11), 1764–1767 (2002)

Brummel-Smith, K., Butler, D., Frieder, M., Gibbs, N., Henry, M., Koons, E., Scanlon, W.J.: Person- centered care: a definition and essential elements. J. Am. Geriatr. Soc. 64(1), 15–18 (2016)

Dempsey, L., Murphy, K., Cooney, A., Casey, D., O'Shea, E., Devane, D., Hunter, A.: Reminiscence in dementia: a concept analysis. Dementia 13(2), 176–192 (2012)

Dumurgier, J., Dartigues, J.F., Gabelle, A., Paquet, C., Prevot, M., Hugon, J., Tzourio, C.: Time orientation and 10 years risk of dementia in elderly adults: the three-city study. J. Alzheimer's Dis. **53**(4), 1411–1418 (2016)

Hattink, B.J.J., Meiland, F.J.M., Overmars-Marx, T., Boer de, M., Ebben, P.W.G., Blankenvanv, v/d Leeuw, J.: The electronic, personalizable Rosetta system for dementia care: exploring the user-friendliness, usefulness and impact. Disability and Rehabilitation: Assistive Technology, 11(1), 61–71 (2016)

Nijhof, N.: eHealth for people with dementia in homebased and residential care. Universiteit Twente (2013)

Topo, P., Saarikalle, K., Begley, E., Cahill, S., Holthe, T., Macijauskiene, J.: I don't know about the past or the future, but today it's Friday"–evaluation of a time aid for people with dementia. Technology and Disability, 19(2, 3), 121–131 (2007)

Wimo, A., Winblad, B., Aguero-Torres, H., von Strauss, E.: The magnitude of dementia occurrence in the world. Alzheimer Dis. Assoc. Disord. **17**(2), 63–67 (2003)

Prevention of Drug Intake Mistakes Through a Medication Control System for Elders

Diana Herrera-Hidalgo[(⊠)] and Aline Gonzalez-Moreno

Universidad Anahuac, 76246 Queretaro, Mexico
dh.diana@hotmail.com

Abstract. This project seeks to contribute to the health and well being of adults, through a comprehensive system that helps them have better control over the consumption of their medications. To achieve this, a multifunctional product is proposed; that stores, orders and doses the drugs; and that alerts users at the time they should be taken, while helping to keep track of their consumption. This in order to reduce the probability that users have failures in the consumption of their medications and that they suffer from side effects that come with this, and achieve better control over their treatment.

Keywords: Medication · Elder · Control

1 Background

Dementia is a worldwide problem, according to the PAHO (Pan American Health Organization, n.d.), with 6.21% until 2012 it has been the third leading cause of mortality in the population over 60 years, in the region of the Americas. The WHO (World Health Organization) estimates that there are around 47.5 million people in the world suffering from dementia and predicts that the number of those people will increase to 75.6 million in 2030 and 135.5 million in 2050.

Parallely, population is aging rapidly worldwide; between 2015 and 2050 the proportion of the world's population over 60 years old will multiply almost by two, going from 12% to 22% (WHO 2017) of which, between 65% and 90% consume 5 or 6 prescriptions of medicines, in many cases from different specialists. And, up to 50% make errors in the administration of medications, which leads to the increase in the number of prescribed drugs, which can lead to fatal adverse reactions, highlighting urinary incontinence, depression, restlessness, confusion, extrapyramidal symptoms, constipation and falls (Valenzuela, n.d.). This indicates that the market is increasing, and with it, the need to develop design projects that help solve these problem, in order to promote health and wellbeing in elders, and to have a better control of their medication intake.

With all of these data, a target audience was defined, which is people over 55 years of age who are multi-pathological and polymedicated, that is, they suffer two or more chronic pathologies and take five or more drugs a day, a sector of the population that frequently makes mistakes in the management of their medication.

R. Brankaert and W. IJsselsteijn (Eds.): D-Lab 2019, CCIS 1117, pp. 156–160, 2019.
https://doi.org/10.1007/978-3-030-33540-3_16

2 Hypothesis

If a product is designed, to store, order and dose medications; and to alert users when they should take a medication, while tracking their consumption behavior, the likelihood that users have mistakes in the consumption of their medications and suffer the side effects, would decrease, therefore, an increase of the control over the treatment is expected.

3 Methodology

The project's development started through a literature research, followed by a documental analysis, which was presented in the background, and then by an empirical analysis through case study, field research, expert advice and interviews. With this information a diagnosis was formulated and the creative process began, from which a result was defined.

During the case study the following conclusions were drawn: Proper and frequent drug consumption is the main challenge; performing tasks within a routine does not present itself as something complicated; elders seek to maintain an active life and independence; caregivers try to respect the autonomy of the elders; the resulted proposal must be intuitive enough for people over 65, but avant-garde, to attract the attention of people under this age, who in a few years will become the profile of the user. A list of design requirements was defined in order to satisfy the needs of the user and of the caregivers. The result has to be portable, ergonomic, durable, anthropometric and intuitive among many more requirements related to its function, techno-production and use.

4 Results

The system proposed consists of 3 elements, the first one (E1) doses and stores the medications, the second one (E2) reminds the patient at the right moment of the intake, and the third one (E3) helps keep track of consumption. These three elements will be controlled at its full by technology due to the effectiveness of it, by connecting the elements via Wi-Fi, so that they can interact with each other. Parallely to the development of this system, the graphic design studio created the branding for the product to give it an identity.

E1 consists in 3 color coded medicine dispensers, each color is accompanied by a symbol that will make its identification easier, this due to the fact that medicines are usually taken in 3 moments of the day; morning, evening and night. By a mechanical-electrical process it can only be opened at the time interval needed which the user or caregiver can program. An easy weekly refill function was added to it by generating an extractable and replaceable container, though not disposable. Several of this containers can be owned by the user, in order to facilitate the refill process, they can own as many as they wish and can place them in a separate structure which can hold a month of medicines. This containers have a false bottom that helps control the temperature on the inside, this to maintain the chemical properties of the medicines. It counts with 15 cm^3 of internal space; this is enough to store 10 pills (different dimensions). The shape of E1 was defined through a long creative process, sketching some ideas, analyzing the strengths and weaknesses of each one, with the use of a Pugh Matrix, and then merging all their strengths to produce a final proposal. The final proposal dimensions are 131 × 114 × 18 mm, this according to ergonomic features that allow an average adult to hold and interact with the product (Fig. 1).

Fig. 1. From left to right; E1, daily color-coded medicine dispensers, morning dispenser with extracted container, E1's anthropometric ratio.

E2 is a small portable reminder, which notifies the user, by vibration and sound, at the moment for the intake. It also features a panic button that will help the user send an alarm to a pre-designated contact in case they are in need of help. To define the shape of this element, the internal circuit was an important referent, knowing its dimensions was crucial for the design process, for this, the help of a mechatronic engineer was requested. After defining this, the creative process began and the final shape was defined, it has a diameter of 35 mm, and a high of 45 mm. For it to be user friendly, three silicon cases were designed, which will help the user adapt this element to their daily routine. The first one has the same shape of the element and helps protects it, the second one will allow the used to hang the element wherever they want, and the third one helps adapt E2 to the back of any watch with the help of straps and magnets. These cases come in a variety of colors in order to give the user the option to choose according to its personality (Fig. 2).

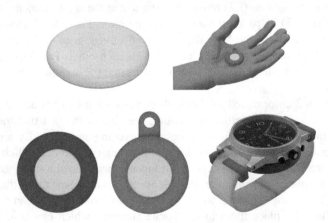

Fig. 2. From left to right and top to bottom; E2, its anthropometric ratio and E2's 3 silicon cases.

It's needed to measure data to know if and how effectively E1 and E2 are working. For this, E3, which is a mobile application, allows setting up the specific date and time a medicine should be taken, also the day the weekly refill should have place, the extension of the treatment, among others. This will help the user or caregiver have an overview of the medication history of intake, because E1 will send via Wi-Fi a notification when the dose was taken. E3 also features a tracking function, which will help the caregiver know where the user is in case they activate the panic button in E2 (Fig. 3).

Fig. 3. From left to right; E3 main page, configuration page and intake daily overview.

5 Conclusion

Drug intake mistakes can lead to fatal adverse reactions, in order to prevent this there has to be more control over the dose and time of intake. Even though there are existing products that aim to fulfill this urgent need, it seems that none of them has worked properly. The research and analysis made through the protocol led to the system described in the results of this document, which proposes a complete and functional solution to the medication intake control problem that elders encounter in their everyday life.

References

Pan American Health Organization (PAHO): Estado de salud de la Población; Salud del adulto mayor. [Population's state of health; Senior health] 29 January 2019, from Organización Panamericana de la Salud (OPS) (n.d.). https://www.paho.org/salud-en-las-americas-2017/?post_t_es=salud-del-adulto-mayor&lang=es

Valenzuela, E.: Uso de fármacos en el adulto mayor. [Use of drugs in the elderly] 22 January 2019, from Pontificia Universidad Católica de Chile (n.d.). https://medicina.uc.cl/publicacion/uso-farmacos-adulto-mayor/

World Health Organization (WHO): La salud mental y los adultos mayores. [Mental health and the elderly] 29 January 2019, from World Health Organization (WHO) (2017). https://www.who.int/es/news-room/fact-sheets/detail/la-salud-mental-y-los-adultos-mayores

World Health Organization (WHO): Informe mundial sobre envejecimiento y salud. Ginebra; 2015. [World report on aging and health. GINEBRA; 2015] From World Health Organization (WHO) (2015). http://apps.who.int/iris/bitstream/10665/186466/1/9789240694873_spa.pdf?ua=1

REsilience Monitor for INformal Caregivers in Dementia (REMIND): Digital Monitoring of Informal Caregivers Wellbeing to Prevent Crises

Dorien L. Oostra[1,2(✉)], Minke S. Nieuwboer[2],
Marcel G. M. Olde Rikkert[2,3], and Marieke Perry[2,3]

[1] Radboud University Medical Center, Radboud Institute for Health Sciences,
Nijmegen, The Netherlands
Dorien.Oostra@radboudumc.nl
[2] Department of Geriatric Medicine Radboud, Radboud University
Medical Center, UMC Alzheimer Centre, Nijmegen, The Netherlands
[3] Department of Geriatric Medicine, Donders Institute for Brain Cognition
and Behaviour, Radboud University Medical Center, Nijmegen, The Netherlands

In collaboration with Medworq, digital healthcare innovators

Abstract. Societal dependency on informal care for people with dementia will grow. Informal caregiving causes a considerable burden on caregivers, often a direct reason for crisis admission of the person with dementia. Close monitoring the wellbeing of caregivers and early intervening may prevent crisis admissions. Therefore, our aim is to develop a user-friendly application for informal caregivers and a dashboard for case managers to monitor wellbeing and resilience of the caregivers to provide timely support and prevent crises. A human centered design method was used to identify wishes and needs. End users invited to participate were informal caregivers and healthcare professionals from different disciplines. Experts were researchers, clinicians, innovation experts and application designers. Three end user meetings and multiple expert sessions took place. Wishes and needs were identified during the first end user session. During a second meeting functionalities of the application were discussed. It emerged to ask questions frequently to assess deterioration of caregiver's wellbeing. During a third meeting, concept screens of the application and dashboard were presented and discussed. Questions were reviewed covering the topics: social support, reciprocity, burden/competence, mood, own activities, person with dementia, and small crises. End users indicated they want to fill in approximately seven questions per week. Several challenges will be faced: making the application and dashboard easy to use, useful in practice and tailor-made. This methodological approach will result in a product that best meets the needs and wishes of caregivers and case managers in order to prevent crises.

Keywords: Informal caregiver application · Informal caregiver wellbeing · Monitoring

© Springer Nature Switzerland AG 2019
R. Brankaert and W. IJsselsteijn (Eds.): D-Lab 2019, CCIS 1117, pp. 161–168, 2019.
https://doi.org/10.1007/978-3-030-33540-3_17

1 Introduction

A vast majority of people with dementia live at home, resulting in complex care situations in the primary care setting [1, 2]. In most cases persons with dementia receive informal care as an addition to regular care. Informal care is nonprofessional care provided by people from a person's social environment, usually a partner or child [3]. Informal care is a large and crucial part of necessary care for people with dementia; societal dependency on informal care will grow [4]. Providing this care causes a considerable burden on informal caregivers [5, 6].

In the Netherlands, thirteen percent of informal caregivers for people with dementia are overburdened [5]. Caregivers frequently feel stressed and frustrated, and are depressed or have depressive symptoms [7–9]. Caregivers perceived burden can increase the risk for institutionalization of people with dementia [9]. It is of considerable importance that informal caregivers are willing and able to provide care and maintain the care situation for as long as possible. It is suggested that informal caregivers might benefit from monitoring their health status [7]. Previous research showed that short-term digital self-monitoring increased levels of competence and decreased levels of perceived stress [10]. Close monitoring the wellbeing of informal caregivers and early intervening may therefore prevent crisis admissions. We defined a crisis as an situation where a quick decision (within 24 h) for an unplanned admission to a hospital or nursing home is necessary from someone's own home [11].

Our aim is to develop a user-friendly application for informal caregivers and a dashboard for case managers to monitor wellbeing and resilience of the informal caregivers to provide timely support and prevent crises.

2 Methods

2.1 Design

The application will be developed according to the method of human centered design. Wishes and needs of the end users are key elements of this methodological approach. Therefore, meetings with end users took place regularly between November 2018 and July 2019 and new sessions will be scheduled. We started with the design process in the summer of 2018 and at the end of 2019 a first test version will be ready to carry out a pilot.

In the inspiration phase the wishes and needs of end users were inventoried and the goal of the application was determined. During the ideation phase, concrete ideas and prototypes were iteratively developed with the end users and experts. We worked according to the scrum methodology: after short building trajectories the application and dashboard are shown to the end users and project team to make adjustments when needed.

2.2 Participants

End users invited to participate are informal caregivers and healthcare professionals from different disciplines (especially case managers); the group of experts consisted of researchers, clinicians, innovation experts and application designers.

Potential end users were nominated to participate in the sessions using purposive sampling, based on the following criteria: (1) working regularly with persons with dementia (in the primary care setting), (2) working in the region Nijmegen or surroundings and (3) having a proactive attitude. End users who met these criteria were invited via email. To ensure representativeness, we balanced the number of participating professionals from each discipline. Experts were selected based on their involvement in the project; all were employees of the Radboudumc or Medworq.

2.3 Sessions

Three end user session took place, each session had a duration of two hours. The sessions had a mixed group of professionals and informal caregivers. The overall structure of the sessions was similar; started plenary with an introduction and purpose of the session, thereafter the topic was discussed in a separate group of professionals and informal caregivers, the session ended with a plenary discussion to reach between group consensus. Moderators were present to lead the group- and plenary discussions. The sessions were audio recorded and verbal consent was asked.

3 Results

3.1 Participants

Between ten and fifteen end users participated in the sessions. Informal caregivers and health care professions from different disciplines were present: case managers, general practitioners, practice nurses, community nurses and welfare workers. Table 1 describes the characteristics of the participants per session.

Table 1. Characteristics of participants, defined per session.

	Session 1	Session 2	Session 3
Number of participants	13	10	15
Female, n (%)	12 (92%)	6 (60%)	14 (93%)
Dominant background, n (%)			
Healthcare professional			
Case manager	3 (23%)	4 (40%)	3 (20%)
General practitioner	1 (8%)	1 (10%)	1 (7%)
Practice nurse	1 (8%)	-	1 (7%)
Community nurse	2 (15%)	2 (20%)	2 (13%)
Welfare worker	2 (15%)	-	1 (7%)
Informal caregiver	4 (31%)	3 (30%)	7 (46%)

3.2 Outcome Sessions

Three meetings with end users and multiple expert sessions took place and new meetings will be scheduled.

The purpose of the first meeting was to identify wishes and needs. Four informal caregivers and nine professionals (general practitioner, district nurses, welfare workers, case managers and practice nurse) attended this meeting. It emerged that most informal caregivers find it difficult to acknowledge they feel overburdened. If a case manager is not able to notice when an informal caregiver becomes overburdened, support cannot be provided in time. Although case managers visit regularly, the moment an informal caregiver becomes overburdened often happens at a different time. Based on this information, the aim of the application was specified: to monitor wellbeing and resilience of the informal caregiver to reduce crisis situations for the person with dementia to be able to continue living at home. During expert sessions we translated this aim to a concrete idea. In order to provide case managers with more insight into the wellbeing and resilience of informal caregivers, we want to measure this regularly via the REsilience Monitor for INformal caregivers in Dementia (REMIND) connected to a case managers dashboard. Hereby, both informal caregivers themselves and their case managers obtain better insight into the wellbeing of the informal caregiver. When wellbeing of the informal caregiver deteriorates case managers can offer support in time.

In a second meeting with end users concept screens of the application and dashboard were presented, to verify and optimize the idea in order to build a suited prototype. It was well received by the end users. Detailed information on the application and dashboard can be found in appendix I and II. Three informal caregivers and seven professionals (general practitioner, district nurses, welfare workers and case managers) attended this meeting. Also, the content of the app was discussed and the idea emerged to frequently ask informal caregivers questions. By analyzing the answers over time, deterioration in wellbeing will be noticed. These questions should be about perseverance, stress, coping, physical and mental condition of the person with dementia and the experienced social support. During expert sessions, standardized questionnaires were collected and additional questions were formulated.

In a third meeting with end users adjusted concept screens of the application and dashboard were presented and discussed. Seven informal caregivers and eight professionals (general practitioner, district nurses, welfare workers, case managers and practice nurse) attended this meeting. During the session questionnaires and self-made questions able to asses resilience and wellbeing of informal caregivers were discussed and evaluated on their relevance. Questions and questionnaires covered the following topics: social support, reciprocity, burden/competence, mood, own activities, small crises, person with dementia. Informal caregivers and professionals agreed on suitable questions and questionnaires. Furthermore, end users indicated they would be willing to fill in approximately seven questions per week. During an expert meeting we used the output of the session to construct a set of questions, including standardized questionnaires to measure resilience and wellbeing: perseverance time [12], EDIZ [13], Sociale Steun lijst [14], 4DKL [15], GDS-8 [16], IDEAL [17] and Brief Resilience Scale [18].

Construction of the prototype has started. During this process, prototypes will be presented to the end users to assess relevance and user friendliness.

4 Discussion

4.1 Challenges

During the further development process we will face several challenges, first to make the application and dashboard easy to use and useful in practice. Therefore, it should be user friendly. Connection of the case manager dashboard to other patient information systems is essential. In terms of content, the application and dashboard must be innovative and have added value to existing applications and support systems.

Second, in terms of feasibility we face another challenge. An informal caregiver must get the feeling that they are heard. Therefore, a case manager must review the data frequently; we hope this is feasible in practice. We want to create an overview in the dashboard to make the review process as simple as possible. It will be a challenge to make the app relevant for informal caregivers without an urgent request for help. The app and dashboard aim to notice the moment of deterioration of informal caregivers' wellbeing and therefore needs to interact with the informal caregiver over a long period of time.

Third, informal caregivers will not express burden similarly, i.e. some will withdraw from social life and others will actively look for fellow caregivers to share their experiences with. To overcome the challenge to make the application partly tailor made, informal caregivers will be asked during the app set-up to select questions that best characterize their burden. This will make the application more tailored to the user. During the further development process we will continue to focus on the tailor-made aspect, the end-user sessions are an ideal platform to test whether the application is suitable for informal caregivers of for example different ages.

4.2 Strengths and Limitations

Certain limitations of the methodology need to be acknowledged. It is very time consuming process to schedule and carry out end user sessions. However, we believe it is essential to achieve an end results useful for practice. The human centered design methodology is therefore a major strength as well. A limitation for the spread is the context-dependency of the application and dashboard. The product is designed to fit guidelines and existing applications and support systems in this region. For translation to other regions or even countries adjustments are necessary.

Performing mixed group sessions, sessions with professionals and informal caregivers, is a major advantage due to the possibility to interact and reach consensus between both groups, outcomes are therefore of more value. Furthermore, we were able to include opinions from a diverse group of people, as there is a large diversity in caregivers ages and roles (child or partner) and professionals' backgrounds.

4.3 Practical Implications

With this methodological approach, we aim to develop a product that best meets the needs and wishes of caregivers and case managers in order to prevent crises. We hope to provide caregivers and case managers with a product that is a valuable addition to regular primary care. Focusing on informal caregivers wellbeing through monitoring will provide case managers with more insight and earlier warning of deterioration, a safer feeling for informal caregivers and fewer admissions of people with dementia. We are aiming for a wide-scale implementation of the tool, although adjustment might be needed for usage in other regions of the Netherlands. Further development process and pilot testing will provide insights in the feasibility, applicability and effectiveness of the application and dashboard.

Developers

This project is initiated by DementieNet, an initiative of the Radboud Alzheimer Centrum (https://www.dementienet.com/dementienet/). DementieNet aims to improve local collaboration among healthcare professionals to provide care for community-dwelling elderly with dementia. Overall, the approach aims to reduce the burden of the disease for all persons involved in dementia care, including healthcare professionals, patients and their informal caregivers. The healthcare professionals consult with all healthcare professionals involved (medical, care and welfare), thereby coordinating the care to the needs of the patient. This personal approach allows patients to live at home longer and we all get a better grip on dementia.

DementieNet collaborates with Medworq to develop the application and dashboard (https://medworq.nl/). Medworq is a company of healthcare innovators. It is specialized in healthcare solutions, making them better, faster and cheaper. They develop and implement healthcare programs for chronic diseases, combining medical, financial and IT knowledge.

Appendix I - REMIND Application

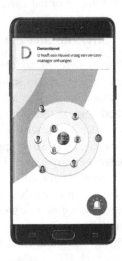

The REMIND application will be used by informal care-givers on their smartphones. When setting up the app, informal caregivers will enter some general information about themselves, including their own social network, see Fig. 1. One question per day will be sent. To notice deterioration in wellbeing, data over time is needed. If an informal caregiver becomes overburdened, interventions or support can be offered by case managers. A questionnaire will also be sent every few months the people in the informal caregiver's social network. Thereby, we identify whether the caregiver is being too optimistic about his or her wellbeing.

A red emergency button can be pressed, in case an informal caregiver is feeling overburdened.

Fig. 1. Concept screen of the REMIND application

Appendix II - Casemanager Dashboard

The case manager dashboard will be used by case managers through their web browser. The dashboard will show an overview of each dementia patient with all involved health care professionals, the informal caregiver and the data from the REMIND application, as shown in Fig. 2. Measurements will be shown in the overview, e.g. perseverace time will be displayed in a graph. A meter indicates the perseverance time by showing an arrow in the red orange or green area. This is an indication of informal caregivers' overburden. An overview will show all informal caregivers in need of support.

Fig. 2. Concept screen of the case manager dashboard

References

1. (VTV), V.T.V.: Ouderdomsziekten zorgen voor grote druk op de zorg (2018)
2. Francke, A., et al.: Een samenhangend beeld van dementie en dementiezorg: kerncijfers, behoeften, aanbod en impact. Themarapportage van de Staat van Volksgezondheid en Zorg (2018)
3. Wimo, A., et al.: Time spent on informal and formal care giving for persons with dementia in Sweden. Health Policy **61**(3), 255–268 (2002)
4. Ministerie van Volksgezondheid, W.e.S., Programma Langer Thuis (2018)

5. Heide, I., Buuse, S., Francke, A.: Dementiemonitor Mantelzorg 2018: mantelzorgers over ondersteuning, zorg, belasting en de impact van mantelzorg op hun leven (2018)
6. Chiao, C.Y., Wu, H.S., Hsiao, C.Y.: Caregiver burden for informal caregivers of patients with dementia: a systematic review. Int. Nurs. Rev. **62**(3), 340–350 (2015)
7. Baumgarten, M., et al.: The psychological and physical health of family members caring for an elderly person with dementia. J. Clin. Epidemiol. **45**(1), 61–70 (1992)
8. Butcher, H.K., Holkup, P.A., Buckwalter, K.C.: The experience of caring for a family member with Alzheimer's disease. West. J. Nurs. Res. **23**(1), 33–55 (2001)
9. Brodaty, H., Donkin, M.: Family caregivers of people with dementia. Dialogues Clin. Neurosci. **11**(2), 217 (2009)
10. van Knippenberg, R., et al.: An experience sampling method intervention for dementia caregivers: results of a randomized controlled trial. Am. J. Geriatr. Psychiatry **26**(12), 1231–1243 (2018)
11. Litjens, M.-J., Van der Marck, M.: DOSSIERANALYSE Crisisreductie binnen de Dementiezorg (2018)
12. Richters, A., et al.: Perseverance time of informal caregivers for institutionalized elderly: construct validity and test-retest reliability of a single-question instrument. J. Am. Med. Directors Assoc. **17**(8), 761–762 (2016)
13. Pot, A., Dyck, R.V., Deeg, D.: Ervaren druk door informele zorg-Constructie van een schaal. Tijdschr. Gerontol. Geriatr. **26**(5), 214–219 (1995)
14. Eijk, L.V., Kempen, G., Sonderen, F.V.: Een korte schaal voor het meten van sociale steun bij ouderen: de SSL12-I. Tijdschr. Gerontol. Geriatr. **25**(5), 192–196 (1994)
15. Terluin, B.: De vierdimensionale klachtenlijst (4DKL). Een vragenlijst voor het meten van distress, depressie, angst en somatisatie [The four-dimensional symptom questionnaire (4DSQ). A questionnaire to measure distress, depression, anxiety, and somatization]. Huisarts & Wetenschap, **39**(12), 538–547 (1996)
16. Jongenelis, K., et al.: Construction and validation of a patient-and user-friendly nursing home version of the Geriatric Depression Scale. Int. J. Geriatric Psychiatry: J. Psychiatry Late Life Allied Sci. **22**(9), 837–842 (2007)
17. Richters, A., et al.: The International Dementia Alliance Instrument for feasible and valid staging of individuals with dementia by Informal Caregivers. J. Am. Geriatr. Soc. **64**(8), 1674–1678 (2016)
18. Smith, B.W., et al.: The brief resilience scale: assessing the ability to bounce back. Int. J. Behav. Med. **15**(3), 194–200 (2008)

Babbelbord: A Personalized Conversational Game for People with Dementia

D. S. Nazareth[1,2]($\boxtimes$), C. Burghardt[1], A. Capra[1], P. Cristoforetti[1],
W. Lam[1], J. B. van Waterschoot[1], G. J. Westerhof[2],
and K. P. Truong[1]

[1] Human Media Interaction, University of Twente, Enschede, The Netherlands
d.s.nazareth@utwente.nl
[2] Psychology Healthy and Technology, University of Twente,
Enschede, The Netherlands

Abstract. We present a demonstration of the board game named "Babbelbord" that stimulates narrative reminiscence in a novel interactive, personalized and entertaining way for people with dementia. Narrative reminiscence is part of reminiscence therapy which is often used in dementia care as it reduces neuropsychiatric symptoms, and therefore improves the quality of life for people with dementia. Stimulating narrative reminiscence entails communicating personal memories with others without intent or evaluation. The Babbelbord game is a newly developed board game that was based on an old-fashioned game that is familiar to people with dementia. The purpose of the Babbelbord game is to reconnect older adults with dementia to their relatives and friends by stimulating narrative reminiscence with a personalized game question approach. The Babbelbord game provides interactive and entertaining conversation starters in a gamified way between people with dementia and their relatives. In this paper, we describe and demonstrate how the Babbelbord was designed to offer an engaging and gamified user experience, tailored for older adults affected by dementia.

Keywords: Dementia · Older adults · Narrative reminiscence · Serious game

1 Introduction

Dementia is a neurodegenerative disease that affects cognitive functions [1] and that can lead to an increase of neuropsychiatric symptoms such as frustration, aggressiveness, anxiety, agitation, apathy and/or delusions in people with dementia (PWD) [1]. A method to reduce these symptoms are by conducting reminiscence therapy (RT). Using reminiscence or life review therapy can have a positive impact on cognition, mood, and behavior of PWD [1]. RT involves the conversation of past activities, events and experiences with another person or group of people, usually with the support of tangible cues such as photographs, familiar items from the past, music and sound recordings [1]. Narrative reminiscence (communicating personal memories in an interactional context with no evaluative or instructive intent [2] frequently sets up or magnifies positive emotions [3]. Using technology that offers many benefits, we aim to

© Springer Nature Switzerland AG 2019
R. Brankaert and W. IJsselsteijn (Eds.): D-Lab 2019, CCIS 1117, pp. 169–173, 2019.
https://doi.org/10.1007/978-3-030-33540-3_18

stimulate personalized narrative reminiscence with PWD. By combining the technology of SoftWare-based Assistive Technologies (SWAT), serious games and narrative reminiscence therapy, a technology driven gamified game can be developed that encourage reminiscence about the past to offer an engaging user experience [4], tailored for people with Dementia, which in turn will stimulate conversations andthereby improving quality of life.

2   Development of the Game

As the aim was to develop a personalized, technology driven game to stimulate conversations by presenting topics and questions from the past, we combined technology to personalize the game and traditional board games. Multiple iterations were conducted to design the technology driven board game.

2.1   Design of the Board Game

From the interviews with an activity expert in dementia care, caretakers and relatives of a person with dementia, we found that the board game had to be familiar and simple in terms of interaction and motor skills. Based on these interviews, we designed a board game named "Babbelbord" which is based on a popular traditional board game named "Game of the Goose". We created pawns that represent the players, a colored dice that matches the squares on the board where the pawns are placed when rolling the dice. Babbelbord is played in a similar way as the "Game of the Goose" is played. Babbelbord can be perceived as familiar, and therefore, simpler to understand especially for PWD who has played lots of board games in their past. In addition, we included a personalization layer in the Babbelbord, by using technology in forms of an arduino and a tablet. This personalization layer includes three separate functionalities: (1) We can display the conversation topics and its game questions to stimulate narrative reminiscence on the tablet, (2) the possibility to filter out conversation topics prior to starting the game, and (3) skip game questions during gameplay. The personalization layer functions as the added value of using technology, by avoiding topics and game questions that triggers negative associations and memories in PWD. Figure 1 shows the finished prototype of the Babbelbord board game.

Fig. 1. Left: The Babbelbord game. Right: A question in the Babbelbord web application shown on the tablet.

2.2 Constructing the Conversation Questions

The developed game questions were based on the book "Dierbare herinneringen" [5]. The book gives examples of well formulated questions about recalling previous memories of different phases in life (i.e., childhood), especially for PWD. Based on findings in the interviews that also focused on the comprehensibility of the questions, we found that game questions have to be formulated in a simple, more closed-ended way to reduce confusion in PWD and makes it for them easier to answer the questions. Although closed questions are less efficient to recall a memory, a balance of closed and open-ended main questions that were further divided into sub-questions were constructed and implemented for the board game. First, closed game questions are asked that are easy to understand and guides the PWD step by step towards the main open question, thereby providing the context of the main question. In addition, giving an indication of time when talking about the past (i.e., childhood or teenage years) is important as it should be clear to the PWD that childhood refers to 0–12 years old and that teenage years refers to 12–18 years old. Lastly, it was suggested in the interviews that providing context for game questions is as important as the question itself. In other words, the PWD should be slowly introduced and guided through a series of easy understandable steps, to eventually understand the situation as a whole. An example of a game question of the category "Love" is shown in Fig. 1.

2.3 Gamified Experience

To introduce a gamified experience to the Babbelbord game, special colored squares have been added that contain various actions, such as making the other player skip their turn. These special squares are inspired by "The Goose Game". In addition, another game element that was added are special colored cards that the players have to collect in order to win. The color on the cards matches to one of the categories, so when players answer a category question, they also receive the corresponding colored card. Each colored card also has the same special power: when a player has two cards of the same color, he/she can decide to discard these cards to obligate the other player to discard their card of the same color.

3 Evaluation of the Babbelbord Game

To evaluate the user experience of the Babbelbord game, two user studies were conducted. The first user study consisted of caregivers and an activity expert at a Dutch care home. The second user study consisted of six older adults with mild-moderate dementia with their relatives or a volunteer at a Dutch care home. In both user studies, a semi-structured interview was carried out with the caregivers, activity experts and relatives at the end of the gameplay. The study was approved by the Ethics Committee of the University of Twente. Prior to the user studies, participants signed the informed consent.

3.1   1st User Study with Caregivers and Expert

The Babbelbord game received positive feedback from the activity expert and care-givers. The activity expert stated that the board game evokes conversation in a gamified way, where the players are potentially entertained and motivated. The activity expert indicated that the competitive game mechanic of the colored cards might be too difficult for people with moderate dementia. He suggested a possibility to implement different versions of the game, including and excluding the new game mechanic. The current game can be played by people with early-mild dementia, and the game without the game mechanic of colored cards can be played by people with moderate dementia. Both the caregiver and activity manager agreed that the personalization layer adds value to the player. According to both, when having a conversation with a person with dementia and a negative memory is triggered, they might get frustrated and will not be able to communicate any further. It is therefore essential not to raise any topics with a heavy negative emotional load. With the topic selection, one is able to filter out topics prior to playing the game. This is particularly essential when the topic also has an emotional effect on the caregiver/relative. Moreover, by giving feedback about the appropriateness of the questions, the system can remember what questions not to ask the next time.

3.2   2nd User Study with PWD

To evaluate the user experience of PWD, a 2nd user study was conducted with six older adults with mild-moderate dementia and their relatives or a volunteer at a Dutch carehome where PWD and a volunteer/relative engaged in conversations with and without the hi-fi prototype of Babbelbord. Two experimenters made observations about the perceived engagement and carried out thematic analyses on the semi-structured interviews that were held with the volunteers/relatives. Observations showed that all subjects involved gave more responses and were more enthusiastic when the Babbel-bord was used. The semi-structured interviews showed that the Babbelbord could support most of the PWD in recalling memories and engaging in conversations. Some mentioned better attention levels with the Babbelbord, and improved listening and conversational abilities. However, it was also mentioned that some PWD were con-fused by the way the questions were formulated (they did not understand the ques-tions), the unclear rules of the game (it was sometimes not clear whose turn it was), and that some PWD showed avoidance of certain questions.

4   Discussion and Conclusion

In general, the reactions to Babbelbord were positive - a physical interactive board game brought back a feeling of familiarity while gamifying and personalizing the reminiscence experience helped improve engagement in conversation. However, attention should be paid to the creation of the questions - these should be easy to understand and should be personalized such that sensitive topics can be avoided.

References

1. Woods, B., O'Philbin, L., Farrell, E.M., Spector, A.E., Orrell, M.: Reminiscence therapy for dementia. Cochrane Database of Systematic Reviews, vol. 3 (2018)
2. Webster, J.D.: Construction and validation of the Reminiscence functions scale. J. Gerontol. **48**(5), 256–262 (1993)
3. Cappeliez, P., Guindon, M., Robitaille, A.: Functions of reminiscence and emotional regulation among older adults. J. Aging Stud. **22**(3), 266–272 (2008)
4. Asghar, I., Cang, S., Yu, H.: Software based assistive technologies for people with dementia: current achievements and future trends. In: 2016 10th International Conference on Software, Knowledge, Information Management & Applications (SKIMA), pp. 162–168. IEEE (2016)
5. Richters, K., Schoonen, C., Korte, J., Bohlmeijer, E., Westerhof, G.J.: Dierbare herinneringen: Interventiebeschrijving en draaiboek [Precious memories: Implementation manual]. Oldenzaal: Schrijverij

Seven Ways to Foster Interdisciplinary Collaboration in Research Involving Healthcare and Creative Research Disciplines

Daan Andriessen[1(✉)], Marieke Zielhuis[1], Kees Greven[1],
Wilke van Beest[1], Berit Godfroij[2], and Remko van der Lugt[2]

[1] Research Group Practice-based Research Methodology, University of Applied
Sciences Utrecht, Padualaan 99, 3584 CH Utrecht, The Netherlands
daan.andriessen@hu.nl
[2] Research Group Co-design, University of Applied Sciences Utrecht,
Utrecht, The Netherlands

Abstract. Making design work in the field of dementia requires interdisciplinary research. However, obstacles are likely to occur when healthcare and creative researchers work together. Analyzing the startup phase of ten interdisciplinary projects in the field of dementia, overweight and loneliness we found seven strategies to overcome these barriers: use boundary brokers, combine theory, combine research approaches, organize for collaboration, joint activities, separate activities, and use artefacts. As many dementia research projects involve exploring new products and technologies, particularly the use of artefacts might be an interesting strategy to foster the collaboration of healthcare and creative research disciplines.

Keywords: Interdisciplinary research · Healthcare · Creative sector · Design research

1 Introduction

Making design work in the field of dementia requires interdisciplinary research with close collaboration between researchers from the creative and the healthcare sector. However, intensive collaboration between different disciplines is often not without obstacles [1–5] and healthcare and creative professionals come from different worlds that do not automatically align. For the success of research projects in dementia it is important to put strategies in place to overcome such obstacles. Although the literature on healthcare and design collaborations is quite voluminous, most focusses on the challenges that designers and design researchers face when working for healthcare practice [e.g. 6, 7]. However, research on additional challenges that arise where the two research disciplines meet is scarce. We will therefore provide a broader overview of barriers and strategies on interdisciplinary health research projects by analysing the research plans and progress reports of ten projects and interviewing the project leaders. In this paper we try to answer the research question: *What strategies do researchers put*

© Springer Nature Switzerland AG 2019
R. Brankaert and W. IJsselsteijn (Eds.): D-Lab 2019, CCIS 1117, pp. 174–177, 2019.
https://doi.org/10.1007/978-3-030-33540-3_19

in place to foster interdisciplinary collaboration in research projects that involve healthcare and creative research disciplines?

2   Research Approach and Context

We applied a multiple case study research approach [8] combining content analysis of research proposals and interviews. We use the theoretical framework of Boundary crossing theory [9, 10] to help us understand the merging of different practices (creative sector, health sector and research). Our sample consisted of ten research projects that were granted by the Dutch funding agency ZonMw within the programme *Create Health – E-health knowledge base for a healthy and active old age*. This is a programme aimed at funding fundamental research on which to base the development or improvement and implementation of e-health applications intended to support the day-to-day functioning of people as they grow older. The programme funds three-year projects in three themes: Living independent with dementia (five projects), preventing overweight (three projects), and preventing loneliness (two projects). A prerequisite of the projects is that they are executed by a consortium made of a research organisation active in healthcare and welfare, a research organisation active in creative industry, representation of the target group and an undertaking.

3   Data Gathering and Analysis

We gathered the research proposals and progress reports of each of the ten granted projects. After coding the proposals and reports we interviewed the projects leader of each project using a topic list based on the coding and we recorded the interviews.

The analysis strategy consisted of five steps. (1) Five researchers performed an open coding [11] of two proposals based on the research question. In a collective analysis [12] we collected quotations and comments from the coders, grouped them and assigned axial codes to each group [11]. Based on this we drew up a coding protocol. (2) Each coder coded two research proposals using the axial codes in Atlas.ti. In a collective coding session we discussed these quotations and their codes to develop a protocol. (3) The five coders coded all the proposals. (4) The corresponding author checked all coding for consistency across all proposals. (5) The interviews were analysed by one author who listened to the recordings, and made notes about relevant remarks, and analysed these notes looking at comments that supported or contradicted the findings of the document coding.

4   Findings

The research proposals contained an average of eighteen quotations related to ways of working to foster interdisciplinary collaboration, with a minimum of six and a maximum of 25. We found seven strategies to foster interdisciplinary collaboration in the project proposals and interviews with the project leaders and/or main researchers:

- **Use boundary brokers**: Many consortium members have experience in different fields, like health and game technology. This indicates experience in crossing the boundaries between fields [9, 10]. These people can act as boundary brokers between disciplines. Some projects create a specific boundary broker position, for example a PhD candidate who takes office at two institutions in order to combine health and creative expertise.
- **Combine theories**: All projects aim to integrate both sectors through the use of theory. Some projects explicitly combine theories from healthcare and design disciplines to create bridges and eight projects combine this with theory from third domains, e.g. psychology or built environment.
- **Combine research approaches**: Projects explicitly combine research methods from different disciplines to tackle core science challenges. For example, one project combined cultural probes, a designerly technique to gather insights into user's interactions and experiences with a series of experimental trials.
- **Organize for collaboration**: All proposals mention organizational measures to improve collaboration. This can include for instance a steering committee or project team in which all disciplines are represented, or the assigning of responsibility to one person or partner for all coordination.
- **Joint activities**: An often used way to collaborate within the ten projects is to organize events and meetings in which members from the different disciplines are involved.
- **Separate activities**: A clear division of roles can contribute to a successful collaboration. When combined with the installation of a project team or steering committee to coordinate the separated activities, this can be an effective way to make responsibilities clear. Explicitly highlighting differences and potential conflicts of interests is also mentioned as a way to deal with differences.
- **Use artefacts to convey meaning**: The seventh strategy we found is the use of artefacts to create understanding. Design researchers use artefacts such as prototypes to explain their way of working and underlying principles.

5   Conclusions and Discussion

We found seven strategies to foster interdisciplinary collaboration in ten cases from the Create Health Programme involving healthcare and creative research disciplines.

This overview of strategies to overcome obstacles in interdisciplinary research projects adds to the growing body of knowledge on collaboration between healthcare and creative disciplines by zooming in on the collaboration between the research disciplines. This study is a starting point for an empirical study of the authors in which the ten projects will be followed to study how these strategies play out in practice and how successful they are.

In light of the theoretical framework of boundary object, the seventh strategy is an interesting one. Using artefacts to convey meaning can be related to the concept of boundary objects: artefacts that cross borders between disciplines by fulfilling a bridging function [9, 13]. In the field of design research, the theory of boundary crossing and boundary objects has gained attention [14, 15]. However, there is little research on boundary objects are not studied yet as means to overcome barriers between design researchers and health researchers. As many dementia research projects involve exploring new products and technologies, the use of artefacts might be an interesting strategy to apply.

References

1. Gavens, L., et al.: Interdisciplinary working in public health research: A proposed good practice checklist. J. Public Health (U. K.) **40**(1), 175–182 (2018)
2. Kumar, K.: Interdisciplinary health research (IDHR): an analysis of the lived experience from the theoretical perspective of identity. Ph.D. thesis, Sydney Med Sch, The Univ Sydney (2012)
3. Smith, P.M.: A transdisciplinary approach to research on work and health: what is it, what could it contribute, and what are the challenges? Crit. Public Health **17**(2), 159–169 (2007)
4. Thompson, J.: Building collective communication competence in Interdisciplinary research teams. J. Appl. Commun. Res. **37**(3), 278–297 (2009)
5. Bruun, H., Hukkinen, J., Huutoniemi, K., Klein, J.T.: Promoting Interdisciplinary Research; The Case of the Academy of Finland. Academy of Finland, Helsinki (2005)
6. Groeneveld, B., Dekkers, T., Boon, B., D'Olivo, P.: Challenges for design researchers in healthcare. Des. Health **2**(2), 305–326 (2018)
7. Van der Lugt, R., Van der Laan, T.: Design facilitators' journeys through the jungle of Co-in healthcare. Des. J. **20**(sup1), S2057–S2067 (2017)
8. Creswell, J.W., Poth, C.N.: Qualitative Inquiry and Research Design. Sage Publications, Thousand Oaks (2018)
9. Akkerman, S.F., Bakker, A.: Boundary Crossing and Boundary Objects. Rev. Educ. Res. **81** (2), 132–169 (2011)
10. Kerosuo, H., Engeström, Y.: Boundary crossing and learning in creation of new work practice. J. Work. Learn. **15**(7/8), 345–351 (2003)
11. Saldana, J.: The Coding Manual for Qualitative Researchers. Sage Publications Inc., London (2015)
12. Sanders, E.B., Stappers, P.J.: Convivial Toolbox. BIS, Amsterdam (2012)
13. Star, S.L.: This is not a boundary object: reflections on the origin of a concept. Sci., Technol. Hum. Values **35**(5), 601–617 (2010)
14. Bergman, M., Lyytinen, K., Mark, G.: Boundary objects in design: an ecological view of design artifacts. J. Assoc. Inf. Syst. **8**(11), 546–568 (2007)
15. Henze, L., Mulder, I.: Networked collaboration canvas: how can service design facilitate networked collaboration? In: ServDes, pp. 451–453 (2014)

Author Index

Printed in the United States
By Bookmasters